What Others Are Saying about
BECOMING GRACE

LOCATED IN BEAUTIFUL WINONA LAKE, INDIANA, GRACE COLLEGE and Theological Seminary have been fixtures on the conservative evangelical landscape for much of the twentieth century. Jared Burkholder, Mark Norris, and the scholars they have recruited for this informative volume explore Grace's fascinating history at the intersection of Pietism, Anabaptism, and Evangelicalism. *Becoming Grace* will appeal to the friends of the college and seminary as well as anyone interested in the history of American evangelicalism. It is a model institutional history that reflects the critical faithfulness of its editors. Burkholder and Norris celebrate Grace's triumphs, but do not ignore its struggles.

> John Fea, author of *Why Study History?: Reflecting on the Importance of the Past* and chair of the Department of History at Messiah College.

THIS IS THE BEST KIND OF INSTITUTIONAL HISTORY: AT ONCE CELEBRATORY and critical, addressed to a particular community and yet also participating in larger scholarly conversations. Beyond its clear relevance for the people of Grace and the Fellowship of Grace Brethren Churches, it is especially valuable for those interested in how Christian higher education has developed at the crossroads of multiple traditions: evangelicalism and fundamentalism, Pietism and Anabaptism.

> Christopher Gehrz, chair of the Bethel University Department of History and editor of *The Pietist Vision of Christian Higher Education: Forming Whole and Holy Persons*

BECOMING GRACE DOES NOT SIMPLY RECOUNT THE HISTORY OF GRACE College and Theological Seminary. It also provides insight into cultural shifts that have influenced collegiate ideology and student life. The contributors' understanding of the historical, political, and theological movements throughout the years allows them to open a window into the decisions and policies that shaped the school into what it is today. This book will be of great interest to academics but also will intrigue other readers as they discover the rich legacy and spiritual landscape surrounding Grace College and Theological Seminary.

Melissa Spoelstra, author of *Jeremiah: Daring to Hope in an Unstable World*

IN THIS WELL-CRAFTED OVERVIEW OF THE HISTORY OF GRACE COLLEGE and Theological Seminary, the various contributors offer timeless stories of the institution that has been the catalyst for the FGBC movement of churches. Their writings capture the heart and history that have been built into the lives of countless families, churches, and individuals. These pages are filled with the detailed development of an academic institution but are written in a way that feels like you are swapping family stories with loved ones as you come to understand and appreciate your heritage.

Mark Artrip, lead pastor of Movement Church (FGBC), Hilliard, Ohio, and Grace Alumnus

I WELCOME THIS WORK. IT SITUATES GRACE COLLEGE AND THEOLOGICAL Seminary within the larger American religious and cultural context and highlights the internal and external forces that have shaped its unique identity. It balances chapters that take a more scholarly and interpretive approach to Grace's place in the Brethren, fundamentalist, and evangelical worlds with chapters that feature informative details about various aspects of Grace's institutional life. As a historian as well as someone who has sought to build bridges between the Ashland and Grace Brethren, I feel this volume will contribute to increased understanding and dialogue between two fellowships that have at times been wary of, if not openly antagonistic toward, one another. May this volume serve to open a new chapter in this relationship.

Dale Stoffer, professor of Historical Theology at Ashland Theological Seminary and author of *A Gleam of Shining Hope: The Story of Theological Education and Christian Witness at Ashland Theological Seminary and Ashland College/University*

BECOMING
GRACE

BECOMING
GRACE

Seventy-Five Years on the
Landscape of Christian
Higher Education in America

Edited by Jared S. Burkholder
and M. M. Norris

Becoming Grace, Seventy-five Years on the Landscape of Christian Higher Education in America
Editors: Jared S. Burkholder, M. M. Norris

© 2015 by Jared S. Burkholder and M. M. Norris
ISBN: 978-088469-312-3

Cover design: Terry Julien

Unless otherwise noted, photos are used courtesy of the Winona History Center at Grace College. Used by permission.

For

Ron and Barbara Manahan

CONTENTS

SKETCHES

PREFACE

THE 2012-2013 ACADEMIC YEAR MARKED THE 75TH ANNIVERSARY OF the founding of Grace Theological Seminary from which the undergraduate college was later established. The college and seminary marked that anniversary by reflecting on the history of both institutions. Banners were hung across campus, and two commemorative issues of the campus magazine, *Two Eight and Nine*, were published during the year. With a special focus on the schools' past presidential administrations, these issues served as a fitting backdrop to then President Ronald Manahan's announcement that he would conclude his service at the end of the spring semester. Homecoming and commencement, imbued with a special sense of meaning, also marked the anniversary with special programming. Additionally, the campus held a series of "Heritage Forums," which were designed to highlight the school's 75 years from a more critical approach. Held over the course of the year in historic Westminster Hall, the forums included several papers as well as formal comments from historians not affiliated with Grace. This volume is a result of the reflection and commemoration of the 2012-2013 academic year, especially the research, oral interviews, and critical assessment conducted as part of the heritage forums.

Long before this anniversary year, however, President Manahan tasked the department of history with the job of writing a critical history of the institution for the occasion. He specifically did not want us to write something that was self-congratulatory or that was relevant only to the Grace "family," but rather something of solid scholarship that would intersect with broader academic conversations. In honoring his desire, we realized that we would need a team of scholars to complete this task and thus invited others to join the project. In doing our work together, we strove to be objective,

i

nonjudgmental, and not to be defensive about our past. Instead, we attempted to look systematically at who we were as an institution and to see how we got to where we are now.

It is worth nothing that although the contributors to this volume have worked hard in their research and labored over their conclusions, we do not see this book as the final word on the topics and tensions it covers. Historical writing is always subject to differing perspectives. It is also important to point out that the conclusions expressed by the authors and editors are theirs and theirs alone. While we have enjoyed working with members of the Grace administration as well as members of the Fellowship of Grace Brethren Churches, this book does not necessarily speak for Grace College or Seminary, its board, its administrators (past or present), BMH Books, the leadership of the FGBC, nor its members. Naturally, readers are free to form their own opinions about the conclusions drawn by the book's contributors.

Though commemorative books are typically meant for a popular audience, our goals perhaps make this book somewhat unconventional as a commemorative volume. Indeed, it has been written primarily with scholars and historians in mind. In looking toward this audience, the book is largely arranged around tensions that have played a prominent role within the seminary and college's past, and which are of particular interest to those who were invited to contribute. From the beginning, we have hoped that this volume would offer something of critical value to the scholarly conversation about Christian higher education in general. In particular, the relationship between evangelicalism and ethno-religious traditions such as the Brethren, the realities of institutional politics, and the challenges of changing social contexts were seen as requiring critical study.

Having said this, we do hope that church leaders as well as many in the FGBC will also be able to glean greater understanding about how Grace College and Seminary has been situated on the landscape of Christian higher education and will come away with a greater understanding of their own denominational heritage. Manahan wanted this volume to uncover fresh angles so we could all learn something from the past without feeling the need to "gloss over" tensions and sticky points. He felt that, as an institution and as a Fellowship, it was time for something like this to be written. In doing this, as editors and contributors, we have wrestled with the past and have gone through a whole range of emotions, and we expect that those of our readers who experienced the history about which we write may go through similar feelings. Though this path has had its ups and downs, we hope that this volume will be a beneficial part of an ongoing journey as we learn from those who went before us.

It is also important to note that the scope of this volume is modest. It is not meant to be comprehensive or a definitive narrative of the history of the institution. There is no question that numerous people, academic programs and departments, campus events, administrative decisions, and financial ups and downs, which helped to shape what Grace College and Seminary has become and which might have been included in this volume, do not receive the attention they deserve. Choices about what to include were largely determined by the main focus and argument of each chapter.

We sincerely hope that we have brought together a volume with scholarly merit. But we also hope these chapters will facilitate healing, honest conversations, and genuine appreciation for the past as we, as well as future generations, continue to become more faithful conduits of God's grace.

Jared S. Burkholder
M.M. Norris

ACKNOWLEDGMENTS

THIS VOLUME HAS BEEN COMPLETED WITH THE HELP OF NUMEROUS individuals, not the least of whom are the contributors who lent their efforts to this work despite their heavy teaching and administrative responsibilities. To them especially, we are grateful. Countless individuals took time to talk with us and the other contributors either informally or to conduct more formal interviews. We are very grateful for their help and for teaching us about the story of Grace College and Theological Seminary. Many are footnoted in the following chapters but we want to acknowledge those who were interviewed below:

Frank Benyousky	Jim Eisenbraun
Ken Bickle	Skip Forbes
Dean and Jean Coverstone	Ron Henry
Jim Custer	Jesse Humberd
Jesse Deloe	Rich Jeffreys
Don DeYoung	Tom Julien
Dick Dilling	Bill Katip
John Davis	Homer Kent, Jr.
Kent and Karla Denlinger	Jim Kessler
Jeff Gill	Joe Lehmann
Bill Gordon	Bill and Ella Male
Michael Grill	Ronald Manahan
Steve Grill	Roger Peugh
Tom Edgington	D. Brent Sandy

Paulette Sauders	John Teevan
Jacqueline Schram	Miriam Uphouse (Christensen)
Tammy Schultz	Greg Weimer
R. Wayne Snider	Nancy Weimer
Dan Snively	John C. Whitcomb
Roy Snyder	Mike Yocum
Tom Stallter	Jerry Young
John Stoll	

Many others reviewed portions or all of the manuscript as it came together. We are especially indebted to Nancy Weimer, Tom Julien, Gary Kochheiser, Carol Forbes, Terry White, Brent Sandy, and Jim Custer for this. Dale Stoffer was immensely helpful in offering his perspective, corrections, and assisting us with the nuances of historical theology in the Brethren context. Conversations with other historians, including Brad Gundlach, Chris Gehrz, Jeff Bach, Devin Manzullo-Thomas, and Tim Erdel have been enlightening and encouraging as well. We could not have asked for a better editor in Jesse Deloe whose personal experience and memory were as valuable as his excellent editing work. We enjoyed the support not only of Liz Cutler Gates and Terry Julien, but also from the Grace administration. A spring 2014 conference on "historic religious roots and the future of higher education" organized by Thomas Mach at Cedarville University provided a forum for the exchange of ideas as did a session at Pepperdine University organized by Devin Manzullo-Thomas and Chris Gehrz, on institutional history at the 2014 biennial meeting of the Conference on Faith and History. A fall 2014 fellowship at the Young Center for Anabaptist and Pietism Studies at Elizabethtown College allowed time for final editing.

President Manahan initially commissioned this work and the administrative support continued from Bill Katip and Jeff Gill, both of whom offered valuable comments on our work, but did not seek to influence what was written. We appreciate immensely the freedom they have afforded us.

Others, including Deborah Raymond, Carrie Yocum, Elma Sherman, and the staff at BrandPoet, have provided invaluable assistance in a host of details both large and small, especially with the Heritage Forums that were so important to celebrating the 75th anniversary year. Of course we are indebted to Bill Darr, Rhoda Palmer, Tonya Fawcett, and Jody Hopper at the Morgan Library as well as David Roepke at the Brethren Church and Ashland University archives. Several of our history students contributed as well and these include Hillary Burgardt, Katherine Marshall, John Forcey, Scott Moore, Betsy Rumley Vastbinder, Lauren Cartwright, Jessica Anton, Joel Zakahi, Andy Clark, Brandy Allen, Tory Sears, Corey Grandstaff, and Carrie Halquist. Finally, we thank our families, for we know that projects such as this also require the sacrifice of those to whom we are closest.

CONTRIBUTORS

Jeff Bach (PhD Duke University) is Associate Professor, Department of Religious Studies and Director of the Young Center for Anabaptist and Pietist Studies at Elizabethtown College.

Frank Benyousky (MA University of California Santa Barbara) is Associate Professor of English at Grace College.

Jared S. Burkholder (PhD University of Iowa) is Department Chair and Associate Professor of History at Grace College.

Perry Bush (PhD Carnegie Mellon University) is Professor of History at Bluffton University.

Robert G. Clouse (PhD University of Iowa) is Senior Research Scholar in Liberal Arts and Professor Emeritus Indiana State University.

Timothy Erdel (PhD University of Illinois at Urbana-Champaign) is Professor of Religion and Philosophy at Bethel College (Mishawaka) and Archivist for the Missionary Church.

Christy Hill (PhD Talbot School of Theology) is Professor of Spiritual Formation and Women's Studies at Grace Theological Seminary.

Shirley Mullen (PhD University of Minnesota; University of Wales) is President and Professor of History at Houghton College.

Steven Nolt (PhD University of Notre Dame) is Professor of History at Goshen College.

M. M. Norris (PhD University of Edinburgh) is Dean of the School of Arts and Sciences and Professor of History at Grace College.

Tiberius Rata (PhD Trinity Evangelical Divinity School) is Assistant Dean in the School of Ministry Studies and Professor of Old Testament Studies at Grace College and Theological Seminary.

Kim Reiff (MFA Azusa Pacific University) is Department Chair and Assistant Professor of Art at Grace College.

Paulette Sauders (PhD Ball State University) is Chair of the Department of Languages, Literature, and Communication and Professor of English and Journalism at Grace College.

Jim Swanson (PhD Western Michigan University) is Vice President for Academic and Student Services and Assistant Professor of Sociology at Grace College and Theological Seminary.

Juan Carlos Téllez (MDiv Grace Theological Seminary) is Dean of the Chapel and Global Initiatives at Grace College and Theological Seminary and is completing a PhD at Trinity Evangelical Divinity School.

Terry White (EdD Indiana Wesleyan University) teaches part time in Communications at Grace College and serves as the lead docent at the Winona History Center in Winona Lake, Indiana.

FOREWORD

Shirley Mullen

IN THE MIDST OF THE TURBULENCE AND SKEPTICISM SURROUNDING so much of American higher education in our day, *Becoming Grace* offers a story of hope. It is the story of one relatively small academic institution, Grace College and Theological Seminary, inspired by the occasion of its 75th anniversary. Unlike many such institutional histories, *Becoming Grace* embraces the complexity, even the pain, of Grace's own history.

The organization around themes and tensions, rather than chronology, inherently communicates the rich texture that characterizes the development of the institution over the past 75 years. We see the impact of key personalities—the presidents, certainly—but also selected faculty and staff whose individual faithfulness to their own callings also shaped Grace's story. We see the ways in which Grace's history is inextricably intertwined with the story of its sponsoring denomination, the Fellowship of Grace Brethren Churches. We also see how the larger Grace history is shaped by stories within its own story—the story of global engagement, of curricular transformation, of expanded co-curricular activity, and of increasing partnership with the surrounding community. We also see how Grace's story has been shaped by those that ran parallel to its own, such as the story of Winona Lake's Chautauqua and Bible Conference.

The incorporation of the voices of outside scholars, invited into the Grace community for an anniversary series of Heritage Forums, further contributes to the sense of authenticity that characterizes this commemorative narrative. *Becoming Grace* truly seeks to provide for the Grace community not only a comprehensive and complex, but also critical assessment of its history.

But *Becoming Grace* is not only a book for the Grace community. It links Grace's story to the larger story of American Christianity in the 20th and 21st centuries. In this narrative, we see the working out of the various religious traditions that came together in its history. We see how, in Grace's story, European Anabaptism and Pietism were reshaped in the context of American fundamentalism and Evangelicalism. Beyond this, *Becoming Grace* reminds us of the ways in which Grace College and Seminary has helped to shape the Christian world beyond its own borders, certainly in its leadership in the controversial creation science movement, but also in its connections through the Winona Lake conferences to such crucial organizations as Youth for Christ, and to such luminaries as Homer Rodeheaver and Billy Graham.

Finally, *Becoming Grace* is a book of value for anyone who cares about the story of Christian higher education. While Grace's story is particular in certain ways, it shares key elements with many of North America's institutions of Christian higher education over the past two centuries: the transition from a curriculum focused primarily on the Bible to a comprehensive liberal arts curriculum, but motivated throughout by the same desire to prepare young men and women to effectively incarnate the Gospel in their world; the tenacious effort to hold onto the essentials of the faith while also staying close enough to culture to have a redemptive impact on that culture; and the all-important and ever-challenging task of imitating our Lord Jesus in keeping Truth and Love in balance.

Becoming Grace culminates in the hopeful account of Grace's accomplishments during the tenure of President Ronald Manahan from 1994-2013. While growing enrollment from 886 to over 1900, President Manahan also developed mutually beneficial partnerships with key industries in the surrounding community, most notably the orthopedic industry. In the spirit of God's instructions to the Children of Israel in Jeremiah 29, Grace has "sought the welfare of the city" in which they have found themselves and in promoting the welfare of the surrounding community Grace has strengthened its own wellbeing. For a community with roots in the Anabaptist tradition, this conscious effort to link its future to the surrounding world shows both remarkable creativity and courage.

I pray that Grace, and all of her sister Christian colleges, universities, and seminaries will continue to have the creative courage to remain faithful to their core mission as they also seek to forge the conditions for long term financial sustainability in an ever more pluralistic and regulated environment.

Congratulations on your first 75 years. May they be only the foretaste of what God has in store for Grace in the future.

Shirley A. Mullen
President, Houghton College

FOREWORD
Jeff Bach

BECOMING GRACE IS A GIFT TO MANY AUDIENCES THAT SURPASSES THE scope and purpose of most institutional histories. Jared Burkholder, M. M. Norris, and their contributors offer a clear and balanced account of Grace Theological Seminary from its origins in Akron, Ohio, through its expansion at Winona Lake and the difficulties of a later denominational division. The story of the seminary, as well as the college, is carefully set in the context of conflicts between professors and their advocates that precipitated its founding. The account explains the deeper Brethren context behind those events while moving forward through the continued religious developments among the Grace Brethren. At the same time, authors set that background in the context of broader cultural movements and developments within conservative Christianity in the U.S. in the early twentieth century. Readers can almost hear the rousing revival preaching, the singing of Rodeheaver hymns, and the passionate teaching of professors at Winona Lake.

The book also offers an excellent introduction to the global reach of Grace College and Seminary while also recounting in sufficient detail its significance in the region around Winona Lake, as well as connections to the wider network of Christian fundamentalism. The writers succeed at putting human life into their story by telling of students, outreach ministries beyond the campus, and accounts of significant leaders. As a result, the book tells real stories about real people, not just lofty ideas bantered by a few larger-than-life leaders. While the various authors work at fairness to the prime movers at Grace, they also offer balanced, respectful insights into the challenging personality characteristics of some of those leaders. Consequently, this book is a truly human story of an institution that has at times struggled, yet also has achieved much. Though this is a more difficult path for writing a good institutional history, the fruits are much more satisfying in presenting a complex picture of the institution and its people, the values important to it, and the influences of external forces along with internal conflicts and achievements. Readers can enjoy the dynamic moments and persons throughout the first 75 years of Grace's history.

The attention to social and political developments during Grace's history likewise adds depth to the story. Changing views on the participation of women in church leadership, both in American society and among the Grace Brethren, views about race, attitudes toward members from around the world, and reactions to challenges in American politics such as the Cold War, cultural change in the 1960s, and new roles for conservative Christians in politics since the 1980s—all show how Grace has responded to changes from the outside and their impact on the inside. By facing into these issues, the authors have narrated a story that is connected to its times from its beginnings on the heels of the Chautauqua movement to the present day. Readers will find here much more than a tepid story of a denominational institution; rather they will discover an engaging account that weaves a textured cloth of cultural context.

The authors provide meaningful historical background that will illumine readers on topics that may seem less familiar, such as Pietism, Anabaptism, and the small movement of Brethren and their distinctive beliefs and practices. For readers who want to understand the Grace Brethren and this deeper context, the writers provide plenty of information. For newcomers to these topics, the account is not overwhelming in obscure detail, yet it is informative. Similarly, the various authors provide theological insight throughout the book. These insights are especially helpful for readers who may be less familiar with the vocabulary of fundamentalism, which is clarified in the narrative. At the same time, readers who are well grounded in these terms will find plenty of description and analysis of refinements and distinctions in the theological developments among the Grace Brethren. Burkholder, Norris, and others are to be commended for doing the additional work to provide this careful, scholarly work to make this story serve the alumni and supporters of Grace Seminary, as well as to deepen the historical and theological understanding of all readers.

Burkholder and Norris have succeeded remarkably in sustaining a clear and credible editorial voice throughout the book. Often institutional histories with multiple contributors can seem like a crazy quilt pieced by a sewing circle. In this book, the pieces fit, and the unique expertise of contributors comes through, yet the completed project stands together as a whole. The author-compilers have crafted a story that gives remarkable detail, yet explains the twists and turns of the plot and sets it within both its specific denominational scope and the much broader American context. Few accounts of denominational histories achieve this balance with the fairness and engaging qualities of this book.

Readers should welcome the gift of *Becoming Grace*, offered in these pages. It is at times a captivating story of human conflict and spiritual aspiration, far more than a dry account of a few leaders and their ideals. The book is also a tale of the dynamics of preserving ideals and responding to cultural change. The pages are filled with characters, some famous, some less known, all woven like strands into the cloth of a compelling story. *Becoming Grace* is an informative and engaging narrative about an institution and its people who have accomplished much. Ultimately it is a story about people of faith and their best hopes to act in response to their perceptions of God at work in their lives. *Becoming Grace* will draw readers of many backgrounds to receive the gift of this story.

Jeff Bach
Director of the Young Center for Anabaptist and Pietist Studies
Elizabethtown College

Introduction

HISTORICAL WRITING OFTEN TAKES THE FORM OF A MONOGRAPH, A single-author book with a unified narrative, which carries through from beginning to end. As an edited collection of essays, this volume is not organized in that fashion. While monographs have their advantages, edited volumes provide opportunity for collaboration among contributors, incorporate multiple efforts, and are usually structured, as this book is, around themes, rather than a single narrative. There has been an attempt to tease out from the various chapters recurring topics as well as to impose a useful structure. Still, rather than a single chronological narrative, there are multiple chronologies that are particular to the themes and overall topic of each chapter. Thus, some readers will want to read all the chapters to get a full sense of the overall chronology of the first 75 years of Grace College and Seminary and the context in which its history has developed. Others may want to skip immediately to chapters that interest them. (In an effort to aid the reader's sense for the overarching chronology, a brief timeline is provided at the end of this introduction.)

It should also be noted that the chapters that follow do not pretend to offer an exhaustive chronicle of events, people, milestones, or initiatives that have been part of Grace's first 75 years. Indeed, there is much that will be left out or mentioned only in passing. Even so, it is hoped that the themes and topics that were chosen for this book capture many of the most important parts of the Grace culture and its intersection with the history of Christian higher education in America. We also hope that sufficient details emerge from these chapters to illustrate those intersections and acknowledge the important work that has taken place in all sectors of this campus.

Part One focuses primarily on distinctive tensions that have arisen throughout the history of the institution. This section begins with a chapter on the Pietist, Anabaptist, and Evangelical heritage of Grace and some of the tensions found therein. Following this, chapter two focuses on "beginnings," and argues for the importance of Louis S. Bauman, a figure of influence within the Brethren Church, but whose connections with the foundations of Grace Seminary have been largely overlooked. In addition, the chapter introduces Alva J. McClain, the founding president, and his participation in the complex "divorce" that took place at Ashland Seminary in 1937. Following this, chapter three argues that after McClain retired from the presidency in 1962, the seminary fostered a more strident fundamentalist and premillennialist culture, primarily as a result of the strong personalities of Herman Hoyt, the second president, and John C. Whitcomb, one of the seminary's most visible faculty members, as they attempted to resist the influence of neo-evangelicalism. Then, Christy Hill probes the desire for a holistic approach to seminary education—one that fosters both rigorous academic output and warm spirituality. This also provides a backdrop for her examination of the passing away of the old seminary and the shift to a new structure and approach under Dean Jeffrey Gill.

In chapter five, Juan Carlos Téllez examines the importance of the global focus that has existed at Grace since the beginning. He lays out the way this originated as part of the missionary impulse within the Brethren Church and early seminary and was then expanded and augmented by the efforts to promote greater diversity awareness and cross-cultural experiences within the undergraduate context. Jim Swanson then focuses specifically on the history of student affairs and its relationship to the culture of the Grace College campus. In chapter six, he sketches the rise of athletics, fine arts, and most significantly, demonstrates the intersections between developments at Grace and the broader trends in higher education across the nation—basically a transition from a model that served "in place of parents" to one focused on personal growth and restoration. Following this, chapter seven explores the ways in which Grace has attempted to build connections with the community in which it has been situated, showing how the earliest attempts were a mixture of community-building and traditional methods of soul-winning. Norris especially gives attention to the efforts since 1994, under the tenure of President Ronald Manahan, to partner with local and regional institutions, industries, historical associations, and community leaders in efforts to build bridges. These efforts, in fact, also mirrored initiatives on campus to foster a community that more fully embodied a spirit of grace.

Part Two then offers two chapters on the contextual background of Grace College and Seminary that have shaped its history—the geographic context of Winona Lake, Indiana, and the "denominational" context of the Fellowship of Grace Brethren Churches. Terry White handles the Winona Lake context, demonstrating that even though Grace Seminary did not move to Northeast Indiana until the fall of 1939, the religious culture of Winona provided a fascinating backdrop against which Grace College and Seminary could expand. Interestingly, this backdrop included many Brethren annual conferences and the formation of the Brethren Foreign Missionary Society. Robert Clouse then examines the content of three doctrinal statements and provides historical analysis that highlights the development of increasing degrees of precisionism.

Finally, Part Three consists of brief remarks from outside historians who were invited to participate in a series of "Heritage Forums," held between fall 2012 and fall 2013, which provided a venue for the Grace campus to revisit its history. All three have familiarity with the Pietist, Anabaptist, and evangelical heritage of Grace College and Seminary as well as experience in writing denominational or institutional histories. Their comments are included to prime the reader's thinking about the way this institutional history intersects with broader historical currents and to provide a glimpse of the themes and topics that emerged from these forums.

To those familiar with the history of evangelicalism in America, parts of this story will represent familiar territory—fundamentalist struggles over orthodoxy, tensions between the seminary model and the liberal arts approach to learning, the search for a balance between discipline and restoration, unity and diversity, and between academic rigor and warm piety. Yet, in the story of Grace College and Seminary questions also emerge that may be less familiar—questions about the way schools with Anabaptist roots have navigated the evangelical landscape, or about the promise and challenges of making a Pietist heritage relevant for the 21st century. Perhaps through these chapters the familiar and the not-so-familiar will converge to illuminate an institutional history that has sought to fuse a cord of many strands around a core desire to faithfully educate students for service, for the academy, and for the Christian life.

Annotated Timeline

1880-1883 - The Brethren tradition in America separates into three main branches; the progressives take the name "Brethren Church."

1888 - The Beyer Brothers establish Spring Fountain Park in what is now Winona Lake, Indiana.

1895 - The Presbyterian Synod of Indiana purchases Spring Fountain Park; Solomon Dickey changes the name to Winona Lake, creates "Christian Chautauqua" and Bible Conference venue.

1900 - The Brethren Foreign Missionary Society is formed in Winona Lake.

1906 - Ashland Seminary (undergraduate) is founded as the flagship seminary for the Brethren Church.

1911 - Billy Sunday, exuberant evangelist, moves his headquarters to Winona Lake, location of the leading Bible Conference in America.

1912 - Louis S. Bauman establishes the Long Beach, California, congregation and becomes a major leader in the Brethren Church and strong proponent of premillennialism and Christian missions.

1920 - Construction begins on the iconic Billy Sunday Tabernacle in Winona Lake.

1921 - Alva J. McClain and J. Allen Miller write the doctrinal statement, "Message of the Brethren Ministry" and hope to tighten theological conformity at Ashland Seminary.

1930 - Alva J. McClain helps establish Ashland Theological Seminary (graduate).

1937 - Schism takes place at Ashland between its seminary leaders, supported by Louis S. Bauman, and the administration, resulting in a new seminary, which was first located outside Akron, Ohio; takes the name Grace Theological Seminary with McClain as first president.

1939 - Grace Theological Seminary moves to Winona Lake, Indiana, and begins classes in what is now Mount Memorial Hall.

1940 - Seminary Articles of Incorporation are filed with State of Indiana.

1948 - The "Undergraduate Division of Grace Theological Seminary" is created with two-year programs and includes four majors: English, History, Greek, and Bible.

1951 - Dedication of McClain Hall, the first building constructed on the Winona Lake campus; it was built to house the growing seminary.

1953 - Campus newspaper, *The Sounding Board*, publishes first issue

1954 - Undergraduate Division becomes four-year liberal arts college with 13 majors: Archaeology, Bible, Education, English and Speech, Greek, History, Latin, Linguistics, Modern Languages, Music, Philosophy, Physical Education, and Science.

1955-1960 - Varsity athletic programs for men and women established; Gymnasium completed; "Lancer" is chosen as mascot, and Grace becomes charter member of Mid-Central Conference.

1958 - Dedication of Philathea Hall, which was built to house the growing undergraduate college.

1960 - The seminary begins publishing *The Grace Journal*, which continues until 1973.

1961 - John C. Whitcomb publishes *The Genesis Flood* with Henry Morris, contributing to narrowing views on creation and moving Grace Seminary to the center of the modern creationist movement.

1962 - Herman Hoyt becomes president, overseeing a building and enrollment boom.

1964 - Dedication of Alpha Hall, the first residence hall and dining commons.

1966 - Dedication of Beta Hall, the first men's residence hall.

1968 - McClain publishes *Greatness of the Kingdom*, his Dispensationalist *Magnum opus*; Grace College and Seminary takes possession of the Winona Lake Christian Assembly and its properties, continues to hold annual Bible Conferences although attendance is dwindling.

1969 - Dedication of the Betty Zimmer Morgan Library; Statement of Faith of the National Fellowship of Brethren Churches adopted.

1974 - William Male and Roy Lowrie begin graduate degree program in Christian School Administration, making Grace Seminary a hub for the growing Christian School Movement.

1976 - Homer Kent, Jr. becomes president, presiding over an era that includes expanding recognition for the seminary within evangelical circles; Grace College becomes accredited by Higher Learning Commission.

1977 - Membership in the Council for Christian Colleges and Universities (CCCU).

1978 - Dedication of the Science Center (renamed the Chester E. Cooley Science Center in 1985); Nursing program begins.

1980 - Seminary revives publication of its journal under the name *Grace Theological Journal*. It continues until 1991.

1982 - Grace Theological Seminary becomes accredited by the Higher Learning Commission; the seminary establishes Institute for Biblical Counseling under Larry Crabb.

1986 - John Davis becomes first president without previous personal or family ties to Ashland Seminary or the Brethren Church; fosters stronger liberal arts focus for the college and reforms in Student Affairs.

1988 - Davis, along with then Academic Dean Ronald Manahan, begins periodic leadership retreats to facilitate thinking on liberal arts identity; annual Bible conferences end.

1989 - Grace College's Student Academic Advising Center selected country's top Outstanding Institutional Advising Program, validating efforts to improve Student Affairs under Deans Dan Snively and Miriam Uphouse.

1989-1991 - Upheaval in the seminary contributes to decreasing enrollment and the seminary is restructured as a graduate division of the college's Department of Biblical Studies.

1992 - Fellowship of Grace Brethren Churches experiences schism; the aging Billy Sunday Tabernacle deemed too costly to maintain and is torn down.

1992 - James Bowling (faculty) and Joel Curry (staff) publish *Values in a Liberal Arts Education*, representing ongoing efforts to define the college's Christian liberal arts identity

1994 - Ronald Manahan, former academic dean and provost, becomes president, ushering in a period of renewed stability, growth, and community partnerships.

1996 - First distance-education classes offered; seminary begins Korean Studies program (expanded in 2009).

1998 - Renovation completed on two historic buildings on the Grace campus: Westminster Hall and Mount Memorial Hall.

1999 - Kent Hall (residence hall) is dedicated.

2000 - Indiana Hall (residence hall and student services) completed.

2002 - Seminary enters rebuilding phase under Jeffrey Gill.

2003 - Gordon Student Recreation Center dedicated.

2007 - Orthopaedic Capital Center completed, representing a tangible testament to new and continuing connections with the local orthopedic industry (renamed The Ronald E. and Barbara J. Manahan Orthopaedic Capital Center in 2013); online education begins (Department of Online Education created in 2011).

2007-2009 - The "Great Recession" creates financial pressures; cuts include the School of Music, German language curriculum, Physical Education Program, Department of Social Work, as well as faculty and staff reductions.

2009 - GOAL (Grace Opportunities for Adult Learners) degree-completion program begins.

2010 - Grace Theological Seminary becomes accredited by the Association of Theological Schools.

2010-2012 - "Reimagine" campaign implemented with new accelerated options, expanded online course offerings, adjusted academic calendar, and "applied learning" credit requirement; Henry and Frances Weber School at Grace College is established; and Grace contracts with marketing firm, Brandpoet to increase visibility for new initiatives

2013 - William J. Katip, formerly provost, becomes president

Part I
Tensions

Chapter 1

Heritage
Pietism, Anabaptism, and Evangelicalism
Jared S. Burkholder

At the start of the fall 2013 semester, Jacqueline Schram, Associate Dean of Students, provided a visual aid to members of the leadership team for the Grace College course, Freshman Foundations—the class designed to help Grace College's first-year students transition to college life. She handed each member a small piece of rope and encouraged the team to think of the "Grace Core" (the liberal arts general education curriculum) as the center strand around which the other components of the institution were bound. With multiple strands woven together around common goals, the core, she implied, would prove a strong foundation for the important endeavor of educating students. The bit of rope was an effective teaching tool.

But the usefulness of this metaphor extends beyond the relationship between the "core" and the rest of the curriculum. Indeed, in considering the historical journey of Grace College and Theological Seminary, one is struck by the many strands that have come together to shape the institution as it stands now. While many Christian colleges and universities enjoy a singular heritage with clear historical identity markers—such as those with Lutheran, Reformed, Catholic or Mennonite affiliation—Grace College and Theological Seminary has evolved within an eclectic heritage.[1]

The two rites, or "ordinances," that have been most important for defining a distinctive Brethren identity are understood as three-fold events. Communion is comprised of the bread and cup, the love feast, and a feetwashing ceremony. Similarly, baptism entails being immersed three times.[2] Another group of three exists with regard to the heritage of Grace College and Theological Seminary: the converging strands of Pietism, Anabaptism, and American Evangelicalism.[3] Today, the evangelical strand is perhaps most meaningful for the majority of individuals within the Grace Brethren orbit—due largely to the fact that this part of the institution's identity has overshadowed the older Pietist and Anabaptist heritage.

The fact remains, however, that each of these three strands, along with the smaller strands included in each, has contributed to the educational heritage of Grace College and Seminary and each holds potential for inspiring a continuing tradition of Christian higher education. In the paragraphs below, this chapter will provide a more specific historical introduction to the Pietist and Anabaptist roots of the Brethren tradition, as well as the way these older movements have intersected with evangelicalism. Together, they provide important context for the founding of Grace College and Seminary.

Pietism

The Brethren tradition emerged within the context of a renewal movement in Europe that began in the seventeenth century and became known as Pietism. In German-speaking areas, the founders of this movement believed the churches of their day were more concerned with human creeds, rational theological debate, and the persecution of religious dissenters. The established Reformed and Lutheran churches, they believed, lacked authentic or truly experiential faith. Although this perception was not entirely true, Protestantism at the time was dominated by what historians call "Scholasticism," which was indeed characterized by a zeal for theological dogma and preserving orthodoxy according to their respective creeds and confessions. Pietists, on the other hand, pursued "heart religion" with gusto, writing practical devotionals, hymnals, and prayer books, experimenting with new modes of worship, facilitating Bible study among the laity, and organizing small groups for fellowship and prayer that met separately from the official church services. Because of these pious pursuits, they were called "Pietists" by their opponents, and regardless of the fact that it was a derisive term, the name stuck.[4]

Although there were earlier proponents of Pietist-style renewal, Philipp Jakob Spener is usually credited as the movement's most prominent founder. Trained in theology, philosophy, and history, Spener served important posts within the Lutheran church at Frankfurt, Dresden, and Berlin. In his best-known work, *Pia Desideria*, Spener outlined a program for spiritual renewal that included, among other initiatives, the organization of small fellowship groups called conventicles. These are sometimes said to have functioned as "little churches within the church." Perhaps the fullest and most far-reaching center of Pietism in the eighteenth century originated under the direction of August Hermann Francke who was an influential professor at the University of Halle, beginning in 1692. As a student, Francke had studied at several institutions including the University at Leipzig, where conventicles had been formed according to Spener's model. Due in large part to Francke's leadership, the University of Halle became a leading and well-known center for the promotion of Pietism. Pietists at Halle operated an orphanage, began new missionary efforts, and worked to give practical training to those studying for pastoral ministry. Halle also organized an extensive printing program which published religious literature for laypeople.[5] Pietism made its way to America in the 17th and 18th century as individuals migrated across the Atlantic for the opportunities that the New World promised. Pietist books also made the journey and in just a short time, they were being printed and sold in the colonies. Pietists also corresponded with each other across the ocean and in that way; Pietism became a significant part of a transatlantic awakening that connected likeminded Protestants in England, Germany, Holland, Scandinavia, and the Americas.[6]

Most Pietists, such as Spener and Francke, were content to remain within the established churches and did not promote doctrines that presented a significant challenge to the religious authorities. Others, however, stretched the boundaries of what the state was willing to tolerate. Those individuals, whom historians sometimes refer to as "radical" Pieists, often separated themselves from the established churches or were expelled. At times, they began their own fellowships and religious "societies." Some became traveling preachers who renounced their worldly possessions and developed networks of little societies. Often, these Radical Pietists compared the established churches to the "Babylon" of biblical prophecy. Many believed that the end times were imminent and that God would soon send judgment to the earth, condemning the established churches, which had become aligned with forces opposed to God and were destined to face God's apocalyptic wrath.

Believing that judgment was coming and that the churches were beyond hope, Radical Pietists separated themselves from the churches, discontinuing their participation, and in many cases church leaders relinquished their offices. Some among the radicals gave up their employment as well. Some moved into the countryside, living in makeshift religious communities. Others pooled their resources, living completely from the common treasury. At times they experienced what they believed was direct divine revelation or religious ecstasy. Influenced by the Christian mysticism of earlier generations, they yearned for experiences of mystical union with God.[7]

The Brethren were one such group of radicals that took shape in the small village of Schwarzenau under the leadership of Alexander Mack. Although raised in a traditional Reformed household, Mack was inspired by the Pietist itinerant preacher Ernst Christoph Hochmann von Hochenau. Hochmann was a charismatic preacher who traveled the countryside, preaching a separatist message and condemning the churches of "Babylon." Traveling through Schwarzenau, Hochmann attracted a large following. As was the pattern for radical Pietists, Hochmann established religious communities of those who renounced their worldly lives, consecrated themselves to God, and moved into camps to await the end times and the impending judgment. Mack may have joined Hochmann on occasional preaching tours, but more significantly, he provided leadership in Schwarzenau for the Pietists there. Mack's group became the nucleus for the Brethren movement.[8]

Anabaptism

Mack's spiritual journey took him from the Reformed context into Pietism. Yet it also took him into Anabaptism, which had begun roughly two centuries earlier as a branch of the Protestant Reformation. Mack came to believe that the traditional rite of infant baptism was illegitimate and he became a strong proponent of rebaptism, even calling for other Pietist groups to adopt believer's baptism. The "ordinance" of baptism quickly became a defining feature of the group.

So in practicing believer's baptism, the Schwarzenau Brethren joined an existing tradition of "Baptist-minded" (*taufgesinnte*) Protestants who were called Anabaptists (literally "rebaptizers"). Anabaptists originated as part of the Protestant Reformation in the sixteenth century. The Lutheran and Reformed (Calvinist) branches of the Reformation are well known to most people, but the Anabaptist branch, or the "radical" Reformation is less familiar, even though it was every bit as significant. The first Anabaptists consisted of a small band of church leaders in Zurich, Switzerland, who believed that local Protestants were not carrying out reform quickly enough or thoroughly enough. Rejecting their own Catholic baptisms, the small group received believers' baptism in January, 1525, and refused to perform any more infant baptisms. Although the movement was persistently harassed by Catholic, Lutheran, and Reformed leaders, eventually Anabaptists spread beyond Switzerland and into many other parts of Europe even as it developed into several branches.

Besides their strong beliefs in adult, or "believer's" baptism, Anabaptists were among the earliest proponents of what we call today the separation of church and state. Since the churches of Europe were extensions of the civil government for the territories in which the church was situated, Anabaptists believed that the established churches were corrupted by secular politics, worldly affairs, violence, wealth, and power. They were convinced that they needed to create congregations that were free from these political entanglements and have, for this reason, comprised a significant part of the "free church" tradition. While the other main branches of the Protestant Reformation retained the church's strong ties with local political authorities, only the Anabaptists rejected both the church establishment and its alliance with the state. Thus they were both religious and political separatists, believing that the teachings of Jesus demanded such a stance as articulated in the Sermon on the Mount.

Along with believer's baptism, separation from the world (sometimes called "nonconformity") became a hallmark of Anabaptism.

Count the Cost:
A Hymn of Alexander Mack

Collections of hymns were important to 18th century Pietists and were foundational to fostering the kind of spiritual life Pietists valued. Hymns were not just sung during times of gathered worship, but were also used as devotional readings by individuals and families. Along with prayer books, a Bible, and perhaps a catechism or collection of biographies, hymnals were an essential part of a family's devotional tools. The Brethren published their first hymnal, the *Geistreiches Gesung-Buch*, in 1720. Included in this collection was Alexander Mack's *Count the Cost*, which was likely sung at baptisms. It represents the emphasis that the early Brethren placed on believer's baptism as well as the important role of devotional practices and personal piety. The translation below was made by Brethren scholar, Hedda Durnbaugh. Although *Count [Well] the Cost* has been adapted for singing in English, Durnbaugh intended this particular translation to capture the literal ideas of Mack, rather than something that could be put to a melody.[1]

"Count the cost," says Jesus Christ, when you will lay the foundation. Are you willing, in your own mind, to risk your wealth, body, possessions, and your honor, in following Christ's example, as you are about to promise?

Through baptism you are buried into Christ's death and will no longer be allowed to be your own, if you are minded to be co-inheritor with Christ's Church and his bride, whom he has created through his word.

If you hate sin from the bottom of your heart, you will succeed; gird yourself with righteousness and you will be able to do battle with your enemy, the god of the world, who is obstructing your path.

The child is formed in the bosom of the church according to the Father's will. His spirit fills it and removed the [old] garments, the childish indecision disappears, and the child becomes an adult according to Christ's mind.

As Anabaptist theology developed, this theology of separation has come to represent a distinct "Two Kingdom" theology. The kingdom of God and the kingdom of the world have existed throughout human history, but their values are diametrically opposed to each other. God's kingdom values are embodied in the beatitudes: love, mercy, peace, and meekness. The world's kingdom values have always been power, corruption, violence, and greed. God's kingdom leads to harmony and fellowship; the world's kingdom leads to war and injustice. Because human governments are the seat of this world's power, they are especially implicated in the evils of the world, and Anabaptists have lived in various degrees of separation from the state, especially choosing to resist participation in the violence and blood-shed of state-sponsored war.[9]

Although they originated as two distinct movements, Pietists and Anabaptists had a lot in common. They were both estranged from the established churches and the existing religious authorities. They both had radical and moderate factions and they both sought a higher order of spiritual commitment that included deep biblicism, godly living, and strong communities. And members of both groups were often forced to flee all over Europe in search of places where their communities would be tolerated. It is not surprising, then, that Pietists and Anabaptists sometimes associated within the same circles and even exerted mutual influence on each other. The Schwarzenau Brethren are a prime example. Mack and Hochmann had rubbed shoulders with Anabaptists and were certainly familiar with the Anabaptist tradition. Although it would be too simplistic to conclude that Mack simply borrowed the notion of believer's baptism from other local Anabaptists, he was well aware that the Schwarzenau Brethren were a "new" manifestation of the Anabaptist tradition. They called themselves "New Baptists" in fact, and referred to the original Anabaptists as "old Baptists." (We should remember that in this context, "Baptist" was synonymous with "Anabaptist" and is not to be confused with the Baptists with which most American evangelicals are familiar today, who have only a small connection to European Anabaptism. The various American Baptist denominations have stronger historic ties to English Puritanism than Anabaptism in continental Europe.)

Many Pietists and Anabaptists made their way to Pennsylvania in the 18th century, taking advantage of the freedom of conscience,

This adult is incorporated [into the church] to grow into a fruitful vine. To this end he will often be offered the bread of fellowship when the church gathers who are Christ's body and members.

They are truly in the house of God where God teaches them through his son, of whom it is said that one should listen to him in all that he teaches which is sealed through his own blood.

His testament is still as valid as it was a thousand years ago with the disciples to whom God had revealed it through signs, miracles, and through power, through which the old was abolished.

When later on it was destroyed, there was no evidence of any sign anymore. When Joshua heard it read, he believed and no longer asked for a sign.

Whoever believes in the word of God will not demand a sign, for Christ reprimanded the evil band whose unbelief became manifest when they demanded a sign. When he did accede, they did not believe it.

O dear soul, remember the words which Abraham said to the rich man who, after he had died, asked Lazarus to tell his brothers about the agony and pain that they might believe it.

Abraham denied him this, he took it as unbelief. Their hearts had to be directed towards faith in God and his word, as the writings of Moses and the prophets directed towards Christ, the light.

Keep your heart from false teachings and do not be deceived by those who pretend that they, too, listen to Christ. If someone does not follow Christ's word in his own teaching, then what such a person says is not true.

Arise, dear soul, the time is now to stem the evil, for Christ himself goes into battle against those who will not listen to him in his outer and inner word. But those who do, have the mind Christ.

1. Mack's *Count the Cost* is reproduced here from William R. Eberly, Ed. *The Complete Writings of Alexander Mack* (Winona Lake: BMH Books, 1991), 107-111. On Brethren hymnody, see Hedwig Durnbaugh, *The German Hymnody of the Brethren, 1720-1903* (Philadelphia: Brethren Encyclopedia, 1986) and Tanya Kevorkian, "Early Brethren Hymn-Singing Practices in Context," *Brethren Life and Thought* 58 (2013), 59-65.

which existed there due to William Penn's commitment to religious tolerance. How did Pietism and Anabaptism fare in the American context? Both movements struggled to retain a sense of distinctiveness, which in most cases, was tied directly to ethnic and therefore cultural/linguistic identity. Pietism contributed much to American Evangelicalism—much more than it often gets credit for, in fact. Anabaptists, however, including the Brethren, were understandably more wary of Americanization as their identity was more fully defined in terms of cultural separation. Retaining distinctive communities, dress, and customs, as well as a general wariness of political involvement, Anabaptists repeatedly divided over cultural issues. Like other Anabaptists, the Brethren movement in America felt these tensions and experienced several splits. The Brethren Church, (not to be confused with the Church of the Brethren) chose a more progressive path in the 1880s and embraced greater degrees of American religiosity including Sunday Schools and higher education, as well as moving toward more cultural assimilation. For many Anabaptists in America, evangelicalism, with its penchant toward generic, revivalist, and nationalist religiosity, has represented a corrupting influence, slowly eroding historic Anabaptist distinctiveness.[10]

Evangelicalism

In a general historical and theological sense evangelicalism can be defined by using a "quadrilateral" defined by historian David Bebbington. According to Bebbington, evangelicals have always emphasized the redemptive work of Christ ("crucicentrism"), the importance of biblical authority ("Biblicism"), belief in the necessity of conversion ("conversionism") and have looked for the fruit of genuine faith to be lived-out in society ("activism"). These four qualities can be seen quite easily in the formative period of American evangelicalism, such as in the First Great Awakening, an eighteenth century phenomenon that laid the foundation for evangelicalism's affinity for revivalism. The impulse toward social activism matured in the nineteenth century and flowered in a myriad of social reform movements that overlapped with the rise of fundamentalism in the 1920s.[11]

Fundamentalism was essentially a response to modern developments that unsettled many Christians in America. As the United States became increasingly involved in foreign nations, barbarism seemed for the first time to threaten western civilization. On the home front, the struggles of urbanization, a sexual revolution, and economic disaster brought tremendous change to the nation. In intellectual circles, Darwinism had for decades seemed to threaten traditional notions of origins. Freud's theories called into question traditional understandings of the human psyche, and German scholars were applying methods of literary criticism to the Bible. Modernity, many Christians came to believe, was not turning out to be a friend to old-time religion.

What was most unsettling for many, however, was in the realm of theology and biblical understandings. Theological "modernists," believing that traditional understandings of Christianity were incompatible with modern scholarship, felt constrained to accommodate to the new understandings, but in the process gave up belief in miracles, traditional understandings of the redemptive work of Christ, and the long-established notions about how the Bible developed as a codified text. A tremendous amount of conflict ensued as conservatives, who styled themselves "fundamentalists," circled the wagons around a short list of essential doctrines on which "true" Christians would never compromise. After decades of struggle, fundamentalists conceded victory to the "liberals" and withdrew from "mainline" Protestantism only to successfully form a large network of Bible Colleges, newly formed denominations, parachurch organizations, media outlets, and charismatic preachers.[12]

These events, to a large extent, framed the beginning years of Grace Theological Seminary and later, the college as well. Alva J. McClain, the first president of the seminary grew up in the last decades of the nineteenth century and was familiar with the schisms within Brethren circles, having experienced them as a child. McClain's family had sided with the Progressive Brethren, so he grew up in an Anabaptist environment that had already decided to move closer to the American—and evangelical—mainstream. The trend would continue as McClain and his colleagues also gravitated toward American fundamentalism. This took place largely through his undergraduate and seminary training as well as the influence of significant people in his life. He studied at the Bible Institute of Los Angeles, a Bible school at the center of the evangelical movement and was influenced by fundamentalist leaders such as R. A. Torrey and dispensationalists such as C. I. Scofield, for example. But while the Grace Brethren churches would move toward the evangelical mainstream, McClain did not intend for the congregations that followed his lead to divorce themselves from their Anabaptist and Pietist moorings. Rather he saw fundamentalism as a means to retain the biblicism within Brethrenism as well as to reform the older heritage.[13]

For much of the history of the Grace campus, the seminary that McClain founded has taken center stage, being viewed as the heart of the institution. Indeed, when the undergraduate program was added in 1948, it was only to serve as a two-year "division" of the seminary and was essentially meant to prepare students for theological training. The first three presidents—Alva J. McClain, Herman Hoyt, and Homer Kent, Jr.—were first and foremost seminarians. McClain and Hoyt had garnered reverent esteem for their connections with what was believed to be a valiant stand for truth at Ashland Seminary, from which they had been dismissed. Additionally, nationally known figures, such as the magnetic fundamentalist John C. Whitcomb brought notoriety to the seminary.

The undergraduate division was founded (1948) as a liberal arts college and its curriculum has always followed this educational model. Early on, however, the curriculum was melded with a campus environment that was not unlike a Bible College. It included a strong emphasis on missions, simple Bible truths, codes of conduct, theological and behavioral "covenants" that had to be signed, and healthy doses of discipline. Although the Bible College Movement, beginning in the 1930s, produced a new vanguard of Christian workers during the first half of the twentieth-century, these institutions often shied away from mainstream intellectual culture, at times failing to engage the broader academic world. Moving more fully into this sort of cultural ethos, and with its Anabaptist roots, the Grace campus has sometimes shared these separatist tendencies.

It was not until the seminary suffered a major setback during 1989 and 1990 that the undergraduate college emerged from behind the shadow of the seminary and fully came into its own as a liberal arts institution. This process began under President John Davis and was carried further through the influence of Ronald Manahan, vice president of academic affairs and provost under Davis and later president. Davis and Manahan, along with faculty members such as New Testament professor Skip Forbes, steered the undergraduate college, which has become the institution's center of gravity, toward a more Kuyperian approach to Christian higher education.

Abraham Kuyper, a Dutch Reformed theologian whose writing is foundational for the commonly cited notion, "all truth is God's truth," believed that if every area of study was under God's dominion, then every area, even if it seemed "secular," could have a Christian interpretation if approached with Christian presuppositions. Kuyper's philosophy, which Reformed schools, such as Calvin College, have successfully applied to Christian education, was of immense importance to what Cornerstone University provost Rick Ostrander has called the "revival" of academic vitality in evangelical higher education in America since the 1970s. This revival included the founding of the Council for Christian Colleges and Universities (CCCU), established in 1976 with 38 member institutions; and today has 100 member institutions, most of which would be somewhere in the evangelical orbit. Grace joined the CCCU in 1977 and more recently has embraced the Reformed model of faith "integration" and "worldview" development, although differences exist among the faculty as to exactly what this means and how it relates to "biblical integration." As it has moved out of fundamentalism and into evangelicalism, Grace College and Seminary, like many CCCU institutions, could also be considered among what well-known historian George Marsden has called "post-fundamentalist" institutions, although Grace is a comparative newcomer to this group.

The Kuyperian model has been beneficial to institutions like Grace where a defensive posture may have at times stifled robust academic engagement. But this shift is not without potential tensions. We might wonder if valuable parts of the Brethren tradition have been lost in the process. Or to what extent is the evangelical strand compatible with the older Pietist and Anabaptist strands? As mentioned above, Anabaptists have often resented evangelical influence since this influence usually goes hand-in-hand with a loss of Anabaptist distinctiveness. Some charge evangelicals, for example, with emphasizing individual religious experience at the expense of communal commitments or for promoting what they believe is a watered-down version of discipleship. For Anabaptists, the "evangelicalization" of their denominations has been difficult to distinguish from "Americanization."[14] American evangelicals have also viewed Anabaptists with suspicion. As evangelicals have increasingly turned to right-wing political activism, the fact that Anabaptists have been critical of the Religious Right and have withheld support for military activity has seemed un-American, un-Christian, and perhaps even threatening. Combined with this is the fact that evangelicals have been surprised that many Anabaptist institutions, with their long history of traditionalism, could embrace a "liberal" social and theological orientation.[15]

Tensions have also existed among evangelicals concerning Pietism. Some evangelicals, particularly those in the Reformed camp, have been wary of what they believe are Pietism's excesses—its separatist tendencies, its enthusiasm, or its experiential theology. Much of the criticism of Pietism by evangelicals can be boiled down to the belief that it has not been intellectual enough, not Reformed enough, or simply too loose on doctrine (essentially the same criticisms leveled against Pietists in the 18th century). Ironically, Pietism has been blamed for the anti-intellectualism in fundamentalism as well as for the existential components of liberalism. In both cases, the problem is a stereotypical conclusion that sentimental faith produces doctrinal compromise, which may be manifest in both emotionalism and rationalism. Some of the most recent criticisms of Pietists among evangelicals have been in regard to higher education. Indeed, for some evangelicals, Pietism has been interpreted as a grave threat to authentic Christian education. As David Dockery charges, Pietism is to blame "for the divorce of faith from teaching and scholarship in universities across the country in the arts, the humanities, the sciences, the social sciences, and all other spheres, including the scholarly study of religion."[16]

In sum, the heritage of Grace College and Seminary is diverse and eclectic. Taken together, Anabaptism, Pietism, and American evangelicalism have included those who have engaged the world and those who fled from it. This heritage has included those who embraced creeds and those who rejected them. There have been radicals and moderates, conservatives and progressives, Calvinists and Wesleyans, as well as dispensationalists and non-dispensationalists.

Given these tensions and difficulties, it could be tempting to see this eclectic heritage, with its variety and even opposing impulses, as something of a curse. Clearly, we are tempted to think, it would be easier to grasp a distinctive identity if we could point to a unified tradition with clear and agreed-upon boundaries. Yet it is likely that the interplay of these three strands, as well as the diverse sub-strands that weave their way throughout, has the potential to shape a robust academic environment. We know that iron sharpens iron and multiple perspectives make for vibrant conversations and creative syntheses. Each of these strands has strengths that can serve the educational enterprise well.

Pietism, for example, has not been opposed to education and academic pursuits as some have argued. Nor has it rejected powerful social engagement. With its desire for spiritual renewal, Pietism's Christocentric, service-oriented approach to the Christian faith can contribute much to our efforts for "holistic" Christian education. What is more, Pietism's emphasis on spiritual dispositions may hold much for elevating Christian scholarship.[17] Anabaptism too, has much to offer. At a time when the hegemony of the "Moral Majority" approach to evangelical witness has largely been eclipsed, many young evangelicals may likely find in the Anabaptist worldview a stronger avenue for "radical" discipleship and intentional community. Instead of fundamentalism's triumphalism, Anabaptism's sensitivity to social justice and its desire to maintain a peace witness within a world of violence and strife may also be welcomed by many younger evangelicals.

Institutions like Grace, says Darrel Tippen, are like mosaics, weaving together sometimes diverse threads that include history, theological approach, and even patterns of ethnicity. Often, the mosaic will include elements that are shared with other institutions. Indeed, we may use many of the same pieces. But the overall picture that emerges in the midst of all these factors is unique to us and can be, as it should, quite distinctive from other colleges and universities.[18] In light of this analogy, rather than a hindrance, this varied heritage should inspire vibrant conversation about how Pietism, Anabaptism, and evangelicalism intersect, why tensions exist, and what these strands have to offer to the Grace mosaic.

Notes

1. Grace is certainly not alone in this regard. One thinks of nearby Bethel College (Mishawaka, Indiana) and its affiliation with the Missionary Church, a denomination that traces its identity from five distinct traditions. The Missionary Church Historical Society has recently devoted an issue of its journal, *Reflections*, to an examination of these five traditions (Anabaptism, Pietism, Wesleyanism, Keswickianism, and Evangelicalism). *Reflections* 13-14 (2011-2012).

2. Various descriptions and defenses of Brethren ordinances have been written in the last century, including that of David R. Plaster, long time Grace Brethren pastor and seminary professor, who wrote *Ordinances: What are They?* (Winona Lake: BMH Books, 1985). For a more recent sociological treatment, see Carl F. Bowman, *Brethren Society: The Cultural Transformation of a "Peculiar People"* (Baltimore: Johns Hopkins University Press, 1995) 51-71.

3. Within each of these are smaller threads. The Pietist tradition includes both "radical" and moderate strands, for instance, and in Anabaptism, we find both progressive and traditionalist strands as well as distinctive ideals such as nonviolence and nonconformity to the world. In American Evangelicalism we find a fundamentalist strand along with dispensationalism and its eschatological handmaiden, premillennialism.

4. Of particular importance is Douglas H. Shantz's recent book, *An Introduction to German Pietism: Protestant Renewal at the Dawn of Modern Europe* (Baltimore: The Johns Hopkins University Press, 2013). A dated, but still wonderfully readable book is Dale W. Brown, *Understanding Pietism*, Rev. ed. (Nappanee: Evangel Publishing House, 1996).

5. K. James Stein and Markus Matthias provide helpful summaries of the importance of Spener and Francke respectively in Carter Lindberg, *The Pietist Theologians* (Malden, MA: Blackwell Publishing, 2005) 84-99, 100-114.

6. For Pietism's transatlantic nature and its North American manifestation, consult W. R. Ward, *The Protestant Evangelical Awakening* (Cambridge: Cambridge University Press, 2002), the essays in F. Ernest Stoeffler, ed., *Continental Pietism and Early American Christianity* (Grand Rapids, William B. Eerdmans Publishing Company, 1976), as well as Parts Five and Six in Christian Collins Winn, Christopher Gehrz, G. William Carlson and Eric Holst, eds., *The Pietist Impulse in Christianity* (Eugene, OR: Pickwick Publications, 2011) 175-284.

7. One of the best reads on radical pietism is Gerald McDonald's English translation of Hans Schneider, *German Radical Pietism* (Lanham, MD: Scarecrow Press, 2007). Recent literature on early American varieties of radical Pietism, namely the Moravians at Bethlehem and the Ephrata Brethren, include Craig Atwood, *Community of the Cross: Moravian Piety in Colonial Bethlehem* (University Park: Pennsylvania State University Press, 2004) and Jeff Bach, *Voices of the Turtledoves: The Sacred World of Ephrata* (University Park: Pennsylvania State University Press, 2002).

8. The definitive study on the early Brethren at Schwarzenau to date is Marcus Meier, *The Origin of the Schwarzenau Brethren*, Dennis Slabaugh, trans. (Winona

Lake: Brethren Encyclopedia, 2008). On Hochmann, see Heinz Renkewitz, *Hochmann von Hochenau 1670-1721*, William G. Willoughby, trans. (Winona Lake: Brethren Encyclopedia, 1993). Alexander Mack's works have been translated and compiled in William R. Eberly, ed., *The Complete Writings of Alexander Mack* (Winona Lake: Brethren Encyclopedia, 1991). It is unclear if Mack accompanied Hochmann on preaching tours. Several authors state that he did, although according to Jeff Bach, there is no documentary evidence of this.

9. Helpful texts on Anabaptist history and distinctives would include William R. Estep, *The Anabaptist Story* (Grand Rapids: Wm. B. Eerdmans Publishing Co., 1995), Steven M. Nolt and Harry Loewen, *Through Fire and Water: An Overview of Mennonite History* (Scottdale, PA: Herald Press, 1996), and Stuart Murray, *The Naked Anabaptist: The Bare Essentials of a Radical Faith* (Scottdale, PA: Herald Press, 2012.)

10. On the Brethren relationship and tensions with American society, see Bowman, *Brethren Society*. These issues are explored within a broader Anabaptist context in Jared S. Burkholder and David C. Cramer, eds., *The Activist Impulse: Essays on the Intersection of Anabaptism and Evangelicalism* (Eugene, OR: Pickwick Publications, 2012).

11. David Bebbington lays out his "quadrilateral" in *Evangelicals in Modern Britain: A History from the 1730s to the 1980s* (Rutledge, 1989). A readable history of evangelicalism in America is Barry Hankins, *American Evangelicals: A Contemporary History of a Mainstream Religious Movement* (Rowman and Littlefield Publishers, 2009).

12. Amid the increasingly large body of specific studies, George Marsden's *Fundamentalism and American Culture: The Shaping of Twentieth-Century Evangelicalism 1870-1925 (Oxford: Oxford University Press, 1980)* remains the defining history of fundamentalism. This narrative is continued in Joel A. Carpenter, *Revive Us Again: The Reawakening of American Fundamentalism* (Oxford: Oxford University Press, 1997.)

13. On McClain and the events that surrounded the beginnings of the Grace Brethren movement, see M. M. Norris, "A Cord of Many Strands: Reexamining Grace Brethren Identity and the Fundamentalism of Alva J. McClain" in Burkholder and Cramer, *The Activist Impulse*, as well as Dale Stoffer, *A Gleam of Shining Hope: The Story of Theological Education and Christian Witness at Ashland Theological Seminary and Ashland College* (Ashland, OH: Ashland Theological Seminary, 2007).

14. See Richard Kyle, *Evangelicalism: An Americanized Christianity* (New Brunswick, NJ: Transaction Publications of Rutgers University, 2006).

15. On this transition, see Ervin R. Stutzman, *From Nonresistance to Justice: The Transformation of Mennonite Church Peace Rhetoric, 1908-2008* (Scottdale, PA: Herald Press, 2011).

16. Dockery took a similar dualistic line in a presentation at Grace College and Seminary, listing Pietism along with the Enlightenment, "Specialization," Liberalism, Fundamentalism, Pragmatism, Civil Religion, and Postmodernism, and blaming them for derailing Christian higher education. Renewing Minds Faculty Lecture, August 24, 2010.

17. For engaging essays on the potential for the Pietist tradition to inspire excellence in Christian higher education, see Christopher Gehrz, ed., *The Pietist Vision of Christian Higher Education: Forming Whole and Holy Persons* (Downers Grove: IVP Academic, 2014).

18. Darryl Tippens, "Scholars and Witnesses: the Christian University Difference," in *The Soul of a Christian University: A Field Guide for Educators* (Abilene, TX: Abilene Christian University Press, 2008), 26.

Chapter 2

Beginnings

Revisiting the Departure from Ashland

M. M. Norris

WHATEVER COMPETING INTERPRETATIONS ABOUT THE FOUNDING OF Grace Theological Seminary that have emerged since 1937, there is no disputing the fact that the school was born amid a nasty struggle in Ashland, Ohio. In the late nineteenth and early twentieth centuries, this small Midwest town was the center for the Brethren Church in America and home of its flagship institution of higher education, Ashland College and Seminary (now Ashland University). Although Ashland began as an undergraduate institution in 1878, the graduate seminary was not founded until 1930 by Alva J. McClain (who would later become Grace's first president) and his friend and senior colleague, J. Allen Miller. McClain had hesitations from the start about the seminary's being housed on the Ashland campus. He believed that the culture of the undergraduate campus and internal politics might prevent him from building a truly distinctive Brethren seminary. Still, McClain took the position as its first academic dean, but by 1936, a rift was developing between the seminary faculty, including McClain, and Ashland's senior administration. The rift widened into a chasm in 1937 and the disgruntled seminary faculty were fired after they refused to step down. They soon founded Grace Theological Seminary.

Given the fact that today the number of students who attend Ashland University number around six thousand,[1] it is important to note that the college was quite small in 1937 and had experienced its share of challenges. Prior to 1900, financial pressures twice forced the college to close its doors. Then, in 1934, Ashland lost its North Central Accreditation, resulting in another financial downturn.[2] As for the graduate seminary in 1937, it was only seven years old and had just four full-time faculty members. Average enrollment was less than twenty-five.[3] This is important since the schism was not a split *within* the seminary at Ashland. It was rather a departure, albeit forced, of the founding seminary faculty cohort from the institution. This was devastating for Ashland's attempts to build a seminary because in such a fledgling program the departure of its primary faculty members was as if the seminary was torn out before it had any real chance to blossom. Adding insult to injury, most of the students followed the departing faculty members. Only two seminary students, in fact, remained at Ashland. This happened within one of the worst economic times in American history, deep within the Great Depression.

McClain later acknowledged that the schism was tantamount to a wholesale removal of the seminary when he stated that he and his compatriots simply carried on the work of "the wrecked seminary reorganized under a new name."[4] As late as 1951, Grace Seminary was actually back-dating their founding by using 1931[5]—the first full year of *Ashland* Seminary's existence—as the beginning of their own institution, not 1937, the year of their departure from Ashland and "reorganization." Indeed, the Grace yearbook for 1951 was a special commemorative edition because it was celebrating the seminary's supposed twentieth anniversary. (If this dating would still be in use, at the time of this writing we would be celebrating 81 years, rather than 75!)

Eventually, the controversy at Ashland led to a schism in the Brethren Church, as individual congregations aligned themselves with either the Ashland or Grace side. In some cases, members of a tradition that represented peace and reconciliation resorted to arguments and even lawsuits to settle property disputes when divided congregations could not make peace. The battle also extended to annual conference gatherings, when emotions ran high and both sides felt betrayed by the other. The uproar was particularly devastating since the Brethren Church was small at the time. It numbered just over 30,000 members—smaller than some mega-churches today.[6]

The great majority of what has been written about the split that gave rise to Grace Theological Seminary was authored by seminary and church leaders who were close to the events. While this proximity provided certain obvious advantages, it has also meant that the events have often been infused with spiritual meaning, and the individuals involved occupy a hallowed place in the narrative. Not at all uncommon, historians refer to this sort of writing as hagiography, or "saintly accounts." A perfect example of this was Norman B. Rohrer's 1986 biography of McClain in which the title alone represents the kind of narrative it contains: *A Saint in Glory Stands: the Story of Alva J. McClain, founder of Grace Theological Seminary.*[7] These accounts have tended to focus on the Ashland/Grace split through theological lenses and sometimes left out important players, as will be shown. On the Grace side, such theological interpretations have also made use of the language of the fundamentalist/modernist debates. Ashland is painted as an institution that was "lost to liberal forces" and had set aside its biblical roots.[8] This is represented well in Homer A. Kent Sr.'s *Conquering Frontiers: A History of the Brethren Church* (1972).[9] One exception, however, is Todd Scoles' *Restoring the Household* (2008), which weighs perspectives and actions on both sides of the controversy with more nuances.[10]

For their part, historians on the Ashland side have viewed the Grace group as having been co-opted by the fundamentalist movement and as a result, gave up much of their Brethren identity. The classic work here is Albert T. Ronk's *The History of the Brethren Church* (1968).[11] This interpretation has been softened through helpful nuancing in Dale R. Stoffer's *A Gleam of Shining Hope: The Story of Theological Education and Christian Witness at Ashland Theological Seminary and Ashland College/University* (2007), but even this relies on a fundamentalist/Brethren dualism.[12]

Although there is no doubt that the fundamentalist/modernist debates did frame part of the context of the schism at Ashland and that the founders of Grace Seminary were influenced by American fundamentalism, this does not fully account for the events that transpired. This chapter seeks to re-examine those early controversies with a more critical eye than previous treatments, providing a greater sense of nuance. It argues that although the schism was imbued with theological meaning in its aftermath, a critical look at the sources reveals that the controversy had much to do with institutional politics, competing visions of Christian higher education, and strong personalities. Although theological wrangling was clearly part of the situation, the events were more complex than has sometimes been recognized. As a means of accomplishing this, we begin with a description of Louis S. Bauman, who has traditionally been overlooked, but who was one of the most significant players on the Grace side.

The Progressive L. S. Bauman and His Protégés

In such a small educational institution as Ashland and in such a minor body as the Brethren Church, it is not surprising that a few personalities were dominant. Louis Sylvester Bauman (1875-1950) was one of those personalities. Today at Grace College a commemorative plaque honoring Bauman is affixed to a wall outside of Ashman Chapel in McClain Hall, but there is little else left to his memory. Understandably, most narratives about the founding of Grace Theological Seminary have focused on Alva J. McClain, the school's first president. McClain helped define the new Grace Theological Seminary, but earlier, it was perhaps Bauman who represented the most significant driving force behind the circumstances that led to starting a new institution. Indeed, Bauman's unlimited energy, highly focused sense of purpose, and sheer doggedness, even in the midst of personal suffering and obstacles, enabled his protégés, including McClain, to lead the new seminary to set out on its own, forge something new, and begin to grow. Bauman was, in fact, not unlike the Roman *paterfamilias*—the male head of an extended family who held authority as well as supported and protected the family. Herman Hoyt, in fact, eulogized Bauman by saying, "No one will ever be able to compute accurately the contribution made by Dr. Louis S. Bauman to education in general and theological education in particular within the Brethren Church and outside until we reach that golden shore...humanly speaking, perhaps no one had more to do with the support of the school [Grace Seminary] than Dr. L. S. Bauman." Bauman was a patriarch who fostered a circle of younger men who were sometimes called "Bauman's boys"[13] The group included three instrumental individuals, Alva J. McClain, R. Paul Miller, and Homer Kent Sr.

Bauman was not a newcomer to Brethrenism. His father, William J. H. Bauman (1837-1922), served as a Brethren pastor for the whole of his adult working life. A highlight of his career was in helping to organize the Brethren Church at Dayton, Ohio, in 1883, and then he moved his family in 1888 to Indiana where he also served. Louis followed in his father's footsteps. As a child, therefore, Louis's family was in the midst of the 1881-1883 split of the German Baptist Brethren into the Old German Baptists (Old Orders, 1881), the German Baptists (Conservatives—later renamed the Church of the Brethren), and the Progressive Brethren (or the Brethren Church, 1883).[14]

Louis overcame early hardships, such as having his foot severed at age 9 when it was caught in a mowing machine. He thereafter wore a prosthesis, which caused him some discomfort throughout his life.[15] At eleven, the precocious young Bauman wrote a letter to the editor of his denomination's lead publication, *The Brethren Evangelist*.[16] The letter, which warned of the evils of smoking, thus began two strong currents that flowed throughout his life: a call for Christians to reform and a prolific writing career that included several books and hundreds of articles and letters to denominational publications as well as several thousand more unpublished letters (often very lengthy) to friends, acquaintances, missionaries, and colleagues.

His preaching career began at the young age of seventeen and he was ordained two years later. Although he had a high school diploma, as a teacher and minister he was self-taught. He became a teacher in Kansas and then in Illinois where he also pastored. His first wife, Mary Melissa Wageman, was an ordained elder, and she increasingly filled the pulpit for him as his prophecy ministry grew. However, the death of his son, Glenn, in 1907 left him in despair. He found answers to his depression through Bible prophecy, which was a major focus of his preaching and writing. In addition to holding prophecy conferences, Bauman authored books on the subject, such as his 1934 *God and Gog or The Coming Meet between Judah's Lion and Russia's Bear*.[17] He also contributed numerous articles to the Bible Institute of Los Angeles' *The Kings Business*, one of the best-known premillennial fundamentalist journals.[18] His wife, Mary, contracted typhoid fever and died in 1909 leaving him with a daughter,

Iva Muriel, and a son Paul R. Three years later he married Retta Virginia Stover, who gave him a more permanent sense of stability in his ministry.[19]

Although we may be tempted to see Bauman as larger than life, he was as complicated a figure as anyone. He had a very passionate and driven personality that could at times be volcanic and impulsive. Once he resigned from his church only to be asked to be reinstated. After a church board meeting, he apologized profusely for having discredited a brother. At times he could be cross with both his children and his missionaries in the foreign field. He resigned from the board at Ashland in a fit of fury only to put his name forward for nomination soon after. Yet the driven personality of this rugged trail blazer and builder provided an amazing degree of focus that helped to forge a new seminary.

Bauman was also very progressive within the Brethren context. He believed in racial integration, for example, and he saw no biblical reason to bar women from preaching. Unlike others, he had no qualms about raising money—first for Ashland and then for Grace— and was a tireless fundraiser, in fact. [20] He even speculated in early oil exploration in Southern California. Foreign missions, another mark of progressivism, was a dominant theme in Bauman's life. At the General Conference of the Brethren Church in 1896 he was first inspired about missions by a Methodist seminary dean. J. C. Cassel and his brother, H. C. Cassel, influenced him as well. Bauman soon helped pioneer modern missions in progressive Brethren circles. In 1900, Bauman, A. V. Kimmell, and J. C. Cassell were unsuccessful in persuading the Brethren General Conference to organize a denominational foreign mission society so they went outside of the conference meeting and with others organized the Foreign Missionary Society of the Brethren Church (FMS) and made it autonomous.[21] H. C. Cassell was one of 53 charter members[22] of the FMS in 1900 and Bauman joined their board of trustees in 1904. He would then serve as the board's secretary from 1906 until 1945. He was an itinerant field secretary for the FMS and the Missionary Board in Ashland, Ohio, from roughly 1907-1912. In addition, he was financial secretary and treasurer for the FMS from 1918 until his death in 1950. He served as a guest editor for special missions pieces in *The Brethren Evangelist* (1935-1939) as well as editor for mission-related sections of *The*

Brethren Missionary Herald (1940-1950). He thus came to embody foreign missions as much as anyone in Progressive Brethren circles.[23]

Defining Fundamentalism

Bauman's progressivism was linked with his involvement in the growing fundamentalist movement. Today, we don't often think of ties with fundamentalism as something progressive. But in a Brethren context, this was indeed the case—because such participation represented increased involvement with mainstream religious currents, which the Brethren have traditionally been hesitant about. For good or for ill, "fundamentalism" is a term that has evolved since first used in the 1920s. In its original historical context evangelical Christians coined the term themselves, proclaiming that they would do "battle royal" for the essential "fundamentals" of orthodox Christianity in the face of theological "modernism," which many believed sacrificed too much in an effort to harmonize traditional belief with modern ways of thinking.[24] Beyond an emphasis on safeguarding doctrinal purity, fundamentalists also created a tangible subculture, especially as they became marginalized by the ascendency of mainline theological currents after the 1925 Scopes "Monkey Trial."[25] This subculture coalesced around a web of charismatic leaders, radio programs, publications, conference gatherings, and parachurch organizations, including the Bible conferences at Winona Lake. In more recent years, however, fundamentalism has been used in comparative discourse to identify any manner of radical religious behavior or belief in any religious context.[26] Although there is merit to this usage, it has made it more difficult to talk about fundamentalism in its original context. While fundamentalism has always been viewed in a negative light by its opponents, its use as a comparative category of religion has imbued it with additional layers of pejorative meaning. If this is the case, why employ it here?

However broad the meaning of fundamentalism has become, it still represents an historic movement within American Protestantism that historians and other scholars study and write about. The fact that it remains an established category within American religious history means that a substantial body of literature has been constructed, and if we use the term skillfully, new studies—such as this one—can engage with a preexisting conversation. In this chapter then, and in those that follow, fundamentalism refers merely to this defined historical movement and is not used as a label meant to imply judgment, whether positive or negative.

Like others in his circle, Bauman's ties with the fundamentalist movement did not eclipse his Brethren identity. He affirmed the doctrine of nonresistance, for example, and was critical of Ashland for allowing an early ROTC program on campus to help recruit soldiers for World War I.[27] The US Department of Justice even warned him in 1918 that he may be in violation of the Espionage Act because of his nonresistant statements in *The Faith Once for all Delivered unto the Saints* (1906-1909).[28] He also did not believe in the swearing of oaths and had a strong belief in the necessity of the Brethren ordinances of feetwashing and trine immersion for the obedient believer. All of these points became part of the Grace Seminary Covenant of Faith.[29]

His prophecy ministry established a progressive Brethren presence in Southern California. At the time, California was becoming one of the fastest growing states in America and Bauman decided to hold evangelistic tent meetings in both Los Angeles and Long Beach, California, in 1911 and 1912. He was so successful that these meetings led to the establishment of the First Brethren Church of Long Beach. This became the largest and most powerful congregation in the Brethren Church, and eventually shifted a significant portion of influence within the Brethren Church from the Pennsylvania and Ohio regions to California. This would later contribute to the schism at Ashland since Bauman represented a substantial, but far removed geographic base of Brethren constituents. He pastored in Long Beach until 1948, two years before his death. In California, Bauman came into contact with R. A. Torrey and the Bible Institute of Los Angeles, and he soon established a generation of leaders. He and his circle would grow to help define progressive Brethren theologically, missionally, and to an extent even educationally. Bauman's circle had as a well-defined goal to transform the work of the Brethren for the cause of Christ. R. Paul Miller was instrumental in helping Bauman establish Brethren Home Missions. Homer Kent, Sr. became one of the first faculty members at the new seminary after he moved his family from Washington D.C., including his son, Homer Jr., Grace's third president. Kent Sr. also became a vice-president at Grace as well as the author of *Conquering Frontiers*.

Alva J. McClain

Bauman's greatest pupil, however, was McClain. Alva was born in 1888 in Aurelia, Iowa, to Walter Scott McClain and Mary Ellen Gnagey McClain. Walter was from a Scottish background and was both a preacher ordained by H. R. Holsinger and a pig farmer.[30] His mother was from Swedish ancestry and was raised in a Pennsylvania German community. Moving west, the family lived for a time in the Arizona Territory and then Los Angeles before settling permanently in Sunnyside, Washington, where McClain's father purchased land. Walter and a partner organized the Yakima-Sunnyside Nursery Company where they grew pedigree fruit trees.[31] McClain's father gave him a lot of freedom as a teenager, and he was somewhat of a maverick as a youth. In Washington, the young "Mick," as his friends called him, was a star athlete. A baseball injury, however, left him sickly the rest of this life.[32]

McClain experienced a profound conversion while at one of Bauman's prophecy conferences and then, after attending Washington College, he followed Bauman's advice and enrolled in the Bible Institute of Los Angeles from 1911-1915 where he studied under R. A. Torrey. At the same time, he worked as a Sunday school teacher at Bauman's church in Long Beach and Homer Kent, Sr. was one of his students.[33] Later he entered Xenia Theological Seminary in Ohio, founded by the United Presbyterians, finishing his Th.M. by 1918. He took undergraduate courses at Antioch College at the same time and completed his B.A. with highest honors at Occidental College, Los Angeles, also a Presbyterian school. He was ordained in the Brethren Church in 1917. He still enjoyed sports, though the more recreational type, and frequently went camping, fishing, and swimming.

Looking back in time, McClain is often seen as a conservative, but like his mentor, he was a progressive reformer. When he went to Philadelphia to serve as a pastor in 1918, he was already contemplating what reforms were needed at Ashland. This was just a few years after his conversion. When McClain's health grew weak in Philadelphia, he was given advice from his doctor to leave for fresher air. He seriously believed that if he did not go to a more temperate climate he might die.[34] So to save his life, he left for California and rejoined Bauman's congregation. Bauman, in fact, had for some time been attempting

The Mediating Influence of John Allen Miller

M.M. Norris

Specific individuals and their personalities often help to determine whether competing factions are able to overcome their differences. John Allen Miller is a good example, as he bridged the gap between the seminary faculty and college administration at Ashland. An Indiana native born just after the Civil War (1866), Miller could relate well with both faculty and students in the college and seminary and also members of the surrounding community. His Pietist outlook and sense of responsibility for community involvement was rooted deeply within the Brethren tradition. Indeed, his father was a Brethren school teacher and his mother was the daughter of a German Baptist Brethren minister. As a Progressive Brethren, Miller was well educated[1] and an Ashland College insider. He served as president between 1894 and 1896 and, after the College temporarily closed for financial reasons, he and his wife, Clara Worst Miller, were urged to re-open Ashland, and Miller again served as president from 1899 to 1906. As president, he often urged the Ashland faculty to get involved in the local community.[2] After his tenure as president, Miller then became the dean of the Theology Department.

Miller was a fine exegetical scholar with a deep commitment to biblical authority. In addition to his academic credentials and his identity as a classic liberal arts scholar, however, he was also a strong churchman.

He served as a pastor at various congregations, including the prominent First Brethren Church at Ashland, where he pastored while serving at the college. Church leaders, including McClain and Bauman, respected Miller as well. He served with Bauman in the 1916 conference in drafting the resolution regarding the infallibility of the Bible. He, also, was a charter member of Bauman's Foreign Missionary Society. Later, in 1921, Miller played an instrumental role, along with McClain, in crafting the "Message of the Brethren Ministry," and remained a close friend of

to entice him back to Long Beach to help lead a new Bible Institute there. But in 1925, McClain went back to the Midwest and began teaching undergraduate Bible classes at Ashland College—only to move back again to California where he taught theology at the Bible Institute of Los Angeles from 1926 to 1929. The Bible Institute model made a profound impression on McClain. Then, in 1930, McClain again joined the faculty at Ashland, this time to help establish the graduate seminary and to serve as the institution's first academic dean.

The 1937 Schism: Simply a Matter of Orthodoxy?

There is unanimity that modernism and liberalism existed at Ashland College and within the progressive Brethren in the early 20th century as it had in virtually every other Christian denomination. John L. Gillin (1871-1958), for example, who became president of Ashland in 1907, was an influential liberal in Brethren circles. Like other cultural progressives of the era, Gillin was an advocate for the social gospel and believed that Christ's Kingdom was being constructed on earth through social reform and the spread of American democracy. It was largely under Gillin that modernism gained a foothold at Ashland, including among the faculty. This continued after Gillin left the presidency in 1911.[35]

Finding Ashland's theological direction under Gillin troubling, L. S. Bauman and Alva J. McClain led the charge against modernism. Their efforts culminated in the creation of "The Message of the Brethren Ministry" (1921). McClain is often credited as the author, but J. Allen Miller, and a third unnamed minister worked with him in creating it.[36] This was not to be a creed, but rather a statement of what one could expect to be preached from Brethren pulpits. It reflected traditional Brethren views, largely owing to Miller's influence. Miller was earlier president of Ashland and was always a wise, steady force during turbulent times, as he proved to be here. McClain's contributions reflected a shift away from strict non-creedalism. He felt non-creedalism was theologically immature and with the new threat of modernism, he felt that the Brethren needed to reform themselves and have a more sophisticated response to liberalism rather than just to say that their creed was the "Bible, the whole Bible, and nothing but the Bible." Since the Brethren church lacked a "systematized statement of Christian truth," their young people were not being

McClain. When the seminary at Ashland was reorganized in 1930, Miller remained dean, and McClain was called back from California to be his associate dean. Miller was often a moderating figure as the tensions developed, but in 1933 the aging Miller asked to be relieved of his duties and was replaced by McClain as dean. Taking Miller's courses at Ashland was Herman Hoyt who could not have been more different as a teacher from Miller. While Miller was a seasoned peacemaker, Hoyt was young and was already known for his rigid personality.

When Miller died in March 1935, McClain gave the eulogy at his funeral, saying that he never had a truer friend. McClain also remarked that only those who were close to him would note "the loss sustained" by the institution and denomination.[3] Perhaps McClain had in mind Miller's mediating personality and his ability to help lead a private institution during difficult financial times and controversy and to deal with strong personalities. For in less than two years after Miller's passing, the peace at Ashland was shattered. It is arguable that with Miller's passing, there was no one capable of preserving the peace that would be lost following the contentious board meeting of 1936.[4]

1. He received a BA in 1890 and DD in 1904 from Ashland College. Miller also did graduate work at Hillsdale College, Hiram College, and the University of Chicago. See "Miller, John Allen" in *The Brethren Encyclopedia*, Vol. 2, 839.

2. Martin Shively, *The Brethren Evangelist*, Number XXXVIII "Some Brethren Church Leaders of Yesterday as I know Them, J. Allen Miller, pp 5, 6. Under Miller Ashland became more local and regionally focused while at the same time, the future Grace group was embracing national fundamentalism. See also Dennis Martin, "Ashland College Versus Ashland Seminary."

3. From the eulogy by Alva J. McClain as it appeared in: *Ashland Times-Gazette*, March 27, 1935, "Dr. J. Allen Miller, Dean of College Seminary 30 Years, Dies at Age of 68," 1.

4. While there is little doubt Miller would have remained loyal to Ashland had he lived long enough to see the split, two of his pallbearers (Herman Hoyt and Norman Uphouse) did depart from Ashland with the Grace group. See, "Tributes Paid to Useful Life of Dr. Miller," *Ashland Times-Gazette*, Volume XXXIII, umber 228, March 30, 1935, 1, 7.

grounded in the truth.[37] "The Message" was the solution. What is most important for our purposes here is the fact that the statement did not allow for any shades of theological liberalism. It was a statement that both fundamentalists and traditional brethren would have been comfortable with and it represented traditional orthodoxy. "The Message of the Brethren," therefore, constituted a firm win for orthodoxy within the Brethren Church and at Ashland.

Thus, the real battle between fundamentalist orthodoxy and liberalism did not take place in 1937 as is often believed. Rather, it happened between 1907 and 1921, well before the split that resulted in Grace Theological Seminary. There is little irrefutable evidence indicating that liberalism existed at Ashland in the 1930s as it had prior to 1921. Those supporting the Grace side, for example, have pointed to a 1937 survey of Ashland students commissioned by the Brethren General Conference that seemed to provide evidence of modernism. However, conference decision makers were divided over whether the survey had been conducted impartially.

McClain's strongest desire was to forge greater doctrinal precision and train students in practical Christian ministry. His primary doubts about Ashland at this time revolved less around the question of modernism and more around evidence that students were engaging in such "worldly" activities as smoking, dancing, or going to movies. Though these practices were prohibited on campus, McClain felt that there was not a strict enough enforcing of the rules, and he kept notes on any morally questionable behavior he learned about. In one such instance, he kept anecdotal evidence from a student:

> Mrs. Stead ridiculed two girls for wanting to go to church to hear [Louis] Bauman instead of attending party ... Mrs. Stead spoke slightly of the Day of Prayer ... Girls compelled to attend house councils where the proposition of Theater parties are discussed ... Some girls remark that they had some religion when [they] came to dormitory but lost it since coming here.[38]

As for Bauman, there was no hint that he was anything but pleased about the direction Ashland was headed by the end of the 1920s and he continued to be a steadfast fundraiser. In 1927, he proclaimed that the institution was the safest institution for young men and women in the country and that it was "growing better every day."[39] In this year he was even instrumental in helping to reorganize the institutional board by giving the denomination more control over board selection.[40] Even as late as 1935, he told his California congregation from the pulpit, "the work of the college was fundamental" and they needed to give to Ashland even above the missions fund.[41] In December of the same year, Bauman wrote an encouraging letter to Ashland's president, Charles Anspach: "How I do rejoice to know that the city of Ashland is standing by you so loyally! ... certainly the Church ought to show the same spirit of loyalty to the college that the city of Ashland shows." Prejudices that existed will not be "wiped off the slate in a day! But you are going to win out, and Ashland College is going to be an honored name among all Christian peoples in the very near future, if our Lord shall tarry." In his letter, Bauman even wondered if it was absolutely essential for him to include the upcoming board meetings into his busy schedule. In so doing, he shows his confidence in Anspach's administration: "Apparently, the machinery is well oiled now in the College, and possibly it makes very little difference whether the [West] Coast shall be represented there this coming year."[42] Anspach soon returned the complements: "I want to thank you for your presence and lecture on our campus. I feel that your work with the seminary students was very well received. I have had many fine compliments."[43] We know that tensions did develop, however. In just a matter of months, in fact, these words of mutual affirmation between Bauman and Anspach would turn sour. It is also important to note that the steady hand of J. Allen Miller, former president and seminary dean who had worked closely with Bauman and McClain, was lifted with his death in March of this same year (1935).[44]

So what exactly was the source of the tensions? Rather than an overwhelming presence of liberalism, the relational breakdown resulted from the political and personal fallout created by Anspach's attempts to revise the institution's constitution, which he believed was necessary to save Ashland from impending bankruptcy. The solution to the school's financial problems involved following the Wheaton College model, which would include plans for more robust community outreach, student internships with local businesses, and changing the makeup of the board of trustees.[45]

As mentioned above, the composition of the board in 1935 had been formed with the help of Bauman and did have more denominational control. The proposed adjustments, however, increased the number of board members so that it included more community members—from 36 to 42. The six new members would be comprised of three members of the Ashland community, two members at large appointed by the board, and one member from the alumni. These changes would weaken Brethren control and create a quasi "self-perpetuating" board.[46] A final proposed change to the board particularly offended Bauman and his group in that dissident districts would now no longer have membership on the board. Bauman saw this as evidence that Anspach was planning to shut out his colleagues. While the proposals angered Bauman, who recognized the shift in power, Anspach was motivated by the fact that the institution was in dire financial straits and they needed more help from the community. What is more, Anspach was reinstituting a means of board selection that had historical precedence since his changes were consistent with selection methods between 1910 and 1927.[47]

Two additional developments in this board meeting offended Bauman and his circle and would also be used later as evidence of modernism on the campus. Anspach sharply criticized a pre-seminary group for passing out tracts on campus, which he believed was condescending and offended undergraduate students. In addition, Anspach allowed a double standard for student body conduct. Those preparing for pastoral or missionary service had a stricter code of conduct, and a more lenient standard was applied for those going into secular professions (though all would abide by the same standards on campus). Anspach argued that it was impossible to require the large number of commuter students to live a completely separated life when they were under their parents' authority at home.[48]

Whatever financial merits Anspach's efforts may have had, the adjustments to the board was a political bombshell for Bauman and McClain. Ashland was to be first and foremost a denominational institution, and their seminary had a mandate to train pastors and missionaries for Brethren congregations. They believed it was essential for Ashland to retain strong influence from the Brethren Church, yet Anspach was threatening to push aside the Church and its representative board members, including those from Bauman's California district. There was little doubt Anspach was attempting to give more control to non-Brethren "outsiders." In April, 1936 McClain wrote to Bauman about his concern over Anspach's constitutional proposals. Note here the political, as opposed to theological, language:

> It is the opinion of the Seminary faculty that if it should be carried through, the move will mean eventually entire loss of church control over the whole institution... According to the plan, as outlined by Anspach to me the other day, the local outside group will be given ten seats on the board. The Alumni will get three. That makes thirteen members who are practically certain to be outsiders who are not in sympathy with denominational[49] control. Then the Brethren Church Districts are to be cut to one member each, instead of three. Then the remaining number, about a third of the board, are to be elected by the board itself, but from among members of the Brethren Church. Now the joker in this scheme is very obvious. It would be easy, in this last group, to get people wholly out of sympathy with denominational control. You could get the whole group out of the First Brethren Church at Ashland ... Now my opinion is that if at the coming board meeting it should appear a possibility that such a proposal might pass, we should demand that the whole scheme be referred to national conference for consideration to find out whether the church wants any such change.[50]

It is telling that McClain recommended that Bauman get "as many members from the West [California] here at the board meeting as possible."[51] With McClain and Bauman rallying the denominational troops, debates over the constitution came to a head at the board meetings as McClain had predicted. Anspach was unaware of how stridently Bauman would oppose his efforts. It is ironic that he entered the meeting feeling assured of Bauman's enthusiastic support, since he had attached his constitutional proposals to an earlier letter to Bauman (the letter quoted from above). In reality, Bauman came ready to counter Anspach, fueled on by his correspondence with McClain, even feeling it necessary to leave the bedside of his dying daughter to do so. Bauman's efforts failed, however, and Ashland accepted a nondenominational settlement that weakened Brethren denominational control and sidelined Bauman's own California Brethren contingency. Defeated, Bauman stormed out of the meeting.[52] Later, Bauman claimed that Anspach would not let him respond to the proposal at the meeting and in a note to the president, Bauman criticized Anspach for not confiding in him earlier. "I honestly believe, Brother Anspach," Bauman lamented, "that if I could have gotten off in a corner with you … and we would have all 'laid our cards on the table,' so to speak, and discussed problems before the board meeting, that some things might have been done differently."[53]

But the damage had already been done. Indeed, this should be seen as the defining skirmish that would eventually lead to the split of the institution, the denominational schism, and the beginning of Grace Seminary.

The Road to a New Seminary

After this 1936 board meeting, the gulf between the seminary and the administration continued to widen. Bauman explained to Anspach that he, like McClain, was also concerned about worldly behavior. Indeed, he cited evidence that a residence director was even selling tickets to the theater. He also complained that Homer Kent, Sr., one of Bauman and Hoyt's church-related allies, was turned down a position at the seminary, while at the same time, money was invested in athletics. (From Anspach's perspective, this decision had more to do with the financial stress of the college owing to loss of accreditation and the realities of trying to maintain the institution deep within the Great Depression.) He then called for a political solution—an appeal to the national conference.[54]

At the next national conference, the Southern California District, not surprisingly, petitioned the Ashland Board to reinstate Bauman as a trustee, but the board refused, prompting Bauman to claim that while he was refused reinstatement, one or two on the board were not even Christians. After all, he had written the popular *The Faith Once For all Delivered Unto the Saints*, and had grown his California congregation from a vacant lot to one of the largest congregations in the Brethren Church at the time. Clearly he was incensed that someone with his church credentials would be sidelined by the Ashland administration.

45

In 1937, tensions continued to escalate when McClain pushed to make it mandatory for all faculty members, including undergraduate faculty, to sign a statement of faith that he had composed and which was first adopted by the seminary faculty.[55] This attempt to exert seminary control over the rest of the faculty was the last straw for the administration. McClain and his strongest ally, Herman Hoyt, were given the choice of resigning, but they declined and were fired. Hoyt later noted that they chose not to resign because they hoped that being forced out would create a stronger sense of indignation among their church-based constituents and provide more leverage within the denomination.[56] In the middle of the summer of 1937, members of the seminary group, along with Bauman, met for two days of strategy planning and prayer near Akron, Ohio.[57] After their two days together, Bauman rose and drafted from his private account the first check for a new seminary.[58] Thus the new seminary began with classes at the Ellet Brethren Church in Akron, Ohio, with McClain's 1921 "Message of the Brethren Ministry" serving as its statement of faith.

In the months after the schism, the Grace group moved quickly to communicate with their constituents about the nature of the conflict at Ashland, sending out a critical pamphlet that made their case against Ashland. Though "liberalism" and "modern trends" are listed as important factors, they are tangential to the issue of governance. The overwhelming majority of the pamphlet focused on political control—that the administration was incrementally replacing board members with ties to the Brethren Church with those who did not have such ties. Although the school worked hard to fool church leaders, the pamphlet charged, in reality the administration had no loyalty to the church and operated according to its own interests. Ashland's Brethren affiliation was merely a painted facade. In making the case for a new seminary, the pamphlet offered testimonials from Brethren Church leaders.[59] "The Brethren Church needs a seminary under sympathetic control," Russell Barnard stated "… No house is big enough for two families. No institution is big enough for two educational agencies especially when there is opportunity for as great a difference in policies and ideals as between a Seminary and a [Liberal] Arts College."[60] Herman Koontz declared,

> I want a Seminary that is actually and legally (not sentimentally) owned and controlled by the churches and members

of the Brethren denomination. Then the church can dictate its policy and I can be assured that as long as the Brethren churches remain true to the fundamentals of the Christian faith, the Seminary will be kept true to the same faith … I want a Seminary that is separated from the compromising atmosphere of a college which has opposing standards of living and where students are discouraged and checked in their zeal to win the lost to CHRIST.[61]

From California, Bauman would continue to represent stridently the interests of the Grace group at future national conventions, but the denomination remained divided, and the Grace contingent was sidelined. Two years later, in 1939, Grace Seminary moved to Winona Lake, which was, ironically, the location of that year's national conference—a conference that has sometimes been referred to as the "Winona Lake battle of 1939."

Anticipating that tensions would run high, a local sheriff was in attendance, along with his stenographer. Bauman's group countered by including their stenographer. Throughout the proceedings, Bauman repeatedly and publically demanded that he and his delegates be seated. He even threatened to take the fight "outside." All his attempts were rebuffed, however, and the delegates loyal to the Grace group finally relented, indeed holding a meeting outside.[62] This would be the final break. Eventually the division spilled into local churches culminating in four lawsuits initiated by the Ashland group, which also escalated outrage.[63]

The Early Institution

With the denominational split becoming more solidified, the Grace group continued to organize their new institution. After moving to Winona Lake, classes were held in what was then the Free Methodist Publishing House (now Mount Memorial Hall), which had long been used for educational purposes since the days of Winona's Chautauqua programs. A library was cobbled together using primarily the holdings of the Winona School of Theology. They would remain in the Free Methodist building until McClain Hall was built in 1951.[64] The purpose and ideals of Grace Seminary were threefold. Students were to receive a theological education and were to enter Christian ministry, foreign missions work, or other types of Christian service. Second, the seminary was to have proper graduate standards. Though McClain had been influenced by a Bible Institute model, he was clearly interested only in graduate theological education. Third, its mission was "To Know Christ and Make Him Known as the only Savior and Lord of Life." In doing this, the curriculum was to be Bible-centered, and professors were to teach competent and believing scholarship. Grace, from its beginning was to have a "spiritual and prayer-charged environment." It was to have a "missionary and evangelistic spirit." Students would also experience a spirit-filled and separated life as well as a "premillennial hope" and view point. Expository preaching and teaching were emphasized, and like the Covenant of Faith, these "cannot be changed or diminished."[65]

Faculty increased slowly but surely until, by the end of McClain's presidency, there were about a dozen full-time professors. Under McClain student enrollment increased from an initial few dozen to a high of 490 graduates and undergraduates. Also, at a time when other seminaries denied women enrollment, Grace had, from its start, a strong contingency of female students, many of whom felt called to foreign missions. Students attended from many denominations and a strong contingent of Baptist students emerged alongside the Brethren students.

McClain's quiet charisma provided the leadership and inspiration for the new Seminary. He was good looking and a meticulous dresser. Contemporaries would have considered him "dapper." He was a clear, focused, and methodical teacher, though somewhat of a loner. He was also a good actor. He always entered the room fifteen seconds before the bell rang and began his lectures right away. In the early years, McClain memorized the biblical texts he used in class and quoted them out loud. Later, he had students read for themselves because he realized this was better pedagogically.[66]

At meetings he had an uncanny ability to command attention. He listened for some time and then, when he felt he had something to say, he addressed the audience softly so that people asked him to speak up and address the audience. McClain was dearly loved for his ability to teach complicated biblical passages in a clear and precise manner. He always wore a coat and tie, and a hat when outdoors—even at home when he was raking leaves. He and his wife, Josephine had no children, and spent a great deal of time alone. They were frequently seen pulling out with their camper and heading for a weekend get-away.[67]

McClain believed that what formed him was independent inductive and empirical Bible study in tandem with the Holy Spirit's guidance. He believed that he was persuaded in his views from a careful study of Scripture, which developed over the course of his career. He was even willing to modify his views in class based on deeper understandings of Scripture.[68] But McClain's dispensationalism was influenced by C. I. Scofield, his connections with Philadelphia School of the Bible (now Cairn University), as well as his time at the Bible Institute of Los Angeles (now BIOLA). His *Magnum opus*, the *Greatness of the Kingdom* (1959), one of a proposed seven-volume series, integrated dispensationalism with a mild form of Calvinism. McClain situated his theological system under the over-arching theme of the Mediatorial Kingdom of God, which represented a new brand of theology for the Brethren and a new twist for other dispensationalists.[69] McClain's unique brand of revised dispensationalism was central to the new seminary and left a lasting legacy.

Financially, the new seminary benefitted tremendously from Bauman's experienced fundraising as well as the windfall from the sale of a local farm (the Busey property), the proceeds from which were donated to Grace. Bauman invested in annuities, and he garnered gifts for the seminary from his Southern California constituents. By 1940 they had a net worth of $60,000 and were making several relatively large loans with interest to various Brethren Churches. They reached half a million dollars by the late 1950s. From the very start, the board authorized a marketing campaign. Advertisements were sent to area Brethren churches and placed in newspapers. When Paul Bauman, son of L. S., was called to the seminary, he was not only appointed professor of apologetics, but also Grace's first public relations officer.[70] This policy of advertisement, fund-raising, and dealing with the public seemed only natural to these progressive Brethren. Faculty were also instrumental in visiting local Brethren churches. This helped with Grace's initial building programs. Besides the aforementioned McClain Hall, major building projects included the Lancer Gym and Philathea Hall.

Framing the Controversy in Theological Language

Throughout the controversy at Ashland, the early Grace group felt betrayed and, convinced of the righteousness of their cause, they interpreted the break-up through theological lenses. As early as 1937, in fact, Bauman wrote to McClain and began to place the blame for the schism on Ashland's modernistic past—which was in stark contrast to the positive statements (referenced above) he was making about Ashland before the split. The implication is that perhaps these heresies did not really die out, but rather smoldered under the surface.[71] In a "public forum" article in 1939, we get a sense for the many interpretations that were circulating at the time about why the split took place. Some said it was over the question of eternal security. Others said it was a debate over legalism and "cheap grace," Brethren identity, or even certain individuals. Bauman denied that any of these issues were to blame, however, and became even more explicit that the disagreements were over the presence of modernism at Ashland College. In fact, he boldly writes, "It is sheer nonsense to say that through these years Ashland College has kept herself free from Modernism…For years upon years, the writer has fought against Modernism in Ashland College."[72]

This view—that Grace Seminary began as a stand for truth against Ashland's modernism—would then become the standard interpretation and served as the primary means of establishing a sense of identity for the Grace group. This can be seen in the seminary and college catalogues for some time after the schism, and it makes sense, given the fact that toward mid-century Grace Seminary increasingly took on the cultural elements of American Fundamentalism. In 1941, for example, the catalogue painted a dualist interpretation of the schism in which the founders were pious saints and Ashland had fallen prey to a "coalition" of ungodly forces. Although the description mentions liberalism, worldliness, and legalism, clearly the charges of liberalism have, by this time, become the key point of the schism. All mention of Bauman's power struggle with the Ashland administration has disappeared.

> The conception of Grace Theological Seminary arose out of an informal and unpremeditated gathering held early June of the year 1937. Deeply concerned regarding the inroads

of modern unbelief in the general field of higher education, and especially about the recent victory of a coalition of "liberal," worldly and legalistic forces over an institution which they had been supporting, a number of Brethren pastors and laymen had come together in a private home for earnest prayer and Christian council... plans were laid for founding of an institution of higher theological education where positive Biblical Standards of Christian faith and life could be established and maintained without hindrance from destructive modernistic elements, and also where it might be possible to make effective certain educational ideals which the founders were firmly convinced would greatly increase the practical and spiritual values of ministerial training... included in the new institution were the teachers save one, and all the students except two, from the school which had been lost to liberal forces... The circumstances under which the school was founded, its clear Christian testimony, as well as its educational ideals, aroused widespread interest among Christian leaders and schools of "like precious faith" throughout this country, bringing many expressions of friendship and encouragement from which the founders are deeply grateful.[73] (Italics added for emphasis.)

As recently as 2003 the departure from Ashland was represented as a Brethren "version" of the fundamentalist/modernist debates.[74] Grace Brethren writers make much of Gillin's liberalism, for example, as evidence to argue that the separation from Ashland was a separation from liberalism. But Gillin had not been in the picture since 1911 and in fact, by the 1930s, he had actually recanted his liberalism and returned back to the Brethren fold. In addition, research at the congregational level has suggested that there were few theological differences between the Ashland and Grace Brethren.[75] Like the Grace group, Ashland continued to believe their institution was biblically-based and even largely kept in place McClain's statement of faith (except for a few years in the 1940s) up to the present.[76] McClain's name still appears on the Ashland campus, engraved in a granite stone tablet that commemorates important leaders in its past, and Ashland's seminary handbook continued to reflect much of McClain's theological language. It is ironic that at Ashland Seminary, little of the theology being taught changed as it regrouped after the departure of the Grace group and at the new Grace seminary, the curriculum was largely what had been taught at Ashland since it was mostly written by McClain, himself. So the substance of teaching at both seminaries after the schism was not all that different, though McClain's revised dispensationalism would have a growing influence.

Perhaps due in part to the tensions they felt at Ashland, the Grace administration was cautious about adding an undergraduate program. The initial impetus for the college division stemmed from enrollment concerns—the seminary was losing potential students who needed pre-graduate preparation before they could do seminary level work. Started as a two-year program of undergraduate liberal arts study in 1948, this was expanded to a four-year liberal arts degree in 1953.[77] Clearly suspicious that an undergraduate program might undermine the position of the seminary and compromise denominational identity, as they believed it had at Ashland, the seminary leadership at Grace kept the young college firmly under seminary control. Even with a four-year curriculum, the undergraduate program was officially nothing more than the "college division" of the seminary. The 1953 policy statement for the college was clear about where the undergraduate program stood. It was merely to provide pre-seminary education for Christian workers, and "not to establish a college of arts and sciences as an end in itself."[78] Although students not intending to enter the seminary could be admitted, if they agreed to the purpose of the college, the number of these students was to be limited so that seminary and pre-seminary students would always be in the majority. It is also telling that the seminary and college division were not to have separate administrations, a move that would prevent the college from ever challenging the position of the seminary as they believed had happened at Ashland.[79] What is more, the college was not to seek accreditation in organizations controlled by non-Christians, and professors were to be either seminary graduates or were to have had specified seminary course work.[80]

It is worth noting, however, that whatever hesitations the Grace administrators had about undergraduate liberal arts education, they did not let this inhibit the depth of course offerings, which were full-fledged and amounted to a robust liberal arts curriculum that could rival the Grace College of today. The 1954-5 academic year was organized under the following departments: Archaeology, Bible, Education (this would later include Psychology), English and Speech, Greek, History, Latin, Linguistics, Modern Languages, Music, Philosophy, Physical Education, and Science. Each department had numerous and solid classical liberal arts courses.[81]

In ensuing decades, some at Grace condemned Ashland in harsh terms. According to a former Grace Seminary student, to hear Herman Hoyt speak of Ashland one would almost get the impression that "the Antichrist had set up headquarters" there.[82] But this was not the case with McClain. In reflecting on the schism at Ashland, McClain seemed to have less animosity than others. He was also adamant that he never wanted the split to start a new denomination. He considered himself fully part of the Brethren Church. This is clearly revealed in a letter that McClain wrote to Albert Ronk in 1961, just before McClain retired as president of Grace. Ronk had earlier sent him a draft of a manual on the faith of the Brethren Church, which he was writing. McClain noted in response that he found "no doctrinal point" with which he had serious disagreement and even remarked that, in hindsight, this would render "much of the litigation we have suffered meaningless." In fact, McClain's only cause for concern was that he disagreed with a statement Ronk made that there was a new Grace Brethren denomination! McClain still considered himself and the Grace group as part of the Brethren Church. McClain closed his letter by saying, "I trust that this misstatement will be corrected in the near future, so as to lessen rather than widen the breach between us; a breach which I deplore just as sincerely as you do."[83]

In McClain's later years, his reputation as a teacher, theologian, and Christian leader grew. He was ever popular among students (a number of whom protested to the board when his writing and speaking engagements took him away from the classroom) and he remains a revered figure to this day.[84] Meanwhile, Herman Hoyt took on more of an executive role. America was also beginning to go through tremendous upheavals at home and abroad. In these new paranoid Cold War years, Hoyt exhibited a disposition that was comforting to a new and narrower breed of fundamentalists, and Grace would see impressive growth. As in many divorces, both sides experienced a sense of betrayal, anger, pain, self-righteousness, and disbelief. Still, the rift forged new directions by creating fresh institutions and new identities. It energized powerful convictions that are still meaningful today. As we look back after more than 75 years of higher education at Grace and Ashland we can benefit from having a certain amount of distance from the heat-filled controversies of that era and as a result, we can see the fuller human drama. What eventually rose from the strife and anger are two fine institutions that found new and expanding constituents and were re-energized to embrace the future. Today, both Ashland and Grace Seminaries share space on the same evangelical landscape.[85] At the same time, this story allows us to see that our successes (and there were many) were less about the talents, heroism, or saintliness of our founders, and more about the grace of God, which so often transcends human conflict. If there is a lesson to be learned from a schism such as the one described here, perhaps that is it.

Notes

1. Office of Media and Public Relations, Ashland University.

2. Dennis Martin, "Ashland College Versus Ashland Seminary (1921-1937): Prelude to Schism," *Brethren Life and Thought*, XXI:1 (Winter 1976), 45.

3. The collegiate program rose to 340 students in 1930-1 but by 1934-5 dropped to 252 students. See Dale R. Stoffer, *A Gleam of Shining Hope*, 104-105, 108.

4. *1951 Χαρις, The History of Grace Theological Seminary 1931-1951*, ed. John Whitcomb, 29.

5. This is the dating of the graduate seminary. An undergraduate seminary was founded in 1906. See Stoffer, *Gleam of Shining Hope*, 75 and 103.

6. Following the split, The Brethren Church fell to 18,737 by 1952 and by 2009 was at 10,227. Membership in the Brethren Church never recovered from the split. By 1942 the Grace group had 16,590 members; in the early twenty-first century this hovered around 30,000 members. See The Association of Religious Data Archives: www.thearda.com/Denoms/D_1053.asp; www.thearda.com/Denoms/D_1369.asp; and www.thearda.com/Denoms/D_1452.asp

7. Norman B. Rohrer, *A Saint in Glory Stands: the story of Alva J. McClain, Founder of Grace Theological Seminary* (Winona Lake, IN: BMH Books, 1986).

8. Grace Theological Seminary and Grace College catalog, 1954-1955, Winona Lake, Indiana, 14-15.

9. Homer A. Kent Sr., *Conquering Frontiers: A History of the Brethren Church* (Winona Lake, IN: Brethren Missionary Herald, 1958 and 1972). Here I am using the 1972 version. Kent's history is still a standard and important work as

it gives the perspective of an early founder of the Seminary. This is revised and continued in David R. Plaster, *Finding Our Focus: A History of the Grace Brethren Church,* (Winona Lake, IN: BMH Books, 2003).

10. Todd Scoles, *Restoring the Household: The Quest of the Grace Brethren Church* (Winona Lake, IN: BMH Books, 2008). Scoles gives an interesting and helpful perspective of both a pastor of note in the Fellowship of Grace Brethren Churches and a graduate of Ashland Theological Seminary.

11. Albert A. Ronk, *History of the Brethren Church: Its Life, Thought, Mission* (Ashland, OH: Brethren Publishing Company, 1968). For the latest history of the denomination see Scoles, *Restoring the Household.*

12. Stoffer, *Gleam of Shining Hope,* 45-128.

13. Ibid., 62. Herman A. Hoyt, "Dr. L. S. Bauman and Brethren Theological Education," Brethren Missionary Herald (January 6, 1951), 21-22.

14. Homer A. Kent Sr., *Conquering Frontiers,* 171

15. *The Brethren Encyclopedia,* Vol. I (Philadelphia, PA, and Oak Brook, IL: The Brethren Encyclopedia, Inc., 1983), 96. In the Bauman Papers, there are numerous advertisements for prostheses that Bauman received and also some letters from doctors indicating that this was often on his mind.

16. *The Brethren Evangelist,* 21 July 1886.

17. Louis S. Bauman, *God and Gog or The Coming Meet between Judah's Lion and Russia's Bear* (Long Beach, CA: Alan S. Pearce, 1934).

18. Warren L. Vinz, "King's Business" in *The Conservative Press in America,* edited by Ronald Lora and William Henry Longton (Westport, CT: Greenwood Press, 1999), 122-27.

19. *The Brethren Encyclopedia,* Vol. I, 96-97.

20. Bauman Papers, passim. Archives and Special Collections, Grace College and Theological Seminary, Winona Lake, IN (hereafter Grace Archives).

21. Dennis Martin, "Ashland College versus Ashland Seminary," 37-38.

22. Plaster, *Finding Our Focus,* 83-4.

23. *Brethren Encyclopedia,* Vol I., 96, 97.

24. There are numerous helpful treatments of fundamentalism in America. The definitive treatment remains George M. Marsden, *Fundamentalism and American Culture.* Marsden has also written a less technical treatment: *Understanding Fundamentalism and Evangelicalism* (Grand Rapids: William B. Eerdmans Publishing Co., 1991). See also David O. Beale, *In Pursuit of Purity: American Fundamentalism Since 1850* (Greenville: Unusual Publications, 1986).

25. The best treatment of the trial of John Scopes, who was charged with teaching evolution in a Dayton, Tennessee, school, is Edward Larson, *Summer for the Gods: The Scopes Trial and America's Continuing Debate over Science and Religion* (Cambridge, Harvard University Press, 1998). Also consult Marsden, *Fundamentalism,* 184-88, as well as Barry Hankins, *American Evangelicals,* 59-67. The post-Scopes fundamentalist resurgence can be seen particularly well in Joel A Carpenter, *Revive Us Again.*

26. See, for example, the series of volumes published between 1991 and 2004 as part of the "Fundamentalisms Project" led by R. Scott Appleby and Martin Marty

(University of Chicago Press). For a reflective piece on fundamentalism and labeling, consult a 2009 interview with evangelical historian John D. Woodbridge: "The 'Fundamentalist' Label," *Trinity Magazine* (spring 2009).

27. In a letter to Jacobs, Bauman wrote, "The matter of militarism in the College two years ago came before the Trustees. I asked the (then) President of the College if I might appear before the board in protest to such action. The answer assured me that I had no business before the board... Surely, my brother, a vote of 'confidence in the school' could hardly be expected from me, nor honestly given, no matter how great I might wish to grant it..." Louis S. Bauman to Edwin E. Jacobs, April 2, 1920. Bauman Papers, Grace Archives. Although Bauman was vocal about his nonresistant convictions, the Grace group did not consider themselves pacifist. They were uneasy in allying themselves with other less biblicist groups and organizations such as the World Council of Churches and were not at ease in demonstrating against war.

28. Stoffer, *Gleam of Shining Hope*, 66. See L. S. Bauman, *The Faith Once Delivered Unto the Saints* (Winona Lake, IN: BMH Books, ninth edition, 1977). Bauman had self-published this from 1906 to 1909 and several editions appeared after this.

29. Bauman and his circle, however, did modify their views over time, especially after the 1930s. They came to hold a version of dispensationalism that was somewhat distinct from traditional Brethren views as well as that of more classical dispensationalists. Unlike other dispensationalists, Bauman and McClain believed that The Sermon on the Mount was not wholly relegated to a future Kingdom and was still relevant. Yet they did not elevate the Sermon on the Mount to the same level as the gospel or see it as a "canon within the canon" as more traditional Brethren and Anabaptists sometimes did. The issue was not over whether the Sermon on the Mount applied to the believer, but over whether or not it was part of the essential gospel message. For more on these theological developments, see Dale R. Stoffer, *Background and Development of Brethren Doctrines (Brethren Encyclopedia Monograph Series,* No. 2, (Nov 1989), 227, 229. Note also Bauman's article, "Public Forum: What Has Divided the Brethren Church?" in *The Brethren Evangelist,* Sept. 2, 1939, 15-21.

30. *Brethren Encyclopedia*, Vol II, 772.

31. Rohrer, 30-32.

32. Ibid., 36.

33. Thanks to Homer Kent, Jr. for offering feedback on this and other points within this chapter.

34. Bauman Papers. Grace Archives, passim.

35. Stoffer, *Gleam of Shining Hope*, 53-54. After leaving Ashland in 1911, Gillin became professor of sociology at the University of Iowa from 1912-1942.

36. Stoffer, *Background and Development of Brethren Doctrines*, 192, 288 note 99. See also Plaster, *Finding our Focus*, 92.

37. McClain to Dr. Jacobs, June 3, 1919, Alva J. McClain Papers. Grace Archives.

38. McClain Papers. This appears in M. M. Norris, "A Cord of Many Strands" in *The Activist Impulse*, 156-184. On the differing perspectives of the student survey, see Kent, *Conquering Frontiers*, 143-145 and Stoffer, *Gleam of Shining Hope*, 120-121.

39. Louis S. Bauman to Lester J. Miller, June 4, 1927. Bauman Papers. Grace Archives.

40. Stoffer, *Gleam of Shining Hope,* 115.

41. Louis S. Bauman to President Anspach, July 3, 1935, Bauman Papers. Grace Archives.

42. Louis S. Bauman to President Anspach, December 30, 1935, Bauman Papers. Grace Archives.

43. President Anspach, to L.S. Bauman, April 4, 1936, Bauman Papers. Grace Archives.

44. Bauman Papers, Grace Archives, passim. "Tributes Paid to the useful life of Dr. Miller," Ashland Times Gazette, Ashland, OH, XXXII:228 (Saturday March 30, 1935).

45. Stoffer, *Gleam of Shining Hope*, 108-123.

46. Ibid., 113-116.

47. Ibid.

48. Ibid., 115-116.

49. Here McClain uses the word "denomination," indicating that the Brethren at this time were comfortable with the term. The Grace Brethren would later react against this term and distinguish themselves as a "fellowship" rather than a "denomination." In fact, historians recognize that many American denominations are uneasy with the term "denomination." The term itself merely means "of or from the name." Brethren, however, had a highly decentralized form of denomination and tend to be unified more because of extended family-like relationships rather than by a hierarchy. It is with this definition that the term "denomination" will be used in reference to the Grace Brethren.

50. Alva J. McClain to Louis S. Bauman, April 16, 1936. Bauman Papers. Grace Archives.

51. Ibid.

52. Louis S. Bauman to President Anspach, July 25, 1936, Bauman Papers; James Sweeton interview in, "A Denomination Torn Asunder: transcription of Dennis Martin's 1973 oral history interview with participants in the 1930s Ashland/Grace Brethren Church division," 4-7, transcribed by Corey Grandstaff. Grace Archives.

53. Louis S. Bauman to President Anspach, July 25, 1936. Bauman Papers. Grace Archives.

54. Ibid.

55. Although this statement was not the "The Message of the Brethren Ministry," McClain did attempt to get the Brethren General Conference to adopt "The Message." He was unsuccessful, however, and even Bauman, owing to his non-creedalism, voted against it. See Stoffer, *Gleam of Shining Hope*, 110-112.

56. Herman Hoyt interview in Dennis Martin, "A Denomination Torn Asunder," 12-13.

57. This was in the home of J. C. Beal (d. 1944), business manager of *the Brethren Evangelist*. See Kent, *Conquering Frontiers*, 152-15.

58. Robert Culver, public interview, June 2013, Winona Lake Grace Brethren Church.

59. "It's All Right to Paint the Walls, But how about the Foundation?" Grace Archives.

60. Ibid.

61. Ibid. Herman Koontz and Russell Barnard would become members of the first Board of Trustees for Grace Seminary. Homer Kent, Sr. was also quoted in this pamphlet.

62. "A Stenographic Report of the General Conference of the Brethren Church 1939," Brethren Church Archives, Ashland, OH.

63. James Custer, interview by author, August 2014. Hoyt and McClain ended up testifying in court. The suits were over which side had the best claim to the property, and thus which side was the "most Brethren." The suits themselves were in violation of the historic Brethren position of not suing a brother in a court of law, but Grace took the position that they were "appealing to Caesar" like the Apostle Paul. Ashland won suits in Peru and Meyersdale and the Grace group in Dayton and Leon. For a full account, see Kent, *Conquering Frontiers*, 210-216.

64. On the development of the Grace campus, including use of buildings, see Terry White, *Winona at 100: Third Wave Rising* (Winona Lake, IN: BMH Books, 2013).

65. Grace Theological Seminary, Articles of Incorporation, 1940, 1-2. Grace Archives.

66. See for example, James Sweeton, interview in Dennis Martin, 8-22.

67. Ibid.

68. Custer, interview.

69. McClain's theological allies were thrilled with *Greatness of the Kingdom*; however, others were more cautious. Though classical dispensationalists would maintain that the Sermon on the Mount was for the future Kingdom of Christ, McClain and others from Grace Seminary saw Christ words as transcending all ages, which was more in line with Anabaptist interpretations. However, McClain did say that he believed readers would find some of the Sermon on the Mount impractical for the church age. The net result was that the Grace group moved from an Anabaptist hermeneutic to a subtle de-emphasis of Christ's words in the Sermon on the Mount over time. This was parallel to a shift toward inerrancy and a literal historical-grammatical hermeneutic. It is ironic that many Brethren interpret this shift as weakening Brethren distinctives, though evangelicals saw this as a way to defend the Bible against modernism and higher criticism.

70. Minutes, Board of Trustees Executive Committee and Full Board June, 1937 thru August 1959, *passim*. Grace Archives.

71. L. S. Bauman to Alva J. McClain, December 31, 1937, Bauman Papers. Grace Archives.

72. L. S. Bauman, "Public Forum," 15-21.

73. *Grace Theological Seminary Catalog, 1940-41*, 9.

74. Plaster, *Finding our Focus*, 89-125.

75. Jerry Young, *The Relationship between Local Grace Brethren Churches and Their Denominational Leadership* (DMin thesis, Dallas Theological Seminary, May 1996). Young suggests that what ensued in the 1930s was an internal fight among evangelical Brethren.

76. Dale Stoffer, interview by author, July 2014. Dale Stoffer and James Custer noted to me that in recent times, leaders of both The Brethren Church and the FGBC assembled at Ashland College to discuss the split within the Brethren Church and to apologize to each other for the manner in which this transpired.

77. Herman Hoyt interview in Dennis Martin, "A Denomination Torn Asunder," 12, 13. Grace Brethren Pastors brought a resolution at the national conference to start a college in 1948. So after eleven years they started a two-year collegiate division. But it failed to grow, however, since students often left after one year and did not come back. The collegiate division dwindled to twenty-five students by 1953.

78. Faculty and Administrative Committee Minutes, August 12, 1952 – August 29, 1958, Grace Archives; "Statement of Policy," Faculty Meeting, March 12, 1953, 32-33. Grace Archives.

79. Faculty and Administrative Committee Minutes August 12, 1952 – August 29, 1958, 33. Grace Archives.

80. Ibid.

81. *Grace Theological Seminary and Grace College Catalogue 1954-5*, 68-82.

82. James Sweeton, interview in Dennis Martin, 19.

83. McClain to Albert T. Ronk, February 14, 1961. Brethren Church Archives, Ashland, OH.

84. Tom Julien, et.al., "Petition to the Board of Trustees," December 15, 1955.

85. Stoffer, interview. See Ashland Seminary's website: Seminary.ashland.edu/about/our-values/#core-values. Ashland continues to maintain an evangelical and a Brethren presence. For example, one of their four core values is "Scripture" and under this they write: "Ashland Seminary believes God's saving revelation has been supremely made in Jesus Christ. The Bible is the complete and authentic record of that revelation. We are committed to both the Old and New Testaments as God's infallible message for the church and the world. The Scriptures are foundational to the educational process at Ashland Seminary." The seminary's mission statement is: "Ashland Theological Seminary integrates theological education with Christ-centered transformation as it equips men and women for ministry in the church and the world." Under its "Operating Philosophy," is written: "In order to carry out its mission, Ashland brings together a faculty with shared commitment to biblical, evangelical faith…" While both Grace and Ashland are evangelical, Grace Seminary is more conservative evangelical and Ashland sees itself as more neo-evangelical. Both accept students from a variety of denominational backgrounds. See Grace's Doctrinal Statement at: http://www.grace.edu/academics/seminary/about-seminary/doctrinal-statement. I am grateful to Dale Stoffer for his helpful comments on this topic.

Chapter 3

Vigilance
The Fundamentalism of Herman Hoyt and John Whitcomb

Jared S. Burkholder

By the time Alva J. McClain rounded his wooden desk for the last time, packed up his personal belongings, and retired from the president's office in McClain Hall in 1962, many American Christians believed the nation faced grave threats from outside as well as inside its borders. Over the summer, the United States Supreme Court had ruled in favor of several New York families who believed standardized prayer should not be allowed in public schools.[1] Then, just after fall convocation, President Kennedy and Russian premier Nikita Khrushchev narrowly avoided nuclear war over the deployment of Soviet missiles in Cuba, just 90 miles off the Florida coast. Three years later, after years of escalating US involvement in Vietnam, combat missions began in earnest, expanding a war that would rend the nation apart. During the same period, tensions over segregation boiled over in the American South while protests erupted throughout the nation. Challenges to traditional notions of gender, hierarchy, and sexuality came in the form of throngs of hippies, psychedelic drugs, and a burgeoning rock and roll culture. Looking around them, many American Christians would have agreed with Herman Hoyt (1909-2000), McClain's successor as president, when he declared to the Grace campus in his 1971 convocation message, "the world is falling apart."[2]

Responding to this era of uncertainty in the 1960s and 70s, the young seminary, even as it gained momentum and continued a period of robust expansion, would turn in a new and narrower fundamental-

61

ist direction. To be sure, McClain, Bauman, and the others who made the journey from Ashland to Winona Lake had begun this turn in the 1930s. But, as described in the previous chapter, the impulse for the initial years at Grace Seminary was a desire to hold the Brethren tradition and American Evangelicalism in creative tension. In McClain's mind, for example, although evangelicalism offered a means to improve or reform the Brethren Church, it was not to replace it—preserving the Brethren heritage was of paramount importance.[3] By the 1960s, however, new tensions over Biblical inerrancy, ecumenism, and concerns about the "new" direction of mainstream evangelicalism pushed many conservatives, including individuals within the orbit of Grace Seminary, toward a stronger theology of vigilance that eclipsed the founding era and overshadowed much of the Anabaptist and Pietist heritage. As Tom Julien, veteran missionary and pastor in the Fellowship of Grace Brethren Churches would later tell a group of pastors, fundamentalism had become the new unofficial position for many of the fellowship's leadership. He counseled, "The attempt to infuse neo-fundamentalism into our fellowship has been an element of the current controversy that we have not easily recognized. It has, however, created much tension and provoked a great deal of personal suffering …" The extent to which this (neo)fundamentalist posture of the Fellowship defined the seminary as a whole is open to interpretation, but for president Hoyt and legendary Old Testament professor John Whitcomb, the struggle to vigilantly guard the gates against the threats of secular society and what they perceived to be the compromises of the evangelical mainstream was of utmost importance.

As with any subculture, fundamentalism has at times exhibited pervasive dispositions, such as a penchant for separatism, militant discourse and attitudes, and among other tendencies, a dualistic approach to intellectual matters. These cultural elements have always existed within fundamentalist circles but have evolved in response to developments and trends within American society. Around 1950, for example, several influential evangelicals, among them theologian and author Carl F. H. Henry and Boston Congregationalist minister John Ockenga, began to question the defensive and militant posture that represented the fundamentalist movement. Charting a course that retained a commitment to orthodoxy yet avoided the intellectual separatism of many fundamentalists, they fashioned a vision that would eventually represent mainstream evangelicalism. Known at the time as the "new" evangelicalism (neo-evangelicalism), this more irenic and intellectually integrative approach would come to be represented by popular spokespersons such as Billy Graham, and was embodied in the creation of new initiatives such as *Christianity Today* and the National Association of Evangelicals. After this point, those who self-identified as fundamentalists routinely condemned neo-evangelicalism and especially Graham's more ecumenical approach to evangelism. This new threat called for a new form of fundamentalist activism that committed itself to finding, showcasing, and defeating not just overt infidelity, but shades of suspected infidelity within the evangelical camp that were sure to lead to grosser heresies.[5]

During the same period, Cold War fears wreaked havoc on the American psyche. Many fundamentalists believed the rise of modernism, the threat of communism, the trends toward secularization, as well as moral declension constituted a perfect storm that seemed to threaten the very foundations of Christian America. Although popular evangelicalism has increasingly eclipsed the fundamentalist subculture, those who have continued to self-identify as fundamentalists remain in relatively small pockets across the country. Continuing to fix their attention on all that seems to threaten the pure gospel, they have come to relish their position on the margins of America society, taking pride in their separatism and suspicion.[6] It is largely for this reason that many conservative evangelicals today, including many at Grace, would acknowledge continuity with (classical) fundamentalism's original definition of orthodoxy, but would distance themselves from the cultural dispositions and defensive postures within more recent forms of fundamentalism.

Fundamentalism has a history in various evangelical denominations such as American Baptists or Presbyterians, as well as in nondenominational contexts. But as a cluster of tendencies, the fundamentalist mentality can surface in almost any religious context, including Anabaptist groups, of which the Brethren are a part. Among American Anabaptists, fundamentalism has sometimes included expectations for rigid adherence to particular Anabaptist cultural and theological distinctives such as dress expectations or requirements for nonresistance. Such is the case with the Mennonite fundamentalism found in the pages of the *Sword and Trumpet*, a periodical published by Virginia Mennonite Bishop George R. Brunk in the 1930s. It may also lead, however, to a loss of Anabaptist distinctives if it is aligned with the larger fundamentalist movement with its ties to broader American denominations.[7]

With this introduction in place, we now turn to the role that Herman Hoyt, John Whitcomb, and, to varying degrees, the seminary as a whole has played within American Fundamentalism.

Strong Theology, Strong Personalities

Those who remember McClain agree that he did not have the militant and separatist dispositions associated with much of the fundamentalist movement. Still, McClain believed there was reason to be uneasy with the direction that the "new" evangelicals were taking after mid-century. In response to a probing 1956 *Christian Life* article, "Is Evangelical Theology Changing," McClain wondered whether, in an effort to gain a more irenic reputation, evangelicals were too hesitant to condemn theological error and were becoming comfortable with mild forms of liberalism. "As history plainly teaches," he said,

> ... hobnobbing too closely with the enemy has always cost the cause of Christianity much more than it ever gained. ... It is both curious and disturbing today to find "evangelicals" who, while bewailing the belligerence of historical fundamentalism and advocating a closer rapprochement with the modern liberals, at the same time spend so much effort and time belaboring and fighting against their own side. It looks sometimes as if they might have gotten lost in the dust of the real battle for the faith.[8]

Indeed, although McClain, in his own "younger days," had once been uncomfortable with the "fundamentalist" label, he had by this time made his peace with it. "I found that nothing much can be done about labels," McClain admitted, "except to insist upon proper definitions and safeguards against misinterpretations. Even the name 'Christian' was probably a term of contempt in the beginning."[9] Notwithstanding the elderly McClain's hesitations about the broader evangelical landscape, it was under Herman Hoyt, McClain's successor, that the seminary moved more fully into a fundamentalist reaction to mainstream American society and to neo-evangelicalism specifically.

Hoyt had humble beginnings in rural Iowa where he learned a strong work-ethic. Making the trip over rough country roads from Iowa to Ashland, Ohio, in his father's Model T, the entire Hoyt family moved to Ohio so that Herman could attend seminary.[10] Hoyt became a close associate of McClain while at Ashland and was asked to resign with him. Following McClain to Winona Lake, Hoyt was a strong lieutenant and sometimes needed to assume some of McClain's responsibilities because of the president's ongoing health problems. Taking the helm in 1962, he oversaw a period of strong growth.[11] Greatly respected by many, Hoyt was known for his fiery dogmatism when it came to historic orthodoxy and Brethren distinctives. Yet those who worked closely with Hoyt also found him to be rigid and uncompromising, perhaps partly due to family problems during his upbringing.[12] Even students who were bold enough to disagree with him could find themselves at the receiving end of his brash style of dogmatism.[13]

Like McClain, Hoyt had a strong Brethren background and identity. Early on he contributed to McClain's attempt to synthesize the Brethren tradition with evangelical trends. Prior to 1960, Hoyt's publishing was a mixture of pastoral articles and defenses of Brethren positions, including several books on Brethren ordinances and non-resistance. After 1960, however, Hoyt's writings increasingly revolved around prophecy and were characterized by a pessimistic outlook about the trajectory of American society and education that was typical of dispensationalists who, like Hoyt, often gravitated toward eschatological speculation.[14] Operating with the assumption that the world was on a downward slope to depravity and chaos from which only the rapture would provide rescue, premillennialists have always had a special penchant for aligning worldly strife with biblical prophecy. We have already seen, for example, how end-times enthusiasts in the Brethren tradition, including Bauman and McClain, identified the years of world war with the prophetic writings of the Bible.[15]

As Hoyt made the transition from seminary dean to president, events in the larger world of evangelical higher education seemed especially ominous. Fuller Seminary, which had become the center of neo-evangelicalism, was embroiled in an internal battle between conservative and progressive factions. The year after Hoyt became president, it was clear that the progressives had won as David Hubbard succeeded the controversial Edward Carnell as Fuller's president. In response, several conservative faculty members left and some found their way to the growing evangelical powerhouse, Trinity Evangelical Divinity School.[16] The events at Fuller seemed to validate the fears that evangelicalism was becoming a new version of neo-orthodoxy with a weak commitment to biblical authority.[17] Squaring these events with the growing political unrest and the rise of the New Left, fundamentalists at Grace believed the moral climate of the nation and its churches were signs of the apostasy that would accompany the end times. As Robert Clouse observed three decades ago, Grace Brethren leaders after McClain's era increasingly defined the traditional notion of separation from the world in ways that more closely resembled American Fundamentalism and the emerging Religious Right, than a strictly Brethren heritage.[18]

Founded in 1960, the *Grace Journal* reflected these concerns, becoming an outlet for the seminary and a means of participating in fundamentalist scholarship—as well as providing a view of the intellectual culture of the campus.[19] Articles and book reviews during the 1960s and 70s show a consistent preference for the Bible Institute model of Christian education and a growing concern over increased secularization, especially in American education. The journal spotlighted articles in biblical studies not only by Grace Seminary professors but others within the fundamentalist network, and book reviews were often provided by local fundamentalist pastors. The general tenor of the journal was apologetic, favoring articles that exposed the evils of cults, defended tenets of fundamentalist orthodoxy, and sought to highlight the dangers of secularism, the apostasy of liberals, and the theological compromises of other "evangelicals."[20]

Campus lectures and debates centered on similar themes. In 1960, the seminary held a public forum in which to "debate" Edward Carnell's controversial book, *The Case for Orthodox Theology*. Despite its title, fundamentalists believed Carnell's book was full of compromise and blasted it accordingly. Charles Feinberg, a Jewish convert to Christianity who taught Old Testament at Dallas Theological Seminary before teaching and serving as dean at Talbot Theological Seminary, delivered the 1964 Bauman Memorial Lectures.[21]

Feinberg's addresses were standard hard-hitting dispensationalist fare with strong themes of moral and spiritual declension.

Likewise, such themes also figured prominently in President Hoyt's semi-regular column in the *Grace Journal*, "General Review: Events in Light of God's Word," a column that was not unlike Mc-Clain's earlier column in the *Brethren Evangelist*, "Signs of the Times." In 1964, for example, Hoyt's "General Review" condemned modern trends in public education, referencing, for example, a speech by Max Rafferty, Superintendent of Public Instruction for the state of California. According to Rafferty, gone were the days when students were taught to love America and the founding fathers. Public education now failed to endorse the glory of the Protestant ethic and had yielded to the "burning-eyed, thin-lipped disciples of Dr. Dewey." Sounding not unlike the Religious Right that would rally two decades later, Hoyt commented:

> To get back to the philosophy of education endorsed by our forefathers would be a start in the right direction. This means that the present trend in education which finally culminated in the decision of the Supreme Court to ban prayer and Bible reading from the classroom of tax-supported schools needs to be reversed; it means that the basic philosophy of education which made this nation great needs to be restored; it means that there needs to be a new dedication to the vital and unchanging verities of life if this nation conceived in recognition of the supernatural and determined to explore the benefits of divine beneficence for all shall long endure.[22]

Even national calamities were opportunities for learning theological lessons. Writing in response to the assassination of President Kennedy, Hoyt thought it was ironic that people were suddenly thinking more about eternal things despite the fact that Kennedy and other liberals had conspired to "rid the schools of our land and public life in general of the very thought of religion and God." In His providence, Hoyt believed God had allowed the assassination of the president in order to awaken the American people to repentance, in just the same way as he allowed the death of King Uzziah. "What appears to men to be the untimely termination of the administration of John F. Kennedy

A Quiet Voice for Women and the Arts: Jean Coverstone and the Building of the Grace College Visual Arts Program

Kim M. Reiff

In early 1970, against the backdrop of an ongoing cultural revolution in American society, Jean Coverstone was invited by Grace College to interview for an art faculty position. The Art Department had existed at Grace from 1955 to 1964, and classes were taught by Alva Steffler. In 1964, however, both the art major and minor were dropped. Then, in 1970, the administration decided to revive the department. At that time, Coverstone held a Bachelor of Science Degree in Art Education *summa cum laude*, was teaching art at a local high school, was active in her local church, and was completing her Master's Degree in Art History. As a potential candidate, Coverstone was aware that her role would include building the visual arts program—a rare opportunity for a woman.[1]

As an educated artist, conservative Christian, and a dedicated mother with a professional career, Coverstone was a complex figure. Although she tested the boundaries of traditional feminine spaces, she rejected the broader cultural shifts of her generation and its effects on the art world.

Social activism of the 1960s segued to the feminist movement of the 1970s. Female university professors had begun testifying before Congress in an effort to call attention to the discrimination of women in higher education.[2] Female visual artists were protesting the exclusion of women from standard college art history textbooks, and women's organizations were criticizing major art museums for lack of female representation in their collections.[3]

was in reality the fulfillment of God's wise and beneficent plan for this country, as must be concluded from the study of God's holy word."[23]

According to Hoyt, modernity and the march of "progress" were to blame for much of the unrest of the 1960s. Development and progress, Hoyt believed, "have projected a whole host of new things into civilization ... as a result, new dangers followed swiftly in the wake of these developments." Innovations in communication and travel were removing the "natural barriers of land and sea." Two world wars had "decimated the earth," and Hoyt predicted a third world war "is now in the making." What is more, increasing space travel and industrial automation were increasing the peril and struggle for survival. Intertwined with these rapid changes were "new doctrines" that more than anything else lay "at the root of the perils that threaten society." Through an "explosion of knowledge that is sweeping the world," Hoyt declared,

> The facts of astronomy, geology, and anthropology are outrunning the facts of theology. As a result, men are suffering from a lowering intellectual skyline and a diminishing horizon. Within these narrowing limits and on this lower level of visibility, they are not able to come to a full and rational comprehension of the facts at hand. Unwilling to wait for more light, they rush to faulty conclusions, the first of which is to reject the teaching of the Bible, and the second of which is to construct a new theology.[24]

Like others who resented the victories of social progressives, Hoyt believed one need only to observe the tumult that plagued the nation to see the fruit of America's downward spiral and the results of godlessness. The "insurrection" of student protests on college campuses, the "unbridled excess" of riots "in the name of freedom," and the "gross sensualism into which the human race is now plunging with utter abandon" were all signs of the final days. "The climax of this so-called new morality is yet ahead," Hoyt warned. "This means that the trend is down. It means that the source of this declension is men who are rotten at heart. It means that the course of this declension is progressive through deterrents to lower depths of degradation. It means that the force of this declension grows out of the ever-enlarging moral and spiritual deception."[25]

While women elevated their voices for change in both higher education and the art world, Jean Coverstone quietly led as a change-maker in the world around her. Offered a contract within three days of the interview, her journey began as a visual arts professor and the first chair of the Art Department at Grace College. Upon finishing graduate school, she became the first woman to earn a Master's Degree in Art History from the University of Notre Dame.[4] Her academic and educational achievements remain historically significant, both at Grace and beyond.

Coverstone was the sixth female hired to teach at Grace with professor status since the undergraduate division began in 1948. (The first female professor to hold a Doctorate degree at Grace was Suzanne Royer, who taught Mathematics beginning in 1963.)[5] Facing facility limitations with determination, Coverstone established the new Art Department in an old house located on the northwest corner of campus. She wrote curriculum and designed course content. Drawing, painting, crafts, and ceramics were taught in refurbished spaces, and 3-D design was taught in the basement furnace room. When it rained, Coverstone placed boards across flooded water for students to get to the new department. Although slacks were not considered appropriate attire for professional women (including female faculty at Grace), Coverstone would often be seen wearing them on campus, explaining that it was "practical" for the studio arts.[6]

The first six art majors were taught in the old house, while *Introduction to Fine Art*, with more than 100 students enrolled, was taught in Philathea Hall's *Little Theater*. Within four years Coverstone's full-time teaching load increased to 20 credit hours per semester, almost double the credit hours considered full-time today. By the late 1970s, Coverstone felt that art, influenced by changing social and political currents, had become increasingly secular and debilitating. In response, she worked to introduce her students to artistic achievements that influenced western civilization, specifically from a Christian perspective. Her belief

Also at the root of the problem were misguided eschatological interpretations. Making a jab at his ammillennial and covenant opponents, Hoyt declared that both those who provoke the "bold denial of a coming kingdom" and those who interpret the church "in terms of the kingdom were equally to blame because [their views] center upon the efforts of men to establish some sort of kingdom." In short, this entire spiritual decline was part of a general increase of paganism, new manifestations of pantheism, and the growing influence of "evil men and seducers."

The godlessness perceived in all directions seemed to validate the urgency the administration felt to construct an institution that would stand strong against the flood of moral decay and theological corruption within society and among their fellow "evangelicals."[26]

An Expanding Fundamentalist Presence

The nation may have been on the road to hell, but things were looking up at Grace College and Seminary. Under Hoyt's presidency, seminary enrollment increased steadily and the undergraduate college was enjoying similar growth. The construction of campus facilities struggled to keep pace. Philathea Hall was "completed"[27] and was to serve as the college academic building alongside McClain Hall, which housed the seminary. Within a decade of the completion of Philathea, Morgan Library, and the Science building were also standing tall.[28]

Through the 1960s, Grace Seminary gained firm standing among other well-known dispensationalist seminaries. Although the seminary would never surpass Dallas Theological Seminary, the center of the dispensationalist universe, some Grace students were known to jokingly parody 1 Corinthians 13:13: "And now abide these three: Talbot, Dallas, and Grace. And the greatest of these is Grace."[29] Grace seminary drew heavily from the continuing strength of the Bible College Movement, pulling in students from various dispensationalist schools such as Pennsylvania's Philadelphia College of the Bible and Lancaster Bible College as well as Chicago's Moody Bible Institute and Ohio's Cedarville College. The growing strength of the seminary meant that the new undergraduate college, though lacking the academic luster and pedigree of Wheaton College or Cal-

that, "God has given us this ability," and that "Anything that we do should be for the glory of God" led her to take a one-semester sabbatical to research and write an art history textbook with a Christian emphasis.[7]

Coverstone's scholarly endeavor took her to art museums, galleries, and libraries throughout Europe. According to Coverstone, "they were most gracious" in granting her and her husband, who served as her photographer, access to public and private art collections and in giving her permission to reproduce copyrighted works. After designing the layout, typesetting, and funding the initial production, her new textbook titled, *Landmarks in Art: art appreciation from an evangelical Christian's viewpoint*, was self-published in September, 1982.[8]

As Coverstone was building the art program, researching, and authoring an art history textbook, activism for women's equality continued in the foreground of the social climate. Dr. Bernice Sandler, committee chair of the Women's Equity Action League, had testified before Congress "… of 411 tenured professors at Harvard University's Graduate School of Arts and Sciences, the number of women tenured professors is: ZERO."[9] Criticism continued for Janson's college textbook, *History of Art* (1985), which included 3,000 male artists but no female artists. Feminist art courses emerged in academic institutions on the West Coast, and female scholars published textbooks featuring only women artists. The Los Angeles County Museum of Art responded to political demands by including women artists in notable exhibitions.[10] Although, Coverstone was aware that the contemporary art scene intended to reinsert "women's personal experience into art practice"[11] her focus remained on reinserting Christ into all art practice and also to help students to achieve faith-based academic goals. Her initiative in leading cross-cultural trips to study art in Europe enabled students to reflect on creativity that resulted from making art with "God in mind." She taught students to appreciate art forms that transcend time and historical cultural change and to observe closely how art

vin College, would also begin to compete with the same Bible colleges that were sending students on to Grace Seminary.[30]

By 1970, college and seminary administrators had reason for measured optimism. In addition to the aggressive building programs during the previous decade, and despite his wariness of modern progress, Hoyt happily reported to board members that an IBM computer had been installed (the campus' first) and within a few months, the new technology provided a new level of efficiency.[31] Perhaps the greatest reason for optimism, however, was the growth in enrollment. Board minutes throughout these years reveal impressive growth and ambitious projections. The institution's enrollment had doubled since 1965 and, given the "crisis of civilization," Hoyt proposed steps for even more growth. "If the winds and waves of present day conditions frighten us and argue for refusing to launch out in the deep, let us remember how this school started, in the midst of depression; and we launched out in faith and God did not forsake us."[32] Indeed, Hoyt declared "In many respects, in spite of the times in which we are now living, this has been the greatest year in the history of the school."[33]

Others on campus were equally thankful to be working at Grace, in effect building an educational haven from the world. Homer Kent, Jr., dean of the seminary and future president, reported to the board, "In these days of campus unrest throughout the world, it is an increasing source of gratification to work with more than 200 young men whose ideals are conditioned by the Word of God, and who are dedicated to the Lord's service."[34] William Male, academic dean, voiced similar sentiments: "In a day when riot and revolution are common terms on college and university campuses, I am especially grateful for the privilege of working with the kind of students and faculty that make up the Grace College academic community."[35]

One of the milestones of the Hoyt administration was a successful bid for accreditation by the Higher Learning Commission, an effort that proved somewhat controversial among the Grace community and its constituency. For supporters, accreditation would help to sustain ongoing enrollment growth and provide greater legitimacy to the institution. Those who opposed it, however, thought accreditation was sure to bring compromise. Accrediting agencies were no friend of Christian education, and it was thought that an effort to

reveals not only the artist's understanding of the human condition, but ultimately the artist's own spirituality.[12]

Coverstone's individualism did not fit into any one stereotype. As a United Methodist, she might have felt out of place at a Brethren institution, but she quietly dispelled concerns of theological incompatibility by explaining that she was a Christian above all else. Although a female change agent, she did not consider herself a feminist and even showed little interest in the

movement. She was progressive enough to include a few female artists in her textbook, but the presentation of art within her course materials could be viewed as reactionary or even Victorian in nature. Michelangelo's *David,* for example, appears in the textbook only from the waist up.

More than forty years later, as cultural revolutions continue on a global scale, Coverstone's accomplishments are unique. Acknowledging Jean Coverstone is recognition not only for a female artist in Christian higher education, but for all women in higher education. She was able to navigate, in her own way, through the atmosphere of a private conservative Christian college to lead as chair and successfully chart the direction for a visual arts program where students could see art from a Christian perspective.

As a conservative Christian artist, educator, and scholar, she was also proud to be a wife and mother of three sons. Coverstone taught and led by example with humility, selfless determination, and grace. Her vision for providing all students the opportunity to study art from a Christian perspective continues to influence Grace's Art Department and curriculum today. Her legacy remains a part of Grace's history and more importantly a part of American history.

—◆—

1. Jean Coverstone, interview with Kim Reiff and Kerith Ackley-Jelenik, May 2012, Mount Memorial Hall, Winona Lake, IN (audio recording and transcription).

2. Congressional Committee on Education and Labor, *Discrimination Against Women*, 91st Congress, 2d Session (Washington, DC: U.S. Government Printing Office, 1970). See also "A Changing of the Guard: Traditionalists, Feminists, and

secure the endorsement of those who did not share Christian values and worldview would lead to some of the compromises they observed at other institutions. Hoyt, who sometimes wondered if the commission was in fact an enemy of religion, nevertheless believed the advantages of accreditation outweighed the risks. After a lengthy process, accreditation was secured, though it came in the months following the start of Homer Kent, Jr.'s presidency.

John Whitcomb and the Popularization of Flood Geology

There is little question that much of the institution's burgeoning momentum was because of the growing reputation of John ("Jack") C. Whitcomb Jr., one of the seminary's most legendary professors and an individual who, along with Hoyt, represented the fundamentalist turn. Born in 1924, Whitcomb was raised in a family with military ties that went back to the Civil War. Whitcomb's father fought in both world wars, once serving as an officer under George C. Patton. Whitcomb himself had hopes of following in the military tradition, but his poor eyesight kept him out of West Point, and he enrolled in Princeton University to study International Affairs. His chance to serve came in 1944, however, when he was drafted and sent to Europe, where his service included time in an artillery unit during the Battle of the Bulge.[36]

Whitcomb's conversion took place through the ministry of Princeton Evangelical Fellowship (PEF), a campus club founded in 1931 by Donald G. Fullerton, a Princeton alumnus who had recently returned from missionary service in India and Afghanistan. Fullerton held Sunday afternoon Bible classes at Princeton for more than 50 years and frequently met with male students individually (Princeton University did not admit women until the fall of 1969) for Bible study and prayer.[37] John Teevan, a member of PEF who came to Grace Seminary, describes Fullerton as a "Scofield Bible dispensationalist with a holiness feel about him. ... The group [PEF] had an austere atmosphere and a strong sense of fundamentalist separatism. They did not interact or cooperate with other campus ministries such as Campus Crusade or Intervarsity."[38] With his strong personal commitment to Christian missions, Fullerton routinely

75

the New Face of Women in Congress 1955-1976" in *Women in Congress*, 108-223, retrieved at http://www.gpo.gov/fdsys/pkg/GPO-CDOC-108hdoc223/. Sandler's efforts led to the passage of Title IX, which was designed to address gender discrimination in education. She went on to publish government reports on women's equity in education over the next 40 years. See also Bernice Sandler, *On Campus with Women,* Association of American Colleges and Universities. Retrieved from http://www.aacu.org/ocww/volume32_1.

3. See www.aacu.org and http://historymatters.gmu.edu/d/6462/. Also consult Whitney Chadwick, *Women, Art, and Society* (London: Thames and Hudson, 2007); Judy Chicago, *Beyond the Flower: The Autobiography of a Feminist Artist* (New York, NY: Penguin, 1997); Eleanor Dickinson, *Discrimination in the Art Field* (New York, NY: Women's Caucus for Art, 2008); and *The Higher, the Fewer: Discrimination Against Women in Academia* (American Social History Productions, Inc., 1998-2013.) See also Judy Chicago, *The Dinner Party (*New York, NY: Merrill Publishers, 2007), 11. Chicago, a visual artist in Los Angeles, began the feminist art movement in the early 1970s as a result of being told by a male professor that no women had contributed to European intellectual history. She created an art installation titled, *The Dinner Party,* and in recognizing 1,038 women's achievements, the installation was intended to "promote social change." Initially controversial, Chicago's artwork and educational pedagogy are now recognized world-wide.

4. At the time Coverstone was hired in 1970, the small number of women teaching nationally in academic institutions with full-time professorial status was also historically significant. See also Historymatters.gmu.edu; usgpo, 1970. When she attended graduate school at the University of Notre Dame in pursuit of her Master's degree in Art History, female students were allowed to enroll in courses only during the summer months. Additionally, she was the only female in an all-male French language class, and women were not allowed on the campus golf course.

5. Thanks to Hillary Burgart for compiling data on faculty.

6. Women in Congress. H. Doc. 108-223 - Chapter III: *A Changing of the Guard: Traditionalists, Feminists, and the New Face of Women in Congress 1955-1976.* http://www.gpo.gov/fdsys/pkg/GPO-CDOC-108hdoc223/. In the early 1970s, females were not allowed to wear slacks in schools or government institutions. Deviating from traditional dress codes was a way for women to challenge the system. Although, Congresswomen wore pantsuits onto the Congressional floor as an act of defiance, Coverstone's wearing slacks on campus was "accepted" by her colleagues. See also Coverstone interview.

7. Coverstone interview.

8. Jean Coverstone, *Landmarks in Art: art appreciation from an evangelical Christian's viewpoint* (Syracuse, IN: Vintage Instant Print, 1982).

9. Congressional Committee on Education and Labor, *Discrimination Against Women*.

10. Chadwick, 355.

11. Ibid., 356.

12. Coverstone interview.

challenged the men in PEF to enter full-time Christian service and, as a strong dispensationalist, he channeled graduates toward dispensationalist seminaries such as Grace.[39] One long-time Grace faculty member commented, "There were always a few Princeton guys running around the seminary."[40]

Feeling called to the ministry, Whitcomb enrolled in Grace on Fullerton's recommendation and excelled in his studies under McClain, Homer Kent, Sr., and Herman Hoyt. Graduating with a B.D. in 1951, Whitcomb began teaching Old Testament and Hebrew while pursuing further studies in the seminary. By 1957 he had earned both a Th.M. and a Th.D. In the years that followed, Whitcomb served the seminary in various capacities, both in his teaching ministry and duties as a supervisory editor of the *Grace Journal*.[41]

More than service to the seminary, however, Whitcomb's legendary status in fundamentalist circles stemmed directly from his first book, *The Genesis Flood*, co-authored with Henry Morris, a revised version of Whitcomb's Grace Seminary dissertation.[42] The book argued for a universal deluge, rather than a localized flood as other evangelicals were theorizing. The book sought to demonstrate that Noah's flood was the best scientific as well as biblical accounting for the geological record. More significant than debates over the extent of the flood, however, was the fact that Whitcomb and Morris advocated an alternative interpretation of the observable geological record. Like other theories then, flood geology sought to reconcile apparent disparities between the biblical and geologic records—the earth only appeared millions of years old because the Noahic flood had so catastrophically altered the earth's crust. In essence, the book was as much an apologetic for a young earth, based on literal 24-hour days of creation, as it was a book about the Noahic flood.[43]

"Flood geology" was a recent concept but not a new theory. In its modern manifestation, it originated with George McCready Price, a member of the Seventh Day Adventists—a movement Whitcomb did not hesitate to label a "cult" in the pages of the *Grace Journal*.[44] Price's explanation of flood geology had been dismissed by the scientific community as well as evangelical geologists, and public connection with him would be a liability for Whitcomb and Morris, who downplayed any indebtedness there might have been to Price's theories.[45] More directly influential were the writings of Alfred Rehwinkel, a Lutheran scholar who represented a more orthodox advocate for flood geology.[46] Rehwinkel's *The Flood in the Light of the Bible, Geology, and Archeology* was required reading in Whitcomb's classes.[47]

Among the scientific community, *The Genesis Flood* was hardly noticed and among neo-evangelicals, it faced strident criticism—something that came as no surprise to Whitcomb.[48] Among fundamentalists, however, the book was an instant success. Numbers has written, "*The Genesis Flood* forever changed the lives of Whitcomb and Morris. The continuing controversy surrounding their book, which went through twenty-nine printings and over 200,000 copies in a quarter-century, turned them into highly sought-after celebrities, famous among fundamentalists as the Davids who slew the Goliath of evolution."[49]

Whitcomb's ongoing celebrity status among dogmatic creationists has transcended his previous connections with the Brethren tradition. The rise of modern young earth creationism, in which Whitcomb was an important part, has contributed to the polarization of evangelical discourse on origins. For many fundamentalist evangelicals today, especially premillennialists, "belief in creation" is code for a commitment to Whitcomb and Morris' brand of young earth flood geology. Other theories, though based on the creative action of God, are sometimes condemned or explained as a result of a compromised commitment to biblical inerrancy. Indeed, there seems to be an historical affinity between young earth creationism and the catastrophism of premillennialists like Hoyt. Linking Noah's flood with earth's future apocalyptic demise is a "compelling view of earth history," Numbers argues, since it is "framed by symmetrical catastrophic events and connected by a common hermeneutic."[50]

While Whitcomb and Morris "gave George McCready Price's Adventist flood theory a proper fundamentalist baptism and then skillfully promoted it as biblical orthodoxy," it would be wrong to assume that the young earth position had always been the default position among the faculty at Grace Seminary.[51] McClain, in fact, held to the Gap Theory, an old-earth view that posited a chronological "gap" between Genesis 1:1 ("In the beginning God created the heavens and the earth.") and Genesis 1:2 ("Now the earth was without form and void."). While it has less currency today, this view was prominent among such Bible-believing Christians as C. I. Scofield, William Jennings Bryan, and Bob Jones Sr. Thus, while McClain and Whitcomb's teaching careers overlapped, old earth and young earth theories coexisted at Grace Seminary. The presence of multiple theories of divine creation paralleled, in fact, the evangelical landscape of nineteenth-century America and can even be seen in the essays of the twelve-volume *Fundamentals of the Faith* (1915), which was a defining publication for the fundamentalist movement.[52]

A Narrowing Fundamentalist Culture

While championing the young earth cause, Whitcomb was also becoming increasingly vigilant in his opposition to neo-evangelicalism, which can be seen in his approach to the courses he taught. No matter who taught them, theology courses at Grace were based on McClain's course notes and syllabi until the 1990s.[53] These notes were sometimes augmented, however, based on the individual who was teaching. Whitcomb's course materials, for example, came to reflect a significantly harsher tone and a stronger apologetic, particularly against "charismatics" and mainstream evangelicals. He significantly enlarged McClain's treatment of the doctrine of inspiration, which had been comprised of a thorough but basic description of verbal plenary inspiration. To this, Whitcomb added nearly fifteen pages of explanatory and apologetic notes on inerrancy, including photocopied statements and short articles meant to indict neo-evangelicals, especially those at Fuller Seminary, for their compromises.[54] One student, sitting through the lecture, wrote in the margins of his notes, "Beware – This person [a neo-evangelical] could be the worst enemy! Warning Warning Warning."[55]

Appeals to Harold Lindsell's *Battle for the Bible* were typical, and Whitcomb called into question the orthodoxy of Billy Graham, who seemed soft on inerrancy and prone to ecumenical compromise. He also cited the divisions that plagued the Wenham Seminar held at Gordon College in 1966 as evidence of neo-evangelical compromise, declaring, "Thus, while the Lord Jesus Christ insisted on the absolute inerrancy of Scripture (Matt. 5:18 etc.), many modern 'evangelicals' desire to have freedom from such restrictions, and others do not consider the issue to be of sufficient importance to determine lines of organizational fellowship in the fulfillment of the Great Commission of our Lord."[56]

Whitcomb also included a litany of compromised Christian colleges, universities, and denominations and cited the downfall of the Ivy League schools, including Yale, Princeton, and Andover. Lamenting the seminary of his alma mater, he called Princeton's apostasy a "sad collapse."[57] In fact, Whitcomb operated under the assumption that a drift into apostasy was all but inevitable for any Christian institution. We live in a "negative environment," he said in an interview, where Satan's forces are out to destroy churches, denominations, and seminaries through theological compromise. History proves it, Whitcomb said, "There isn't a single Christian college that began in the 19th century that has remained faithful to the Bible." Thus orthodox fundamentalists were required to separate from apostate institutions, start new institutions that are "biblical," then when these decline, yet more separations and new initiatives are required.[58] For fundamentalists like Whitcomb, this perpetual cycle of separation became a foundational principle for operating within the world and in relation to other Christians. As late as 1986, Whitcomb was still using these materials, and he kept a thick file of evidence on Fuller Seminary's theological compromises from which he could provide evidence for students in his classes.[59]

Beginning around 1975, Whitcomb also taught a Philosophy of Religion course designed to accentuate the contrasts between fundamentalist orthodoxy and the errors of neo-evangelical compromise, including the sin of ecumenism.[60] He later changed the name to "Biblical Fundamentalism."[61] The class was also a defense of Whitcomb's theology of "second-degree" separation, which he laid out in a chart of circles. He stated that one of the essential errors of evangelicalism is its penchant to be soft on truth in the name of love. The strongest Christian love, Whitcomb taught students, was only to be reserved for those in a very small "inner circle." Whitcomb taught that Jesus provided an example of how Christians are to operate in society. John was the only disciple in Jesus' "inner circle" and therefore the only person to whom he would fully express love. Matthew, Mark, and Luke were regarded as having positions of "privilege," and the full twelve disciples were those with whom Christ would "fellowship." There were "seventy" alongside whom Christ could serve and

500 that had some degree of faith. Those in unbelief were limitless.[62] For Whitcomb, spiritual intimacy is unique and is to be reserved for only those with whom a person can experience spiritual purity. For unbelievers, whom Whitcomb equated to the biblical Pharisees, love is irrelevant. The way Jesus related to the Pharisees with nothing but cold hard truth is the model for how Christians are to relate to unbelievers, including liberals. Thus the further from this relational "inner circle" one moves, the more truth, and the less love, should be applied to the relationship. At the end of the day, love exists in an inverse relationship with truth.[63]

Whitcomb's course was also based on four clearly defined categories that framed fundamentalist identity in a way that was typical of theology courses at any number of fundamentalist Bible colleges and seminaries across the nation. The foundation is a concrete left-right spectrum that places liberalism on one side and fundamentalism on the other. Neo-orthodoxy is next to liberalism and neo-evangelicalism is then between neo-orthodoxy and fundamentalism. Since fundamentalism is as far as one can go on the right, the implication is that the further to the right a Christian is, the closer he is to biblical purity. The problem with neo-evangelicalism, is that it seems to be a new form of neo-orthodoxy, "drifting" toward liberalism.[64]

The Challenges of Growth

Homer Kent, Jr., dean of the seminary, succeeded Hoyt as president in 1976 and helped to grow combined college/seminary enrollment to 1333 in 1981—the largest enrollment figure until 2006 under Ron Manahan's tenure.[65] Known for his ability to allow for differences of opinion and to preserve peaceful relationships, Kent's leadership style represented a marked break with the more authoritarian model of Hoyt. It also anticipated the broader and more irenic styles of his successors, John Davis, and in turn Ronald Manahan, who began teaching at the Seminary around this time. By the 1980s, seminary enrollment continued to expand—reaching an all-time high of 427 students in 1983—as Grace became a central training hub not only for Grace Brethren students, but for students from the fundamentalist General Association of Regular Baptist Churches (GARBC) as well as the Independent Fundamental Churches of America (IFCA).[66]

The optimism that came with strong enrollment, however, simply masked the fissures that existed below the surface. The increase in students necessitated a growing cadre of new faculty hires, which in turn brought greater diversity. To be sure, the younger professors hired under Presidents Kent and Davis were theologically conservative and embraced dispensationalism, but many were orientated toward a broader evangelical spirit. Among these were Charles Smith, Skip Forbes, Jim Eisenbraun, Ted Hildebrandt, and Herbert Bateman, as well as Brent Sandy and Richard Averbeck. Sandy and Averbeck were Grace Seminary graduates who had gone on to do doctoral studies at top-tier institutions. These hires also included Larry Crabb, who was brought in to create a graduate program in Christian counseling.

Some among the strongest fundamentalist circles in the Fellowship, however, were suspicious about the broader evangelical mentality of the new generation of faculty, believing they represented the infiltration of compromise and neo-evangelicalism. Whitcomb, who came to share this sentiment, complained to Tom Julien, calling the younger faculty members "technocrats" who were more concerned with the technical aspects of biblical languages and literary genres than training men for the pastorate.[67] No doubt disturbing to Whitcomb, in 1985 the same academic year that Davis was appointed president, the undergraduate college had even hired a full time faculty member with a degree from Fuller Seminary.[68] Whitcomb's following among fundamentalist members of the Fellowship remained strong. Keeping up his rigorous speaking schedule, Whitcomb responded to concerns about the orthodoxy of the seminary faculty and at times publically voiced his frustrations with the direction of the seminary among his fundamentalist allies. He was becoming increasingly convinced that his fellow faculty members were watering down "the biblical values we hold dear," especially in the areas of creation, dispensationalism, psychology, female submission, and biblical authority. As a result, Whitcomb spoke with Davis "repeatedly" about the newer generation of faculty, believing this was his duty given his "deep concern for theological and doctrinal purity."[69] Not surprisingly, Whitcomb's colleagues resented his closed-door conversations with the administration and suspected he was attempting to have certain faculty members purged from the teaching roster.[70]

Even after Davis decided to dissolve Crabb's program in 1987, Whitcomb remained critical of the administration (See chapter 4). Davis acknowledged that there was room for some degree of diversity among the faculty and was content to deal patiently and "redemptively" if faculty members needed to be confronted.[71] Yet for Whitcomb, who became increasingly critical of Davis, the president's continuing to allow this academic freedom only compounded the problem. In 1989, he challenged the elders of the Columbus (Ohio) Grace Brethren Church, one of the flagship congregations of the FGBC, to conduct an investigation of the seminary faculty on charges that there remained "serious compromises"—compromises he would later compare to "cancer cells."[72] Adding fuel to the fire, leaders among the Fellowship's churches were experiencing a rift over the question of baptism. (See chapter 9.)

Whitcomb, realizing the tense situation, discussed the possibility of resigning with President Davis. Davis, however, persuaded him to stay on and finish out the 1989-1990 academic year. Yet within a few months, Davis received reports that Whitcomb was part of "clandestine" meetings with others in the area that seemed to indicate to him a new level of dissent.[73] In response, in February of 1990 after an hour-long discussion with Whitcomb, Davis made the controversial decision to remove Whitcomb immediately without the possibility of finishing out the last four months of the semester.[74] In the aftermath, Davis attributed the dismissal to Whitcomb's breach of institutional loyalty (insubordination), which was compounded by "personality" conflicts with other faculty members. Essentially, Davis believed Whitcomb's repeated accusations about Grace Seminary to off-campus audiences, which undermined the school's credibility and demeaned its professors, could no longer be tolerated. Whitcomb, who resented Davis' explanation since it seemed to sidestep the question of doctrine, remained convinced that heterodoxy was on the march and the administration was "sweeping it under the rug." The tension between these competing interpretations was accurately captured in a *Christianity Today* headline, "Trouble at Grace: Making Waves or Guarding the Truth?"[75]

In hindsight, the turmoil may have had more to do with competing approaches to pedagogy and theological certainty than with significant doctrinal differences. While Whitcomb was convinced his charges were not insignificant, most of the "compromises" he believed he saw did not explicitly contradict the seminary's doctrinal statement. Liberalism, in fact, was not actually in play. Three of the charges—that a professor had elevated the Septuagint to the level of the Hebrew autographs, that another had not adequately defined the meaning of "ex nihilo" creation, and that the school was not sufficiently anti-feminist, were issues not even addressed in the seminary statement of faith. Another charge, that one seminary professor did not "fully subscribe" to Dispensational Premilleniallism, was the only issue linked to the statement. Criticisms of Crabb's views on Christian counseling could be only indirectly linked to the statement's insistence on the sufficiency of the Bible.[76]

What is more, Jim Custer's board of elders at the Columbus, Ohio, church had acted on Whitcomb's 1989 challenge to investigate the seminary and had concluded that there were "enormous flaws" in his charges. In 1992, a more extensive investigation, which included interviews with numerous faculty members, revealed similar findings. The elders found Whitcomb's accusations, and those of others either "distortions of the truth" or simply false.[77] It is true, however, that the newer generation of faculty members, as they engaged in more mainstream scholarship and moved in broader circles, sought to bring a greater variety of voices to bear on seminary subjects and used a pedagogical style that allowed for more theological diversity. By its very nature, this represented a challenge to the fundamentalist approach of Whitcomb, Hoyt, and their allies, for whom this was evidence of theological slippage. Younger faculty, such as Charles Smith, for example, acknowledged ambiguity and routinely presented a spectrum of evangelical positions on various issues—thus intentionally stimulating intellectual tension among their students.[78] Others refused to endorse fundamentalist attitudes such as second-degree separation even though they knew Whitcomb was promoting it just a few doors down the hall.[79] In short, Whitcomb's fundamentalist orientation became increasingly out of step with both his fellow faculty members and the administration.

The vigilant and separatist posture of Hoyt and Whitcomb did not define every member of the seminary or represent official positions for the institution. Yet, as dynamic leaders and engaging teachers, these individuals unquestionably shaped the culture of the seminary in significant ways and helped to create tangible intersections with fundamentalist networks across the country. As the controversy in the seminary, along with the ouster of Whitcomb and the departure of Crabb became public, the seminary suffered a significant setback. Having peaked in 1983, enrollment continued to decline and consequently the faculty dwindled as well. Grace Seminary survived, however. Kept open on principle, since Grace was the sole institution of theological training for the Fellowship of Grace Brethren Churches, it was supported during the 1990s by the undergraduate college, which was experiencing continued growth. Although traumatic for those who experienced them, the dynamics, divisions, and passions that contributed to these turbulent years were not uncommon either on the larger landscape of American Evangelicalism or within numerous other evangelical institutions of higher learning. That being said, the Brethren heritage of Grace College and Seminary, with its Anabaptist and Pietist roots, and the institution's passionate leaders, has infused a degree of cultural particularity that has made Grace Seminary's sojourn in American fundamentalism unique.

Notes

1. Engel v. Vitale, June 1962.
2. Herman Hoyt, "Hold Fast the Form of Sound Words," Convocation sermon, Grace College and Theological Seminary, September, 1971. A printed version can be found in *Journal of Grace* (June 2002), 27-36.
3. M.M. Norris, "A Cord of Many Strands" in *The Activist Impulse*, 167-75.
4. Tom Julien, "Identity Shock—A Plea for Consensus," unpublished paper, FOCUS Retreat, 1993, 6-7.
5. See Douglas A. Sweeney, *The American Evangelical Story: A History of the Movement* (Ada, MI: Baker Academic: 2005), 155-180.
6. Hankins, *American Evangelicals*, 139-149.
7. On these tensions, consult essays by Benjamin Wetzel, Nathan E. Yoder, Jared S. Burkholder, and Matthew Eaton/Joel Boehner in Burkholder and Cramer, *Activist Impulse*.
8. Alva J. McClain, "Is Theology Changing in the Conservative Camp?" *The Brethren Missionary Herald*, Feb 23, 1957; "Is Evangelical Theology Changing," *Christian Life* 17:11 (March 1956):16-19.
9. Ibid.

10. Solon Hoyt, "Remembering my Brother" *Journal of Grace* (June 2002), 23-25.

11. Ronald T. Clutter, "Herman A. Hoyt, a Biographical Sketch" *Grace Theological Journal* 6:2 (Fall 1985), 180-186.

12. In a public interview, Robert Culver, graduate of Grace Seminary, seminary professor, as well as Hoyt's brother-in-law, commented that Hoyt's personality was shaped by a "dysfunctional" family background. Robert Culver, interview with Terry White and Jared Burkholder, Winona Lake Grace Brethren Church, June 23, 2013.

13. Skip Forbes, interview, November 15, 2012.

14. Robert D. Ibach, Jr., "The Writings of Herman Hoyt: A Select Bibliography, 1934-1984" *Grace Theological Journal* 6:2 (Fall 1985), 187-199.

15. See chapter 3 in the present volume.

16. George M. Marsden, *Reforming Fundamentalism: Fuller Seminary and the New Evangelicalism* (Grand Rapids: Wm. B. Erdmans Publishing Co., 1987, 1995), 208-224.

17. For fundamentalists, "neo-orthodoxy" was particularly dangerous because it made use of orthodox language for what were considered "liberal" theological positions.

18. Robert Clouse, "Fellowship of Grace Brethren Churches" in Donald F. Durnbaugh, *Meet the Brethren,* 101-113.

19. The *Grace Journal* ran from 1960 to 1973 under the editorship of Homer A. Kent Jr. In 1980 it was revived as *Grace Theological Journal* with John C. Whitcomb and D. Brent Sandy as main editors. It continued until 1991; the final two issues were edited by John J. Davis.

20. Edward Carnell, *The Case for Orthodox Theology* (Philadelphia, Westminster Press, 1959). Recordings of these forums can be accessed in the archives of Grace College and Seminary. On the controversy surrounding Carnell's book, see Marsden, *Reforming Fundamentalism,* 188-192.

21. Charles L. Feinberg, "God's Message to Man through the Prophets" *Grace Journal* 5:2 (spring 1964), 20.

22. Herman A. Hoyt, "General Review: Events viewed in the Light of God's Word" *Grace Journal* 5:2 (spring 1964), 27.

23. Herman A. Hoyt, "General Review: Events viewed in the Light of God's Word" *Grace Journal* 5:1 (Winter 1964), 42-43.

24. Herman A. Hoyt, "The New Doctrines and the New Dangers" *Grace Journal* 7:1 (Winter, 1966), 5.

25. Ibid., 4.

26. Ibid., 5-6.

27. The original plan for Philathea Hall was for a tri-level structure; however, the third floor was never added.

28. For a chronological description of the campus buildings, see Terry White, *Winona at 100.*

29. John C. Whitcomb, Interview by author, August 10, 2012.

30. Steve Grill, Interview by author, June 20, 2012.

31. Executive Board minutes, Grace College and Seminary Archives, February 18, 1970, page 350.

32. Ibid., 316-17.

33. Ibid., 409.

34. Ibid., 320.

35. Ibid., 393.

36. Paul J. Scharf, "A Biographical Tribute to Dr. John C. Whitcomb Jr." in *Coming to Grips with Genesis: Biblical Authority and the Age of the Earth*, Terry Mortenson and Thane H. Ury, eds. (Green Forest, AR: Master Books, 2008), 437-451.

37. Ibid., 439.

38. John Teevan, interview by author, June 26, 2012.

39. Ibid.

40. Steve Grill, interview by author, June 20, 2012.

41. Scharf, "Biographical Tribute."

42. Henry M. Morris and John C. Whitcomb, Jr., *The Genesis Flood: The Biblical Record and its Scientific Implications* (Philadelphia: The Presbyterian and Reformed Publishing Company, 1961).

43. On Whitcomb's role in the rise of the modern creationist movement and the impact of *The Genesis Flood*, see Ronald L. Numbers, *The Creationists: From Scientific Creationism to Intelligent Design* (Cambridge, MA: Harvard University Press, 2006), 211-235.

44. John C. Whitcomb, "Review," Norman F. Douty, *Another Look at Seventh-Day Adventism* in *The Grace Journal* 4:3 (Fall 1963), 41.

45. Numbers, *The Creationists*, 214-229.

46. Consult George McCready Price, *God's Two Books, or Plain Facts about Evolution, Geology, and the Bible* (Washington D.C.: Review and Herald Publishing Association, 1918) and Alfred M. Rehwinkel, *The Flood in the Light of the Bible, Geology, and Archeology* (Saint Louis: Concordia Publishing House, 1951).

47. Tom Julien, interview, October 12, 2012.

48. Numbers, *The Creationists* 214, 229-234.

49. Ibid., 234.

50. Ibid., 371.

51. Ibid., 338.

52. Barry Hankins, *American Evangelicals,* 51-67.

53. Several versions of McClain's theology notes can be found in the Morgan Library at Grace College and Seminary.

54. John C. Whitcomb, class notes for "Christian Theology: God and Revelation," (Fall 1986), in author's possession. It should be noted that McClain was a strong proponent of inerrancy, even if less strident than Whitcomb.

55. Ibid., 107.

56. Ibid., 112.

57. Ibid., 114.

58. John C. Whitcomb, interview by author, August 10, 2012

59. Frank Benyousky, interview by author, April, 8, 2013.

60. Whitcomb interview.

61. John C. Whitcomb, class notes for "Biblical Fundamentalism," circa 1980, Morgan Library.

62. Ibid.; See also John C. Whitcomb, "God's Truth Circles," Unpublished mimeographed paper, n.d.

63. Ibid., 22. Whitcomb's fundamentalist response to evangelical "ecumenism" can be seen in his *Christ: Our Pattern and Plan, an Analysis of Evangelical Missions and Evangelism in the Light of the Great Commission* (Winona Lake: BMH Books, 1976) and in the sermon, "When Love Divorces Doctrine and Unity Rejects Truth: A Response to End-time Ecumenism" (Whitcomb Ministries, Inc., 2011). Online at http://media.sermonaudio.com/mediapdf/730111036595.pdf, accessed 4/17/2013.

64. John C. Whitcomb, class notes for "Biblical Fundamentalism," 133.

65. Enrollment figures obtained from Carrie Yocum in the Office of Academic Affairs.

66. Jeffrey Gill, interview by author, January 15, 2013.

67. Julien, interview.

68. Benyousky, interview.

69. John C. Whitcomb to "Friends and Former Students," April 26, 1990.

70. Ibid.

71. Ibid.

72. Ibid.

73. John Davis, interview by M. M Norris and Jared S. Burkholder, June 11, 2012. Transcription by Hillary Burgardt.

74. Ibid.; Whitcomb to "Friends and Former Students"; Scharf, "Biographical Tribute."

75. "Trouble at Grace: Making Waves or Guarding the Truth?" *Christianity Today*, April 9, 1990, 46.

76. Custer, Augspurger, and Simmons to John J. Davis, December 4, 1992. Interestingly, the *Christianity Today* article that reported on the events at Grace erroneously reported that "The school officially maintains a young-earth, six 24-hour-day view of Creation."

77. Custer, Augspurger, and Simmons to John J. Davis.

78. Ibid. This can also be seen in Smith's theology course notes, which were made available to the author by John French.

79. Thanks to Roger Peugh for helpful conversations about this era.

Chapter 4

Piety
Contours of Spirituality
and Holistic Seminary Education

Christy M. Hill

IN HIS ARTICLE ON THE STRENGTHS OF THE PIETIST HERITAGE FOR Christian higher education, historian Christopher Gehrz argues that Pietism has consistently valued transformative experiences in education—that is, training that moves beyond scholastic exercises and toward education that deeply touches "the whole person."[1] Indeed, with Pietism's rejection of the institutional and intellectual formality of Protestant Scholasticism during the 17th century, its pursuit of "heart religion" within the context of community was a defining feature. Although most, if not all, Christian colleges and universities would promote such a holistic approach, the Pietist roots of the Brethren tradition include an especially robust and multifaceted foundation for promoting issues related to spirituality, sanctification, and personal transformation.[2] Pietism's emphasis on the inner life has also become part of American Evangelicalism.

There are, however, inherent tensions. Individual experience, whether in education or other settings, necessarily injects a subjective element into the Christian faith, and this has been an area in which Pietism has been consistently criticized. Indeed, evangelicals have often disagreed about the extent to which personal experience and Pietism itself are valuable.[3] These tensions can be seen in the history of Grace Theological Seminary with its roots in both traditional Brethrenism and American Evangelicalism. Additionally, the influence of Presbyterianism, including the old "Princeton

Theology" of A. A. Hodge and B. B. Warfield, has often facilitated opposition to subjective experiences and especially the "charismatic" gifts.[4] Tensions have also surfaced around the relationship between traditional notions of Brethren spirituality and the application of modern psychology within Christian counseling as well as around the notion of "spiritual formation." Yet another tension is the relationship between inner transformation and outward expectations of behavior.

In spite of these tensions, or perhaps because of them, the faculty and students at Grace College and Seminary, like those at other Christian institutions, have attempted to foster a healthy balance of warm spirituality, academic rigor, and practical Christianity. This chapter explores these issues with the purpose of highlighting this quest for a holistic education at Grace Seminary. The current mission statement reflects more recent efforts to accomplish this since the seminary began its rebirth in the early 1990s. The campus, it states, is meant to be "a learning community dedicated to teaching, training, and transforming the whole person for local church and global ministry."[5] Although statements such as this, which are meant to provide a target for which to shoot, are neat and tidy, the process of arriving at, as well as achieving these goals, has been less so. Thus, developing its present emphasis has been a journey that has included strong foundations, vigorous building years, shaky controversy, and hopeful rebirth.

Outward Evidences

Homer Kent Jr., president of the college and seminary from 1976 to 1986, recalled the way he experienced the integration of academics, personal faith, and ministry during the early years of the seminary, and the kind of education he sought to inspire as an educator and president:

> Each of our professors was completely dedicated not only
> to teaching his academic material, but in applying it to the
> students. As a student, and later as a young faculty member,
> I remember each professor applying what he taught to the
> personal lives of his students so that they could do the same
> in their own teaching ministries when they graduated. To

separate these two concepts as seems to be the practice today was not an issue in those days. All of the professors attended local churches, many of them often preached or taught Sunday School, and expected the students to be regular churchgoers. We did not regard the development of faithful living on the part of the students as something missing or ignored, but simply as something taken for granted. Furthermore, the school was small enough that there was much interaction between students and faculty outside the classroom.[6]

Other individuals, such as Jesse Deloe, a former seminary student, assistant to President Kent, and present lay-leader in the Fellowship of Grace Brethren Churches, pointed to the seminary's chapel services and the sense of community among the students as factors that helped to develop a healthy culture of spirituality.[7] For those among the early generation, such as Kent and Deloe, a spiritual tone—whether in the classroom, in chapel messages, or among students informally—was an ongoing driving force of Grace Seminary.

Notions of transformation could also revolve around behavioral standards. Though for many in the church today, this may not seem consistent with an emphasis on inner spirituality, following the rules in an effort to maintain a godly life was viewed as "evidence and fruit" of inward maturity and spiritual vitality. The seminary's original 1938 Covenant of Faith attested to this desire to see God's Word reflected as tangible fruit in the lifestyles of faculty and students.[8] Indeed, McClain and those in his circle possessed a strong awareness of the need for personal holiness and growth in spiritual maturity. Reflecting Grace's Brethren heritage, the statement framed the outward evidence of inner transformation in the language of nonconformity and separation from the world, a part of Anabaptist identity that meshed well with similar emphases within American fundamentalism:

> We believe in righteous living and good works, not as the procuring cause of salvation in any sense, but as its proper evidence and fruit (1 John 3:9-11, 4:19, 5:4, Eph. 2:8-10, Tit. 2:14, Matt. 7:16-18, 1 Cor. 15:10); and therefore as Christians we should keep the Word of our Lord (John

14:23), seek the things which are above (Col. 3:1), walk as He walked (1 John 2:6), be careful to maintain good works (Tit. 3:8), and especially accept as our solemn responsibility the duty and privilege of bearing the Gospel to a lost world in order that we may bear much fruit (Acts 1:8, 2 Cor. 5:19, John 15:16); remembering that a victorious and fruitful Christian life is possible only for those who have learned they are not under law but under grace (Rom. 6:14), and who in gratitude for the infinite and undeserved mercies of God have presented themselves wholly to Him for His service (Rom. 12:1-2).[9]

We believe in separation from the world; that since our Christian citizenship is in heaven, as the children of God we should walk in separation from this present world, having no fellowship with its evil ways (Phil. 3:20 ASV, 2 Cor. 6:14-18, Rom. 12:2, Eph. 5:11), abstaining from all worldly amusements and unclean habits which defile mind and body (Luke 8:14, 1 Thess. 5:22, 1 Tim. 5:6, 1 Pet. 2:11, Eph. 5:3-11, Col. 3:17, Eph. 5:3-5, 18, 1 Cor. 6:19-20), from the sin of divorce and remarriage as forbidden by our Lord (Matt. 19:9), from the swearing of any oath (Jas. 5:12), from the use of unbelieving courts for the settlement of disputes between Christians (1 Cor. 6:1- 9), and from taking personal vengeance in carnal strife (Rom. 12:18-21, 2 Cor. 10:3-4).[10]

As these formulations indicate, outward standards of living, based on what were understood as biblical requirements, were linked directly with the transformation of the whole person. In other words, one's behavior as an individual who was set-apart and distinct from the world was a significant litmus test of inner spiritual maturity. By coming to Grace, seminary students were expected to live a different lifestyle than the world, which was assumed would either be evidence of growth and maturity or would lead to it. The rigors of seminary were about more than simply developing the mind—it was meant to be training in personal holiness.[11]

Still, there were times when seminary professors, especially during its strong fundamentalist period, may have had a tendency to place scholasticism above genuine maturity, assuming that intellectual proficiency meant spiritual development as well. But as experience shows, that is not always the case.[12] So while evangelicals today are indebted to earlier efforts to preserve the fundamentals of the faith, in hindsight, we can see that there may have been significant blind spots within the fundamentalist culture and approach to education. By wrestling for orthodoxy, they perhaps neglected to foster one of the fundamentals of both the Brethren tradition and the Great Commission: to disciple.

Discipleship in its very essence implies relationship.[13] Without any intentional emphasis on this, discipleship and spiritual formation were assumed to be occurring in the classroom and through the emphasis on accurate textual analysis of the Bible. For some, the conservative scholasticism of the seminary, with its academic rigor and professional distance, communicated that students were encouraged to respect the academic standing of their professors without substantive personal engagement. Jeff Gill, the current vice president and dean of the seminary, described his experience at Grace Seminary in different terms than Kent or Deloe, as referenced above. His experience during the late 1970s and early 1980s was that academics were strongly emphasized, but student-faculty relationships were not. This led, he believes, to a culture of formality, in which students did not feel comfortable asking honest and probing questions and interacting personally with professors.[14]

While Grace College and Seminary has come to embrace more intentional programs for inner transformation, there seem to have been times during this period when spiritual experience was overshadowed by the belief that encouraging, and even enforcing outward behavior—such as hair length, dress, etc.—was evidence of spiritual maturity. Yet it would seem that this approach neglected the deeper infrastructure of inner life change, where the real beliefs and worldview of students are shaped by the truth of God's Word and the experience of His love. In some cases, the strong fundamentalist identity of the seminary at certain points created an atmosphere that competed with the desire to foster this vibrant inner transformation.[15]

There is much from the past that is worthy of admiration, and there is no question that fostering inner spirituality was important to faculty and students from the beginning. We can also appreciate the important heritage of nonconformity that is rooted in the Anabaptist-Brethren ethic. Still, from today's perspective, the seminary has perhaps found a healthier balance in which outward behavior and living separate lives are integrated with personal experiences of God's love and an emphasis on motivation and restoration. In many ways, the tensions explored above probably contributed to some of the shaky and even controversial years the seminary experienced, especially concerning the place of counseling in the church.

Controversies over Counseling

A greater emphasis on counseling as part of the seminary's commitment to train pastors and ministry leaders was just one of the many contributions of President Kent. This effort was also implemented under the direction of Michael Grill, a Grace College graduate who brought a decade of service as a school psychologist when he began teaching at the college in 1978. Four years later, in 1982, Grill was instrumental in bringing Larry Crabb to the seminary in order to establish a counseling program for graduate students.[16]

Born in 1944, Crabb "stumbled" his way into psychology during college. Then, after completing a PhD and briefly teaching at the University of Illinois, he began private practice in 1973.[17] The validity of mainstream psychology was intensely debated among evangelicals at the time. Jay E. Adams' "nouthetic" approach was a reaction to the influence of secular psychology in Christian circles and his *Competent to Counsel* (1970) called for a complete rejection of psychological principles in favor of the Bible alone. This resonated with fundamentalist evangelicals but was criticized by "integrationists" who saw more compatibility between Christian counseling and secular psychology.

During his career at Grace Seminary, Crabb established the short-lived Institute of Biblical Counseling, hired Dan Allender, who would also become a prominent therapist, and continued his writing and speaking ministry. In a short time, the seminary developed a strong reputation as a training center for Christian counseling. Yet Crabb was soon at the center of the debates over the place of psychology among evangelicals as well as the degree of internal examination through which counselors should be led during their training. While teaching at Grace, Crabb published *Understanding People: Deep Longings for Relationships* and *Inside Out*, using his classroom materials. Both books were highly successful, bringing yet more visibility to Crabb and his increasingly prominent approach to the inner life. As the counseling program continued to attract students, it also attracted fierce criticism from both inside and outside the seminary. Although he steered something of a *via media* between the nouthetic and integrationist poles, critics, including some of his fellow faculty members, believed he leaned too far toward the integrationist side, citing his 1977 publication, *Effective Biblical Counseling* as evidence.[18]

John Whitcomb in particular singled out Crabb for criticism, believing, as we have seen in a previous chapter, that Crabb was part of a new and compromised generation of faculty members who were leading the seminary away from biblical teaching. By many accounts, however, Crabb also had a strong personality and an independent spirit that at times made it difficult for him to work well with conservatives like Whitcomb and their expectations.[19] To compound the situation, some local church leaders believed Crabb was too critical of their conservative wariness of psychology and was teaching his graduates to be equally critical.[20] Crabb's frustration over the controversies and the criticism he experienced surfaced in his introduction to *Understanding People*. He described two competing camps: the "self-love theorists" who promoted the necessities of positive self-esteem, and the "stiff exegetes," who cared more for scholastic exercises than internal transformation. Crabb, who declared he fell into neither camp, did not name names, but his fundamentalist colleagues felt they had little doubt that his reference to "stiff exegetes" was a jab at them.[21]

Not surprisingly, a tangible fissure developed between those in traditional biblical studies and ministry programs, many of whom aligned with Whitcomb, and those in the counseling program, who were attracted to Crabb's teaching and methodology.[22] Clearly, the two most visible and charismatic personalities at the seminary represented incompatible assumptions and aspirations. Many people who were around during this era remember these years with sadness, as they realized that, for those on both sides of the growing divide, pride and ego were at times more at play than spiritual maturity.[23] In an effort to restore a sense of unity to the seminary, then President Davis made the tough decision to close down the very successful, albeit controversial, counseling program in 1987 (though Crabb stayed until his last cohort of students were finished.)[24]

Although Crabb's departure was amid unhappy circumstances, Ron Manahan, who was then teaching Old Testament, proposed to Crabb that perhaps it was God's way of releasing him for a larger audience and realm of influence beyond the campus setting.[25] This perspective proved true, as Crabb has remained highly influential in evangelical circles. While Crabb's tenure at Grace Seminary was brief, his impact was far reaching. Indeed, many who are currently teaching in both the Seminary and Graduate Counseling program have been influenced by him directly or indirectly, and these programs are today among the most robust programs on campus.

Rebirth and Refocus

With Crabb's departure between 1987 and 1989 as well as Whitcomb's dismissal during the same period, (see chapter 2), the seminary lost its two evangelical celebrities. Enrollment dropped quickly and financial challenges followed suit. The seminary would barely survive, kept open on principle. Yet it was clear that the "old" Grace Seminary, with its storied fundamentalist past, was dead. A rebirth was the only path forward and so David Plaster, a much-loved Grace Brethren pastor and denominational historian, was appointed academic dean in 1990. Under Plaster's leadership, the seminary began a shift in thinking about seminary training and what it meant to educate the whole person. Plaster, whose teaching included a course on the seminary's Brethren heritage, sought to revisit the strong spiritual foundations developed by the original founders, as he understood them. He also listened to the needs of a new generation of ministry students. In a strategic move, he cast a new and focused vision for Grace Seminary's future mission. He hoped that Grace Seminary would again develop a strong emphasis on the practical components of training pastors and missionaries in addition to preparing people for the more technical pursuits related to advanced degrees. In 1992, Plaster made the difficult decision to drop the Doctor of Theology program, and the Master of Divinity curriculum was retooled to reflect the change of emphasis. It now included new areas of applied theology, such as ministry leadership and pastoral care. It would also give academic credit for self-study courses fulfilled through students' ministry experience.[26]

The seminary's rebirth did not take place overnight, however, and bad press sometimes hurt momentum. Indeed, a *Christianity Today* article in January of 1993 under the ominous headline "Grace Seminary Cuts Program"[27] referred only to the Doctor of Theology program. Yet some misunderstood the article and thought that the seminary was in fact closing, probably due to the story's final quote in which Old Testament Professor Donald Fowler said, "We are forced to attend the funeral of an institution we loved and believed in."[28] Although Fowler was correct that dropping the Th.D. marked the end of an era, his statement created confusion among *Christianity Today* readers and many influential leaders over the status of the well-known dispensational powerhouse.[29]

The seminary did not, in fact, close its doors, and eventually, with a much smaller faculty and a new focus, it would rebound in time and remain viable both economically and spiritually. Although this was a humbling time for Grace's leaders, a renewed desire to keep Grace focused on its mission came with President Manahan, who was appointed by the board in 1994, four years after Plaster began efforts to resuscitate the seminary. Manahan also contributed a robust vision for holistic education, not just for the seminary, but for the whole campus.[30]

By the turn of the new millennium, Plaster had successfully adjusted the focus of the new Grace Seminary and, in continued partnership with Manahan, its gradual growth could soon support several new hires. In 2002, Jeff Gill, currently vice president and dean of the seminary, was hired to continue efforts to revitalize the seminary and by 2006, three new faculty members were hired, holding degrees from such schools as Trinity Evangelical Divinity School, Wheaton Graduate School, and Talbot School of Theology. Under Gill, mainstays of the traditional seminary education— exegetical, theological, and language components—would continue to serve as the foundation under the leadership of a new cohort of faculty members consisting of full time professors Mark Soto,

Piety at Work:
Women of Grace Schools

Paulette Sauders

Early on in the life of the seminary, women were active members of the Grace community and carved out space for pursuing piety and Christian service through Faculty Women's Club (FWC), a parent organization for various initiatives across the campus. FWC was comprised of female faculty members as well as wives of male faculty and administrators.

One of these "daughter groups" was Seminary Women's Fellowship. Since its founding, the seminary has ministered to seminary students and their spouses, and by the 1960s this fellowship group was thriving. Grace Seminary faculty members offered informal evening classes and instruction in the Bible for the women and covered various topics that were relevant to their future ministries. The costs of childcare and honorariums to faculty members who led the classes were taken from FWC membership dues. Gradually, the club started supporting special projects on campus in addition to the classes for Seminary Women's Fellowship. Projects have included donations to help pay for the sound system in Rodeheaver Auditorium and Grace College's prison program in its beginning.

Eventually, changes were made to make the group more inclusive. Mandatory dues were dropped and membership was opened to all female Grace employees and wives. To reflect this shift, the name of FWC was changed to Women of Grace Schools (WGS),[1] and fund-raising projects, instead of dues, now financed service projects. The group continued to cultivate an atmosphere of prayer and over the years WGS has helped make a variety of campus improvements for the benefit of students—from outdoor benches to bike racks. They have also helped students pay for their required

Roger Peugh, Ken Bickel, Thomas Stallter, Matthew Harmon, Tiberius Rata, and Christy (Morr) Hill. Hill was the first full-time female seminary professor. Gill overhauled the purpose statement, defining core values that created the portrait of a spiritually healthy seminary that reflected a holistic approach: "Grace Theological Seminary is a learning community dedicated to teaching, training, and transforming the whole person for local church and global ministry."[31] The core values of this process of training include being "1) Biblically Rooted; 2) Culturally Sensitive; 3) Ministry Focused; 4) Academically Excellent; and 5) Spiritually Transforming."[32] Further evidence of the seminary's recent shift toward a more robust notion of holistic education appears in the Grace Theological Seminary catalog:

> Intellectual development cannot be the only objective of Grace Theological Seminary for its students. Seminary education must make no less contribution to the student's spiritual life than it does to his or her intellectual growth. The seminary's faculty and administration frankly and humbly recognize that the right kind of spiritual atmosphere can neither be produced nor maintained by human mechanics or techniques. The creation of this atmosphere depends wholly upon the all-sufficient grace of the Lord, flowing through truly regenerated lives—lives that are characterized by walking in His Spirit, submission to His will, and trusting in His power. Therefore, one of the seminary's primary goals is that all institutional activities be surrounded with an attitude of prayer and devotion centered in Him. Not only chapel services and prayer meetings, but also every class, every task, and even examinations, should be, by God's grace, avenues of spiritual blessing through which His presence may be felt and His will realized.[33]

The direction in which Gill has chosen to lead the seminary is in part a response to what he believes were common perceptions by students that the "old" seminary emphasized scholastic rigor to the detriment of spiritual growth and practical ministry and strong mentoring relationships. Thus, Gill has intentionally hired faculty who have a passion to disciple students through the educational process inside

cross-cultural trips. Since 2013, WGS (now Grace Ladies Organization) has supported a mentoring program for women on the Grace campus.

Although names have changed, the overall goal for these organizations has remained the same—to facilitate prayerful piety and service among women associated with Grace College and Seminary.

———

1. Initially, the new name was simply "Women of Grace," but a year later, the national Women's Missionary Council of the Fellowship of Grace Brethren Churches adopted the same name, and therefore, "schools" was added to the title to distinguish the two groups.

and outside the classroom. One of his strongest criteria for new faculty has been evidence that they integrate academic credentials with practical ministry experience. All new faculty members have had significant ministry experience in the field of their expertise, which gives them the ability to walk alongside their students in a mentoring role.[34]

Beyond creating a team of spiritually passionate people, the administration has significantly revised the curriculum. While all of the courses are designed to challenge students spiritually, new classes have been added to the required courses for all programs to provide more practical application in learning. For example, Roger Peugh's passion for the discipline of prayer has been embedded in the program, creating a requirement for students to actually put into practice what they are learning about prayer.[35] Through expectations that students actually practice prayer and by reflecting on one's spiritual growth along the way, Peugh has become known to undergraduate and seminary students alike as a spiritual guide and mentor. A true Pietist, Peugh models deep emotion and godly compassion, and his life is an open book, allowing students to benefit from his honest transparency—something that was no doubt reflected in the campus' decision to select Peugh for the 2011 McClain Award for teaching excellence.

The seminary also rolled out a class specifically on Spiritual Formation. The class, initially designed by Ken Bickel was then expanded in 2006 under the direction of Christy (Morr) Hill, who specializes in spiritual formation. Although this approach to discipleship has made some evangelicals nervous, at the heart of spiritual formation is simply holistic inner-life transformation exhibited in all areas of development: mental, relational, emotional, behavioral, and moral.[36] "From a biblical foundation," according to John Dettoni, "spiritual formation is an intentional, multifaceted process which promotes transformation by which Christ is formed in us so that we can become His continually maturing disciples." [37] This transformation is rooted in a dual emphasis on biblical truth and the unconditional love of God, and is most fully experienced in the context of Christian community.

In addition to new curriculum, faculty-led mentoring groups became a new requirement for students in the fall of 2006. Students still have an opportunity to worship together in a weekly chapel service, but they are now placed in small groups where they are able to share what is going on in their lives and find support and encouragement from the Grace community. These small groups, which give a nod to the Pietist notion of *ecclesiolae in ecclesia* ("little churches within the church"), seek to create an environment where life can be shared together, where students' lives are known in a more interpersonal setting, where truth can be spoken in love, and where prayer is engaged in community. Students are invited into the faculty member's life and in some cases, even their home. These weekly touch points between students and faculty create an opportunity for spiritual involvement beyond the classroom.

Graduate degrees in counseling were also revived. With encouragement from Ron Manahan, then academic dean, Thomas Edgington, who had been teaching in psychology and sociology since 1981, proposed rekindling the MDiv in counseling. Plaster and President Davis were understandably gun-shy about another go-around with a seminary counseling program, and required Edgington to go before the seminary faculty to convince them his program would avoid the pitfalls that had earlier plagued Crabb's program. Successfully making his case, the MDiv in counseling began anew in 1994 and the next year, Edgington also supervised the start of an MA in counseling, although this was housed under the college. Edgington, who is currently dean of the School of Behavioral Sciences, and Tammy Schultz, who led the MA program from 2003 to 2012, effectively steered clear of substantial theological controversy. Wrestling to find a balance between leading students through their own personal transformation as well as providing practical and clinical counseling skills, these programs have been consistent with earlier desires to provide a holistic educational culture and have been buttressed by both Edgington's and Shultz's publishing efforts. One of the graduate counseling program's newest initiatives has been to extend its methodology to a "hybrid" teaching platform with a strong online component.[38]

With the passing of the old seminary, the institution has suffered, then rebounded. The most recent changes have occurred in 2008. Under the leadership of then provost Bill Katip, the seminary was brought in as the primary wing of the newly formed School of Ministry Studies, which was also given oversight, under Gill, of the undergraduate curriculum in Bible and Religious Studies. In 2012, it also moved into a building that it shares with the graduate counseling program, enhancing the sense of identity among these grad students and their faculty. What is more, President Manahan's commitment to the integration of the liberal arts and spiritual formation across the campus also complemented this growth at the seminary over the last two decades. In sum, Grace Theological Seminary, in its efforts to educate and train the whole person and promote genuine transformation, has incorporated various approaches to theological education and the culture of the campus. These efforts have produced various shifts throughout Grace's 75 years. Beginning as a reactionary effort to chart a new course, the seminary came to enjoy numerical success, even as it preserved a persistent fundamentalist flair. Yet, with the rebirth of the "new" seminary completed in 2008, pursuing a vibrant and holistic education remains a vital part of the overall efforts at both the college and seminary—efforts that resemble the yearnings of those within the Pietist movement that helped to shape beginnings of the Brethren tradition more than three centuries ago.

Notes

1. Christopher Gehrz, "Recovering a Pietist Understanding of Christian Higher Education: Carl H. Lundquist and Karl A. Olsson," *Christian Scholar's Review* XL: 2 (Winter 2011).

2. See Michelle A. Clifton-Soderstrom, *Angels, Worms, and Bogeys: The Christian Ethic of Pietism* (Eugene, OR: Cascade Books, 2010).

3. See Douglas H. Shantz, *An Introduction to German Pietism: Protestant Renewal at the Dawn of Modern Europe* (Baltimore: The Johns Hopkins University Press: 2013), 283-290, and Roger Olson, "Pietism: Myths and Realities" in Christian T. Collins Winn, Christopher Gehrz, G. William Carlson, and Eric Holst, eds., *The Pietist Impulse in Christianity* (Eugene, OR: Pickwick Publications, 2011), 3-16.

4. M. M Norris, "A Cord of Many Strands" in *The Activist Impulse*, 168. McClain's theology class notes can be accessed in the Morgan Library holdings and illustrate his use of Hodge and Warfield. Anti-Charismatic sentiments can be seen best in John Whitcomb's class notes, which are also available.

5. Grace Theological Seminary website, http://www.grace.edu/academics/seminary/about-seminary (accessed June 13, 2012).

6. Homer A. Kent Jr., June 28, 2012.

7. Jesse Deloe, interview by author, June 29, 2012.

8. The Covenant of Faith, which became official in 1938 and continues to represent the seminary, was reproduced in the 1951 yearbook, *Xaris*, 6-7.

9. "Righteous Living and Good Works," Grace Theological Seminary Covenant of Faith, 1938.

10. "Separation from the World," Grace Theological Seminary Covenant of Faith, 1938.

11. Ronald Manahan, interview by author, March 12, 2012.

12. Behavior always follows our "deep beliefs," not our professed beliefs. As Dallas Willard has argued, people always live up to their true beliefs—or down to them—whatever the case may be. See Willard's, *The Divine Conspiracy* (New York: Harper Collins, 1998). Klaus Issler and Donald Habermas argue that it is a "misconception" to assume that "students automatically change their conduct once they acquire new information." See *How We Learn: A Christian Teacher's Guide to Educational Psychology* (Grand Rapids: Baker Books, 1994), 22.

13. See Michael Wilkins, *Following the Master* (Grand Rapids: Zondervan, 1992).

14. Jeffrey Gill, interview by author, February 15, 2012.

15. Manahan, interview.

16. Michael Grill, interview by author, February 9, 2012.

17. Larry Crabb, "Sovereign Stumbling: My Life Journey to Date," New Way Ministries, http://www.newwayministries.org/sovstumbling.php, accessed April 18, 2013.

18. Crabb defended some integration in chapter two especially: "Christianity and Psychology: Enemies or Allies?"

19. Michael Grill and Thomas Edgington, interview by author, February 9, 2012.

20. Ken Bickel, email interview by author, January 5, 2012; John C. Whitcomb, open letter to "Friends and Former Students," April 26, 1990; Elders of the Columbus Grace Brethren Church to Dr. John J. Davis, December 4, 1992.

21. Thomas Edgington, interview by Jared S. Burkholder, September 17, 2013.

22. Edgington, interview.

23. Bickel email interview; Kent and Karla Denlinger interview.

24. Kent Jr., interview; Grill and Edgington interview.

25. Manahan, interview.

26. Bickel, email interview.

27. "Grace Seminary Cuts Program," *Christianity Today* 37:1 (January 11, 1993): 46-22.

28. Ibid.

29. Roger Peugh, interview by author, April 2, 2012.

30. Manahan, interview.

31. Grace Seminary Catalog: http://www.grace.edu/files/uploads/webfm/academics/catalog/11-12/7b-Grace_Theological_Seminary_Catalog_2011-12.pdf, (accessed August 4, 2012).

32. Ibid.

33. Ibid.

34. Gill, interview.

35. Peugh, interview.

36. Steven Porter, "Sanctification in a New Key: Relieving Evangelical Anxieties Over Spiritual Formation," *Journal of Spiritual Formation and Soul Care* 1:2 (Fall 2008), 129-148.

37. John Dettoni, "What Is Spiritual Formation?" in Kenneth Gangel and James Wilhoit, eds., *The Christian Educator's Handbook on Spiritual Formation* (Grand Rapids: Baker Books, 1994), 15.

38. Tammy Schultz, Interview by author, April 4, 2012.

Alexander Mack's Rechten und Ordnungen (Rights and Ordinances) was first published in 1715. In this small book, written as a dialogue between a father and son, Mack defends early Brethren views on Christian ordinances, including baptism – a defining feature of the Brethren tradition. This title page is taken from a 1774 edition printed in the American colonies by the well-known Brethren printer, Christopher Saur.

Grace College and Theological Seminary Archives and Special Collections. Used by permission.

Like other Anabaptist groups, the Brethren divided over questions of cultural assimilation in the 19th century. Henry Holsinger (1833-1905) pushed for greater degrees of accommodation and during a three-way split between 1880 and 1883, Holsinger led the progressive group that would become the Brethren Church.

The Brethren Church Archives and Dale Stoffer. Used by permission.

Before becoming perhaps the most famous Bible Conference venue in America, what is now called Winona Lake was an established part of the Chautauqua "circuit" since 1887. Then it was known as Spring Fountain Park and attracted well-known lecturers, such as Judith Ellen Horton, who is shown here on the 1891 program.

Winona History Center, Grace College and Theological Seminary Archives and Special Collections. Used by permission.

Through Solomon (Sol) Dickey's efforts, Presbyterian leaders purchased Spring Fountain Park in 1894. Dickey renamed Eagle Lake "Winona Lake" and took over administration of the Chautauqua grounds. Well-known personalities continued to grace the platform, from Jane Addams to Billy Sunday. Dickey also brought an evangelical vision to the Chautauqua programing and placed greater emphasis on the Bible Conferences for which Winona Lake would become known in the decades to come. Letterhead for Dickey's Winona Assembly and Summer School is shown here.

Winona History Center, Grace College and Theological Seminary Archives and Special Collections. Used by permission.

The Chautauqua grounds at Winona Lake were the location for numerous Brethren Church General Conference gatherings. Panoramic photos such as this one were common for the period and this one shows all those who gathered at the 1920 conference.

Winona History Center, Grace College and Theological Seminary Archives and Special Collections. Used by permission.

William Biederwolf was a well-known evangelist who was converted under Solomon Dickey's preaching. In 1922, he became director of the Winona Lake Bible conferences and brought a stronger fundamentalist flavor to the programming. He was also the one who invited leaders of the new Grace Theological Seminary to relocate to Winona Lake.

Winona History Center, Grace College and Theological Seminary Archives and Special Collections. Used by permission.

I HAVE FOUGHT A GOOD FIGHT.
I HAVE FINISHED MY COURSE.
I HAVE KEPT THE FAITH.   II Tim. 4:7

THE BILLY SUNDAY TABERNACLE

MRS. W. A. (Ma) SUNDAY

REV. W. A. (Billy) SUNDAY

Billy Sunday, the era's most recognizable evangelist, moved his headquarters to Winona Lake in 1911. The family established their home on a hill overlooking Winona Lake and a tabernacle, holding 5000 people, was built in 1920. Since Grace Seminary moved to Winona Lake after Billy died in 1935, it was actually Nell ("Ma") Sunday, herself a well-known personality, who fostered relationships with individuals from the seminary, including presidents McClain and Hoyt.

Miller Hall on the Ashland campus was the location of seminary classes in the 1930s before the departure of the "Grace group."

Brethren Church Archives and Dale Stoffer. Used by permission.

Louis S. Bauman, shown here while visiting a historic slave auction block in Fredericksburg, Va., held progressive views on racial integration. He was a progressive leader in the Brethren Church and mentor of Alva J. McClain, with whom he and his second wife, Retta Virginia (Stover) Bauman are also pictured sometime in the 1940s.

Grace College and Theological Seminary Archives and Special Collections. Used by permission.

This 1937 pamphlet depicts Ashland College's Founders Hall on a shaky foundation while the building is painted over with "historic Brethrenism." Issued by the "Grace group," the four-page publication listed a variety of charges against Ashland and testimonials in support of the group's plans to establish a new seminary with stronger denominational control.

Grace College and Theological Seminary Archives and Special Collections. Used by permission.

McClain, seated at center, is shown with the Seminary class of 1937 outside Ellet First Brethren Church near Akron, Oh. – the first location for Grace Theological Seminary. These students would have begun their studies at Ashland and then left as part of the "Grace group."

Grace College and Theological Seminary Archives and Special Collections. Used by permission.

An upper floor of the historic Free Methodist Publishing House (Light and Light Press and later Mount Memorial) served as the location of the seminary from 1939, when it moved to Winona Lake, until McClain Hall was finished in 1951. The contents of the library, being used by students in this photo, were borrowed from the Winona Lake School of Theology, a summertime seminary on the lakefront. Frequently pictured on postcards like this one, the building's restoration was completed in 1998.

Grace College and Theological Seminary Archives and Special Collections. Used by permission.

Although McClain had health problems later in life, as a young man he was active in sports. He was quarterback for this winning Sunnyside (Wash.) high school football team during their 1906-07 year. Around 18 years old in this photo, McClain is shown in the second row, second from the left.

Grace College and Theological Seminary Archives and Special Collections. Used by permission.

Among Anabaptists, including the Brethren, dress customs have often signaled a traditional or progressive identity. Raised in the progressive Brethren Church, Alva J. McClain dressed with meticulous style. The Greatness of the Kingdom was McClain's theological *Magnum opus* and reflects a distinctive version of Dispensationalism. It was meant to be one of seven volumes in a series, but this was the only volume he was able to complete.

Grace College and Theological Seminary Archives and Special Collections. Used by permission.

This poster was meant to help raise money for what would become McClain Hall (dedicated 1951). Among the students shown are those graduating in 1949; it indicates that 13 of the 24 "will take up foreign mission service."

Pictured in a postcard, the Westminster Hotel is one of several buildings on the Grace campus that date to Winona's Chautauqua days. The college has used the hotel (now Westminster Hall) as a student residence hall intermittently since the 1950s and the building was restored and became part of the Grace campus in 1998. The entrance, shaded by its iconic pergola, is shown here during one of Homer Rodeheaver's popular summer school and sacred music conferences sometime in the 1950s. By the time Grace Seminary moved to Winona Lake, Rodeheaver was already a well-known local celebrity as the songleader for Billy Sunday's evangelistic meetings.

Grace College and Theological Seminary Archives and Special Collections. Used by permission.

Founded first, the seminary at Grace was the institution's original identity and it remained the heart of the campus for many decades. The first three presidents, Alva McClain (center), Herman Hoyt (left), and Homer Kent, Jr. (right), were first and foremost seminarians and greatly revered for their personal or family ties to the founding of the institution. This painting, commissioned by the seminary class of 1976, hung for many years in McClain Hall, the building that housed the seminary. It was painted by long-time – and much-loved – art professor, Arthur (Art) Davis who taught at Grace for 34 years.

Grace College and Theological Seminary Archives and Special Collections. Used by permission.

Grace basketball started in 1955, when games were held at nearby East Wayne School (now Jefferson Elementary School) and the team played as the Ambassadors. Here Grace plays Philadelphia Bible Institute (now Cairn University) around 1956.

Grace College and Theological Seminary Archives and Special Collections. Used by permission.

John C. Whitcomb, Jr., who taught Bible and theology courses and served Grace Theological Seminary in various positions, exemplified a strident fundamentalist contingent that could be found at the seminary and in the FGBC after mid-century. Written with Henry Morris, Whitcomb's 1961 *The Genesis Flood* popularized "flood geology" and empowered young earth creationists.

Grace College and Theological Seminary Archives and Special Collections. Used by permission.

Grace's second president, Herman A. Hoyt was a successful though confrontational leader who oversaw a period of enrollment growth and building expansion at Grace between 1962 and 1976. Beginning his career at Ashland Seminary along with McClain, many of Hoyt's numerous books were about Brethren topics or premillennial eschatology.

Grace College and Theological Seminary Archives and Special Collections. Used by permission.

Promoting a conservative response to the rise of the New Left and protests on college campuses across the country, the Grace campus hosted annual events meant to encourage Christian patriotism during the 1960s and 1970s. Events included special speakers, patriotic songs, contests for children, and prayer for American soldiers in Vietnam. Republican luminaries were sometimes brought in to address the campus including U.S. Senator Mark Hatfield, U.S. Representative Walter Judd, and Indiana Attorney General Theodore Sendak. Here, Hatfield speaks in Rodeheaver Auditorium in 1970.

Grace College and Theological Seminary Archives and Special Collections. Used by permission.

Grace faculty members have often filled multiple roles. Ava Schnittjer, for example, cared for female residents in Westminster Hall as Dean of Women, (shown here) from 1955 to 1963, taught English and communications, and was director for Grace College's plays and musicals.

Grace College and Theological Seminary Archives and Special Collections. Used by permission.

Glen ("Chet") Kammerer who, after a career coaching with the NBA Lakers and with a professional team in Germany, became director of player personnel for the Miami Heat in 2004, was Grace's second athletic director and coached many basketball players at Grace between 1965 and 1975. One of those was Jim Kessler, who has now coached the men's basketball team at Grace for nearly 40 years. At right, Kessler is pictured with Phil Hoskins (seated), who served as the men's basketball coach at Grace from 1975 to 1977.

Grace College and Theological Seminary Archives and Special Collections. Used by permission.

Homer A. Kent, Jr., shown here in the classroom around 1970, served as president from 1976 to 1986. Known for his irenic personality, Kent was the last president of Grace to have personal or family ties to Ashland Seminary. (His father, Kent Sr., was part of the original "Grace group.")

Grace College and Theological Seminary Archives and Special Collections. Used by permission.

Serving as president from 1986 to 1994, John Davis was an experienced archeologist and is shown here as a young scholar showing biblical artifacts to seminary students. During his administration, the liberal arts identity of the undergraduate college continued to grow, while the seminary faced several challenges.

Grace College and Theological Seminary Archives and Special Collections. Used by permission.

Art students pose with items from the first senior art exhibit, sometime in the 1970s. At this time, the art department was housed in the basement of an old house on the edge of campus.

Grace College and Theological Seminary Archives and Special Collections, courtesy of Kim Reiff. Used by permission.

As Dean of Men and Dean of Women respectively, Dan Snively and Miriam Uphouse worked together to bring progressive reforms to student affairs, reflecting national trends during the 1970s and 1980s. They implemented training programs for student leaders, coursework to help freshmen transition to college life, as well as policies that emphasized student "discernment" rather than simply regulating behavior.

Grace College and Theological Seminary Archives and Special Collections. Used by permission.

Pictured here in front of Morgan Library around 1973, Jerry Franks' band Dimensions in Brass represented Grace College and Seminary as it traveled throughout the region. Future president Bill Katip, who played French horn and trumpet, stands in the back, fifth from the left.

Grace College and Theological Seminary Archives and Special Collections. Used by permission.

During the 1980s, Grace College and Seminary was an active member of Concerned Organizations for a Better Winona Lake. The organization provided gifts to meet the needs of the town, including this 1984 Plymouth Gran Fury police car, which was presented to town marshal John Trier in front of the iconic Billy Sunday Tabernacle. Grace is represented by President Kent; also included are Lyle Martin, Dave Wolkins, Lester Pifer, John Zielasko, Phil Dick, and Ron Klinger.

Winona History Center, Grace College and Theological Seminary Archives and Special Collections. Used by permission. Photo by Liz Cutler.

E. William Male served a variety of teaching and administrative roles during his long career at Grace and he was well-known for helping to establish a graduate program for Christian school administrators. In recognition for his work, Grace Seminary recently established the William Male Center for Seminary and Graduate Studies in the former Light and Life Press building, adjacent to Mount Memorial.

Grace College and Theological Seminary Archives and Special Collections. Used by permission.

Richard Jeffreys taught biology and pre-medical courses and built a strong program that sent graduates to various medical schools across the country. In this publicity photo sometime in the 1980s, Jeffreys seems to contemplate the relationship between science and faith as he places a Bible over a textbook on evolution.

Grace College and Theological Seminary Archives and Special Collections. Used by permission.

Larry Crabb, right, well-known author and teacher, established a popular but short-lived counseling program in the seminary that brought to the fore debates among evangelicals about the role of psychology in Christian counseling. Dan Allender, left, taught with Crabb in the counseling program.

Grace College and Theological Seminary Archives and Special Collections. Used by permission.

One of the founders of Biomet, a major orthopedic company in Warsaw, Ind., Dane Miller invested heavily in efforts to restore Winona Lake's resort atmosphere, which benefited the Grace campus. Miller was also a part of Ron Manahan's efforts to foster greater community engagement through the formation of OrthoWorx in 2009.

Grace College and Theological Seminary Archives and Special Collections. Used by permission.

President Ron Manahan brought Grace College and Seminary into the 21st century with a robust vision to build stronger relationships with industry and educational partnerships in the region. The Orthopaedic Capital Center is a tangible representation of these efforts. Soon after this image appeared in Lilly Endowment's 2010 Annual Report, the OOC's name was changed to the Ronald E. and Barbara J. Manahan Orthopaedic Capital Center in honor of the Manahans' legacy.

Lilly Endowment, Inc. Used by permission. Photo by Chris Minnick.

Between 2010 and 2012, President Manahan and Provost Bill Katip initiated significant changes, attempting to define Grace as a forward-thinking institution poised for the challenges they believed would characterize higher education in the future. A new "Grace Core" was adopted in 2010, which is constructed around students' relationships with Christ, His world, oneself, and others. Soon thereafter, a campaign to rethink Christian higher education was put into motion, the result of which was Grace "Reimagined," a series of new initiatives that included accelerated degree options, expanded online course offerings, an adjusted academic calendar, and "applied learning" credit requirement.

BrandPoet. Used by Permission.

William J. Katip, the first Grace College graduate to be named president, was inaugurated as Grace College and Seminary's sixth president, November 1, 2013, as part of the institution's homecoming events.

Grace College and Theological Seminary Archives and Special Collections. Photo by Brandpoet. Used by permission.

Chapter 5

World
Developing an International Impulse
Juan Carlos Téllez

IT IS SAFE TO SAY THAT CURRENT STUDENTS AT GRACE COME WITH THE assumption that college will include opportunities for multicultural experiences. Indeed, it is a significant part of the curriculum, including not only a required cross-cultural component, but also an emphasis in course work across the disciplines. This desire on the part of students, faculty, and administration has been a consistent part of the Grace campus, although, like other areas, it has evolved over time. The desire to serve and learn across cultural boundaries first took shape around the promotion of missions within the seminary. Later, this was supplemented and enhanced by a process of "internationalization" that recognized the ways that crossing borders, whether inside or outside the classroom, could move students closer to the educational goals of Grace College and Seminary.

The Missionary Impulse

The close connection between the Grace campus and the Fellowship of Grace Brethren Churches has meant that there was an early international emphasis, dominated by a strong enthusiasm toward missionary outreach. This was by no means something new that developed as part of the early Grace group. Rather, it was consistent with initiatives within the Brethren tradition for decades. Missionary outreach was an extension of denominational organization and was exhibited in the westward population expansion of the nineteenth and twentieth centuries that included denominational structuring and publishing efforts.[1] By 1910, both the Brethren Church and the Church of the Brethren had broadened the focus of outreach to include international missionary initiatives. This period of both institutional development and missionary outreach paralleled trends in other Anabaptist contexts, particularly among Mennonites in the Midwest.[2]

Ironically, some thirty years before the new Grace Theological Seminary set up shop in Winona Lake, this Chautauqua hub became the site where the impulse for foreign missions within the Brethren Church took shape in a more formal way. (See chapter 8.) The church's 1900 conference included an ad hoc gathering of individuals who met "under the trees" to strategize about missionary initiatives. Here, the Foreign Missionary Society was born. Over the next several decades, Jacob C. Cassel (whose interest in missions had been stirred by such evangelical luminaries as Hudson Taylor, John Mott, and Andrew Murray) along with Charles F. Yoder and Louis S. Bauman provided leadership for the society. They worked to sustain support for foreign missions among Brethren Church congregations and at the denominational college and seminary at Ashland, Ohio.

In the wake of the 1937 divorce at Ashland Seminary, the entire missionary society joined the Grace side, shifting the momentum of overseas outreach toward the new seminary and the congregations aligned with it. This evangelical emphasis was framed specifically in the Seminary's motto ("To know him and to make him known") as well as the Articles of Incorporation.[3] The original seminary faculty members—Alva J. McClain, Herman Hoyt, and Homer A. Kent Sr.—served alongside L. S. Bauman on the board of the Brethren missionary society. Not surprisingly, from the first seminary class, approximately one third of the student body was either already involved in foreign missions or was preparing to go to the field.[4] Early initiatives to raise funds called attention to this group who had the "call" for overseas service.

The training these future missionaries received was not substantively different from that of those who were planning for pastoral ministries within Brethren churches stateside. While missions was held in high esteem, the primary focus was on biblical training, practical evangelism, and theological studies. Their seminary training may have lacked the kind of critical approach to cultural issues seminarians take for granted today, but those alumni who headed overseas were not disappointed with their classes.[5] McClain, Hoyt, John Whitcomb, and Homer Kent, Jr. taught with "enthusiasm" and "passion," and former students such as Roy Snyder and Roger Peugh, both of whom went to the mission field, revered them for their great sense of conviction and "ability to explain the Bible."[6] It was "superb biblical training," not sophisticated missiology that "impacted me very, very deeply" long time missionary Tom Julien remembers.[7] Beyond his abilities in the classroom, John Whitcomb also modeled a commitment to missions by regularly traveling overseas to teach classes on Bible and theology, particularly in Europe and Africa.

Grace Seminary and its graduates quickly established a significant and long-term link between the campus and the Central African Republic (CAR). Begun in 1921 by James Gribble (who was converted at Louis S. Bauman's church in Philadelphia) and his wife, Florence, the ministry was one of the earliest enterprises of the Brethren foreign missionary society and it grew to be the largest.[8] Ruth Snyder left her Johnstown, Pennsylvania, school-teaching job to become part of the first group of seminary students preparing for missionary work in Africa. After graduating in 1941, she left for the CAR and was soon joined by Estella Myers, a classmate from Grace who studied Greek in order to better translate the Bible into the indigenous languages of Africa.[9] Wayne Beaver, along with his wife, Dorothy, both graduates of Grace Seminary, were commissioned by the "Foreign Board" two weeks after their wedding and arrived in the CAR in 1944. The Beavers were instrumental in maintaining the mission's growth, primarily through a growing Christian education program, which Gribble had emphasized from the start. In 1946, the Beavers founded a Bible Institute to train pastors and eventually, in 1981, Don Hocking, another Grace Seminary graduate, would establish a graduate school of theology.[10]

The missionary impulse was strengthened on the Grace campus when, about 1953, both undergraduate and seminary students took it upon themselves to organize the first formal missionary organization on campus, which they called World Missions Fellowship. The group met weekly to pray for missionaries around the world, listen to updates from missionary guests, and raise funds for overseas initiatives.[11] During the spring 1954 semester, the inaugural issue of the

"Go therefore and make disciples": Reflections on Foreign Missionary Service from Grace Alumni
Tiberius Rata

Although it is difficult to measure the overall influence of
Grace College and Seminary alumni in foreign mission fields,
what is certain is that those who interpreted the "go" in the
Great Commission to mean "go overseas" did so with full
confidence that God called them to a specific place. With
their calling sure, Grace alumni have been serving as missionaries for decades on the continents of Asia, Africa, North
and South America, and Europe. Indeed, from its inception,
Grace Theological Seminary came to be known as a place
that prepared followers of Christ for foreign fields of service.
From the members of the first seminary class, a third of the
student body was already involved in foreign missions or
was preparing to go to the field.[1]

What follows is a summary of recollections from various
Grace alumni who are serving currently or have served as
overseas missionaries. Unless otherwise noted, these paragraphs were gleaned from responses they provided when
asked to fill out a survey about their joys and challenges, as
well as how Grace College or Seminary provided training or
inspiration for their service.

Preparation for the Mission Field
All the missionaries who responded mentioned the solid
biblical and theological training they received during their
years at Grace. Roy Snyder recalled that Monday evening
missionary prayer meetings were instrumental as many
of the students who attended these meetings decided to
become missionaries.[2] Allan Frey, missionary to Peru since
1984, mentioned that what prepared him for the mission
field was Grace's "excellent doctrine classes, chapels, and

student newspaper provided updates on the group's activities, which included an aggressive "publicity campaign" designed to increase interest in the organization's "informative Monday night prayer sessions."[12] The following fall, the fellowship began holding daily prayer vigils during the noon hour and organized weekly meetings to hear missionary speakers.[13] The group's size, though modest at about 25 members, had a profound effect, as many of those students involved made decisions to pursue missions.[14] By 1960, the student-led World Missions Fellowship had added an annual missions conference that continues to the present.[15]

Effects of these initiatives by Grace students were felt far afield. Tom Julien, who served as president of World Missions Fellowship in 1956, spearheaded missionary efforts in France, for example. In 1958, he and his young wife, Doris, left for France; their ministry was difficult early on until they realized that the methods of evangelism they had been taught were frustratingly ineffective. Changing their approach in 1964, the Juliens found a new beginning in the "Chateau of Saint Albain," a modest fourteenth century castle in Burgundy. Moving into the historic home, they then sought to influence French men and women based on relationships and discussion groups. Julien occasionally spent time with evangelical thinker Francis Schaeffer, whose relationship model of evangelical influence at L'Abri, Switzerland, was not unlike the Juliens' newfound approach at "The Chateau." The small castle also provided a place for short-term opportunities for students of Grace Seminary, such as Larry DeArmey and Dan Hammers. With guests coming and going as well as regional workshops and ecumenical prayer gatherings, Doris' hospitality would also come to define the Juliens' ministry. The Chateau increasingly became a regional and ecumenical hub of evangelical activity in France and eventually, throughout Europe. It helped to inspire other Grace Seminary students, such as Roger Peugh, who traveled to East Berlin in 1969, and sent back regular reports "from behind the iron curtain" for publication in the campus newspaper. Roger, along with his wife, Nancy, would spend 20 years in Germany before returning to Grace to teach in 1989.

While individual Grace faculty members and students made occasional mission trips abroad,[16] the first campus-sponsored trip took place during the 1966-67 school year when the men's basket-

opportunities for Christian service." Church planter David Schwan, who has served in England along with his wife, Becky, since 1990, is grateful for "good Bible teaching" and the opportunity to develop a disciplined life while at Grace. Kent Good, missionary to France and Cambodia since 1979, reported that Grace "armed me with a good grasp of Scripture and the tools to work out my understanding of truth." Tom Julien, who served in France with his wife, Doris, from 1958 until 1986, recounted that, while the teaching lacked studies specifically in missiology and anthropology, he appreciated the "superb, Biblical training" of Alva J. McClain and Homer Kent, Jr. Julien went on to impact others, such as Kip Cone, who served with his wife, Mary, in Germany between 1994-2004. Kip remembers how Julien's mentoring, along with that of missionary Tom Hickey, helped him set his sights to overseas ministry. Rob Plaster reported that his father David (late theology professor and vice president of academic affairs) "knew about theology in a way you could understand," and taught so that the students could grasp it. "He loved the Lord and had a passion for mentoring." Kent Good especially remembers the teaching of Charles Smith, professor of theology in the seminary, who challenged his thinking.

Like Kent Good, Tom Stallter, missionary to the Central African Republic and Chad from 1979-1997, also appreciated the fact that Charles Smith made theology practical.[3] After coming to teach at Grace Seminary in 1997, Stallter brought a new emphasis to the way students were prepared for the ministry. One former student reported, "The foundation of Dr. Stallter's teaching comes from his long, personal experience working overseas. The presence of his extensive, first-hand experience enables him to better help a student along in the process of moving from theoretical understanding to personal implementation … Dr. Stallter helped me apply missiological principles to ever-challenging contexts." Another missionary had similar thoughts, "Dr. Stallter's cross cultural studies classes were illuminating to give words to

ball team went to Puerto Rico. The trip was organized by Coach Chet Kammerer and a local pastor in Puerto Rico. Mike Grill, later a long-time professor in behavioral sciences, was on the team then. Jim Kessler, a player under Kammerer, retained the emphasis on ministry after becoming basketball coach in 1977.[17] Coach Kessler has led his teams on more than eighteen excursions to places such as the Bahamas, Europe, the Philippines, Kenya, Taiwan, Jamaica, Canada, and Egypt, as well as among Native American communities. Kessler stresses that these trips were not for sightseeing or entertainment. His players have often stayed in dorms or with families, getting a substantive taste of local culture and sharing in daily life. Whether the team was running basketball camps or organizing clinics for local children, these trips always mirrored Kessler's own coaching philosophy and the conviction that basketball is a tool for ministry, not an end in itself. Making connections across cultures is always difficult, according to Kessler, but "sports jumps over those barriers ... you can't always speak to each other but you can play together."[18]

Internationalization

Grace's substantial connections with foreign missions was augmented by a slow but continuing development of "internationalization"—a process of adopting a more thorough global dimension and international emphasis that came to the fore on many Christian campuses soon after midcentury.[19] As the seminary remained strong in the study of biblical languages, the undergraduate division introduced classes in modern languages, offering instruction in French, Spanish, Portuguese, and German by the end of 1951.[20] The Spanish and French minors were created in 1968,[21] became available as majors in 1974, and two years later, French and Spanish teaching education majors were also created.[22]

A more substantive step toward internationalization was the addition of the Study Abroad Program, which was instituted in conjunction with the creation of the French and Spanish majors. Initially, study abroad was "highly recommended" for those studying modern languages, but by 1976, language students were required to spend their junior year "studying in a university located in the country of their target language."[23]

the many confusing and disconcerting experiences in Asia. It also showed me many of my serious mistakes in my reactions to my local brothers and sisters."

Challenges in Overseas Ministry

It is no secret that the work of overseas missions is hard. Learning a new language and adapting to a new culture, for example, are never easy, no matter how skilled and gifted one is. One missionary reported that "language training has not been easy; though we have seen much progress, there continues to be a long climb ahead to the peak of fluency." Missionaries also face challenges when they are not successful in recruiting teammates, when they see people reject the Gospel message, and when they see fellow workers burn out and leave the ministry. Missionaries to Peru, Allan and Diane Frey recall a time in the 1980s when terrorist activity made things unstable in Peru, and yet, they recognized that the safest place to be was in God's will.

As Roy Snyder ministered along with his wife, Ruth, in the Central African Republic, disease was a tragic obstacle: "A combination of malaria and tropical parasites left me crippled in both my feet."[4] For Roy, the scars of personal sacrifice are real.

Challenges come from both the inside and the outside. And sometimes, the inner turmoil is much harder to deal with than outside resistance. Disagreements among team members can result in hurt and hurting words among co-workers. Roger Peugh, missionary to Germany from 1969 to 1990 recalls a time when, following a church split, he battled depression. "I was completely controlled by thoughts of sadness... I began battling against suicidal thoughts."[5]

So what keeps them there?

It seems that God's call, which is clear and personal, is what kept a lot of Grace alumni on the field, in spite of hardship. The Freys recounted a painful time in their lives. "When our five-year old son died while on our first furlough in 1988,

It was not until the 1980s, however, that the college began to make more significant strides toward fostering concern for global issues and cultural awareness independent from the promotion of missionary service. This took place partly in response to globalizing trends during the period. Much of it, however, was the result of the administration's desire, under President John Davis and Vice President for Academic Affairs Ronald Manahan to bring a more robust liberal arts disposition to the institution. A Curriculum Task Force was organized, which helped to construct a new set of educational values around which the school's future curriculum would be based. With help from two Lilly Endowment grants, this effort included workshops and seminars as well as a seventeen-day retreat during the summer of 1988. Under Manahan's leadership, the team (comprised of faculty members Skip Forbes, Jim Bowling, and Richard Dilling) set a new vision that included an "International, Multi-Cultural Awareness."[24] In order for this to take place, Grace would need to "guarantee" that students would find "a structured opportunity to be inducted into an experience outside their own culture through foreign language study, study abroad, inner-city and mission-station ministries, and cross-cultural courses."[25] This was implemented within specific programs as well. For example, the Department of Business began to explore opportunities for their students in China and Russia.[26] The new focus also extended to discussions about pedagogy and educational facilities and resulted in steps to upgrade and renovate classroom space in Philathea Hall.[27] This emphasis continued into the Manahan administration, a component that he has attributed in part to his own teaching experiences in urban, multicultural settings.[28]

The drive toward fostering multicultural elements within the curriculum and campus culture were yet again strengthened through the implementation of a new liberal arts general education "core" in 2002. Spearheaded by Skip Forbes, a strong proponent of the liberal arts approach, this implementation had begun in the fall of 1995, when Forbes was given a sabbatical to begin research for the project.[29] A General Education Revision Committee was formed in 1997, which met regularly for the next three years. The committee's recommendations for an overhauled general education program included a proposed class called "Growing Globally," which would be an "introduction to diversity and multiculturalism." According

some asked us if we would return. Like the disciples, our response was, 'Where else would we go? You (Christ) alone have the word of life.' God is good—always and in all ways!" What kept missionaries to France and Cambodia Kent and Rebecca Good on the field? "God's grace is the simple answer. We felt God's leading so clearly in each of our moves that we could not question His design." Missionaries stay on the field because they are people who are committed to God and his call. Rob Plaster, missionary to France since 2003, continues serving because he has "a deep commitment to the French people ... who, without our presence would probably never encounter who Jesus truly is." One missionary has taken 2 Timothy 2:10 and Romans 8:18 as favorite verses because they counter feelings of giving up.[6] Another missionary, serving in a closed country, stays and ministers in spite of outside and inside obstacles because he knows that "God wants us here at this time. God's love for the people of the country and God's intervention in our lives keep us here."

Highlights of Ministering Abroad

Missionaries follow God's call and keep plowing ahead even though there are hardships and obstacles. Yet, faithful to God and His calling, they experience the mountain peaks of seeing lives changed. When Kent Good looks back, he remembers that seeing churches planted as well as his efforts to develop leaders within France and Cambodia have been true highlights. "Helping pastors in the Central African Republic plant and develop churches," is something for which Tom Stallter is grateful. To provide leadership as Field and Area Director was also a rewarding experience in his ministry, which resulted in new ministries such as the Summer School of Evangelism.[7] Allan Frey found it exciting when graduates from the Fetzer Memorial Christian Academy in Lima, Peru, "became leaders" and were "used in God's service." Likewise, under the Juliens' tenure in France, Le Château de Saint Albain became an important center not just for French Christians but also for other European teams.

to the recommendations, it might include attention to international and "geo-political" issues as well as perspectives on economic, cultural, and social realities within various global contexts. Significantly, the course specified a "required ten-day cultural field experience."[30] Faculty had few concerns about the new emphasis in curriculum or a required cross-cultural experience beyond those related to practical challenges and scheduling. For one faculty member, in fact, the proposal did not go far enough. Why not create an "Office of Multicultural Affairs," he suggested, which could facilitate more comprehensive, institution-wide improvement?[31]

With the introduction of the new core in the fall of 2002, "Global Perspectives" was taught for the first time in the spring of 2003 under the leadership of Jacqueline Schram.[32] Schram, the daughter of Tom and Doris Julien, had spent her childhood in Europe literally growing up in "The Chateau." She joined the faculty at Grace College in 1986, to teach French and has been instrumental in promoting the educational benefits of global and cultural awareness.[33] Under the leadership of a part-time staff person and in partnership with Grace Brethren International Missions (now Encompass World Partners), the required cross-cultural field experience was implemented at the same time, although it experienced some problems in the initial stages. According to Joshua Smith, the student body president in 2007, students understood the intent of the new requirement, but they were "frustrated" about the financial costs of meeting the requirement, and many remained "confused" about the logistical details. As a result, more than a few students found themselves scrambling to fulfill the requirement before they graduated. Believing that these problems could be addressed largely through more concerted administrative oversight, Smith recommended the hiring of a full-time program director.[34] In recognition of these realities, the administration created a full-time staff position in the area of cultural diversity with the intent to improve the process for students. In 2010, the general education core was again retooled and Global Perspectives became an interdisciplinary course, organized around recent works of literature represented by a diverse range of cultural and international authors.

As the undergraduate curriculum began to reflect growing trends in internationalization, the seminary entered a rebuilding phase in the wake of its difficulties between 1989 and 1990. (See chapter 4.)

At a time when Europe was not high on many missionaries' priority list, the Château became a strong prayer, recruiting, and training center.[8] While the Juliens served in France, six churches were started, and today the Château continues to serve an important role for evangelical churches and individuals from all over Europe. In the Central African Republic, it took many years of ministry for Roy and Ruth Snyder to see results, but Roy recalls that the number of churches grew from three to sixteen from 1964 to 1982.[9] For another, "one of the greatest honors" has been to share Christ with "whole households in remote villages who had never heard of the death and resurrection of Christ."

1. Ron Clutter, "The Development of Grace Theological Seminary" in *Grace Theological Journal* 10 (Spring 1989), 56.
2. Roy Snyder interview by author.
3. Tom Stallter interview by author.
4. Roy Snyder interview.
5. Roger Peugh. Grace undergraduate chapel
6. 2 Timothy 2:10, "I endure everything for the sake of the elect, that they also may obtain the salvation that is in Christ Jesus with eternal glory" and Romans 8:18, "I consider that our present sufferings are not worth comparing with the glory that will be revealed in us."
7. Tom Stallter interview.
8. Tom Julien, *Seize the Moment*, 57.
9. Roy Snyder interview. Today there are 40 Grace Brethren churches in and around Bangui, the capital city, alone.

This included developing a more formal missiological approach to cross-cultural ministry that was augmented by anthropological sensitivity and greater efforts in contextualization. The idea was fostered most directly by Tom Stallter, who began teaching in the seminary in 1997. Stallter, a graduate of the college, served in various capacities in Africa, including as field and area director in Chad.[35] This combination of personal experience in cross-cultural ministry and background in missiological nuances was a welcome combination. Recent graduates have attested to the effectiveness of Stallter's "extensive, first-hand experience" and insights into the application of "missiological principles to ever-changing contexts." This greater cultural sensitivity has allowed graduates to make sense of the "many confusing and disconcerting experiences" that are common to cross-cultural adjustment and even toward healing relationships and promoting interpersonal harmony.[36]

An Ongoing Legacy

Through the efforts of Tom Stallter and Jeffrey Gill, along with Grace alumni serving overseas, Grace Seminary has retained an international influence in spite of the setbacks of the 1990s. Missionaries continue to give Grace Seminary credit for providing a strong foundation for faith and ministry as well as contributing to a strong sense of calling—something that has sustained them through difficult circumstances. Some have experienced security risks and political violence. Others suffered the loss of loved ones, experienced bouts with depression, as did Roger Peugh, or, as in the case of Roy Snyder, endured debilitating disease. Yet through the strong sense of personal vocation fostered in part through their education at Grace, they found the strength to remain where they were despite the difficulties. As Allen and Diane Fry have said, "Like the disciples, our response was, 'Where else would we go? You alone have the word of life.' God is good—always and in all ways!"[37]

One of the most encouraging initiatives has been the Korean Studies Program, which was implemented in 1996 to provide South Korean ministers and missionaries the opportunity for advanced graduate training they were not able to find in Korea. Since the 1970s, South Korean churches have sent nearly 20,000 missionaries to hundreds of locations around the world—a result of Christianity's tremendous growth there during the twentieth century. Yet many do not have specialized ministry degrees. Beginning with the Doctor of Ministry degree, the program added the Doctor of Missiology in 2003. Although the program saw virtually no growth for a decade after its inception, and the Seminary contemplated discontinuing the program, after it was reorganized in 2007, it has rebounded significantly.[38]

Designed to bring further professional development to Christian leaders, pastors, church planters, and missionaries who have vocational ministry experience and a foundation of theological studies, the curriculum is built around one-week seminar modules and structured to enable Korean students to complete their degree without leaving their current ministries. With various content tracks available, both degrees are non-research, professional doctorates. After the 2007 restructuring, Stallter and Gill began increased networking with Korean schools and missions training centers, taking advantage of the seminary's contacts around the world and on various mission fields. The program saw immediate benefits as enrollment increased from an average of 15-18 students to 47 in the first summer, and income increased from a small deficit to a modest profit.[39]

Student demand and a history of successfully providing this type of education have been factors leading to the desire to expand this program by offering courses in Los Angeles and other centers around the world. By doing so, the seminary's Center for Korean Studies Program can facilitate degree completion in the Korean language as well as through translation. In May 2010, Stephen Park, a seminary graduate from Korea, assumed the role of Director of the Korean Program under the leadership of Stallter, who functions as the Executive Director of the Center. The Center for Korean Studies continues to offer Masters of Arts and Doctor of Missiology module courses in Australia, Cambodia, France, India, the Philippines, and Thailand.

The legacy outlined above is ongoing. Grace Seminary faculty members have recently taught courses to Korean students around the globe. The ongoing international impulse also continues throughout the undergraduate programs. The Office of Global Initiatives at Grace College organizes cross-cultural experiences and ministry opportunities for nearly 150 students annually through the "Go Encounter" program. In 2012 and 2013, as Grace celebrated its 75th year, these experiences, meant to broaden student perspectives on cultures and augment the liberal arts identity of the institution, took place in nearly 30 locations around the world.[40] Added to this are study abroad initiatives, which, in 2012, arranged for 14 students to pursue coursework or internships in Argentina, England, Fiji, France, South Korea, Portugal, or Spain. Also crossing borders, a handful of students from Handong Global University in Pohang, South Korea, are currently living and studying at Grace College as part of an ongoing exchange partnership. What is more, Grace athletic teams have recently participated in sports clinics and other programs in Costa Rica, Brazil, Cape Verde, Dominican Republic, and the Cayman Islands.[41] Clearly, a persistent desire to serve and learn across cultures continues to provide inspiration for both missionary outreach as well as for multicultural educational experiences.

Notes

1. On Brethren missions in the 19th century, see Carl F. Bowman, *Brethren Society*, 132-143.

2. James C. Juhnke, *Vision, Doctrine, War: Mennonite Identity and Organization in America, 1890-1930* (Scottdale, PA: Herald Press, 1989.)

3. Articles of Incorporation, Grace Theological Seminary, Section 4.

4. Ron Clutter, "The Development of Grace Theological Seminary and the Division of the Brethren Church," *Grace Theological Journal* 10 (Spring 1989), 56.

5. The author and editors are indebted to Tiberius Rata for research and interviews, which provided some of the content for this chapter.

6. Roger Peugh, interview by Tiberius Rata, July 27, 2012.

7. Tom Julien, interview by Tiberius Rata, July 4, 2012.

8. See Tom Julien, *Seize the Moment: Stories of an Awesome God Empowering Ordinary People* (Winona Lake: Grace Brethren International Missions, 2000) 25-33, 45-52.

9. For a detailed account of Estella Myers' life and ministry see Ruth Snyder, *Estella Myers: Pioneer Missionary in Central Africa* (Winona Lake, IN: BMH Books, 1984).

10. Julien, *Seize the Moment*, 28-9. See also Wayne Beaver's memoirs, which he compiled in *God at Work in the Central African Republic* (Self-published, 1995).

11. *The Sounding Board* May 28, 1954.

12. Ibid.

13. *The Sounding Board* 3:1, September 23, 1955.

14. Roy Snyder, interview by Tiberius Rata, August 3, 2012.

15. *The Sounding Board* April 8, 1960.

16. *The Sounding Board*, November 25, 1966; January 28, 1966; January, 29 1968.

17. Jim Kessler, interview by author, October 10, 2012.

18. Ibid.

1. On internationalization within American higher education, see P. G. Altbach and J. Knight, "The Internationalization of Higher Education: Motivations and Realities," *Journal of Studies in International Education* 11:3-4 (2007), 290-305 and P. Dewey and S. Duff, "Reason before Passion: Faculty Reviews on Internationalization in Higher Education," *Higher Education* 58:4 (2009), 491-504.

20. Grace Theological Seminary Catalog, 1951-1952.

21. Grace College Catalog, 1968-1970, 57.

22. Grace College Catalog, 1974-1976, 37; Grace College Catalog, 1976-1978, 35.

23. Grace College Catalog, 1974-1976, 37; Grace College Catalog, 1976-1978, 35.

24. John J. Davis, "Foreword," James E. Bowling and Joel B. Curry, *Values in a Liberal Arts Education: An Examination of Grace College's Liberal Arts Values and How they are integrated into the Educational Process* (Winona Lake: BMH Books, 1992), vii-ix. Ronald Manahan, interview by author, November 21, 2011.

25. Bowling and Curry, *Values in a Liberal Arts Education*, 4.

26. Ronald Manahan interview

27. Joel B. Curry, ed. "Participation & Interaction are Keys: Curriculum, facilities stress international awareness," *Grace Magazine* 5:2 (Winter 1989), 6-7.

28. Ibid.

29. Skip Forbes, "Proposal, General Education Revision," Grace College (April 16, 2001), 1.

30. Ibid., 7.

31. "Ballot on the General Education Revision Proposal," April 16, 2001. The proposal passed the faculty vote 34 to 4. The ballot report includes numerous comments from faculty members with responses from the committee.

32. Faculty meeting minutes, Grace College, October 9, 2003; Faculty meeting minutes, Grace College, October 23, 2003.

33. Schram began part-time, but became full-time in 1992.

34. Joshua Smith, "Towards a Better Institution: A Proposal for the Improvement of the Cross-Cultural Field Experience and the Study Abroad Programs," unpublished paper (March 28, 2007).

35. Thomas Stallter, interview by Tiberius Rata, July 5, 2012.

36. These observations have been taken from a series of surveys administered to Grace alumni by Tiberius Rata in July, 2012.

37. Roger Peugh, undergraduate chapel message, August 26, 2003; alumni surveys, July 2012; Roy Snyder interview

38. Data on the Korean program obtained from Carrie Yocum in the Office of Academic Affairs.

39. Ibid.

40. These locations included Brazil, Fiji, France, England, Germany, Ireland, Israel, Japan, the Philippines, South Korea, Taiwan, Thailand, Cambodia, Benin, Bolivia, Canada, Dominican Republic, El Salvador, Gabon, Guatemala, Haiti, Ireland, Jamaica, Mexico, Nicaragua, Zambia, and Zimbabwe.

41. Information courtesy of the Grace College and Seminary Office of Global Initiatives.

Chapter 6

Students

Student Affairs and the Pursuit of a
Seamless Learning Environment

James Swanson

IN 1937, THE SAME YEAR GRACE THEOLOGICAL SEMINARY BEGAN, THE American Council on Education released its landmark report entitled "Student Personnel Point of View." The report pointed to a "long and honorable history" of higher education in America and the commitment to "the preservation, transmission, and enrichment of the important elements of culture" while maintaining "scholarship, research, creative imagination and human experience."[1] The report went on to challenge educators to guide the "whole student" to reach his or her fullest potential and to be a positive contributor to the betterment of society.[2] In short, it reflected a call to foster the development of the "whole student"—both inside and outside the classroom.

Since the 1930s, this desire has been reflected in the professionalization of student affairs across the educational spectrum as a distinct discipline. Indeed, one would be hard pressed to find any institution that has not sought to intentionally foster an educational setting in which academic growth was just one measure of educational success. The shift toward greater student affairs involvement would also become apparent at Christian colleges and universities after the Second World War, when higher education was entering a period that historian John Thelin has called the "Golden Age" of higher education.[3] Christian higher education would take on a distinct flavor, however, due to the fact that many evangelicals distrusted modern higher education and looked for an alternative to the secular institutions to which they could send their children. They looked to Christian colleges and universities to serve as a place where their children would have Christian professors in an environment with structured behavioral standards.[4]

In examining student life and the parallel development of student affairs over the history of Grace College, we find that the educational structure reflected a desire for a seamless educational environment as well as conservative social and behavior patterns that Christian parents expected for their children. This chapter chronicles the history of student affairs at Grace College as it began with an early emphasis on lifestyle regulation and then evolved to include a focus on moral discernment and student services. Finally, the chapter offers more personal reflections on developments since 1994.

Much of the research for this chapter is based on the college newspaper, *The Sounding Board*, which offers a window into the student life side of campus throughout the years. The paper began in May of 1953, and its first issue was a single page publication printed on a mimeograph machine. Costing a nickel, the newspaper was a vital part of "telling the institution's story" during those historic years. While the paper nearly dissolved in 1969, it eventually became a weekly publication in the early 1970s.[5]

"In Loco Parentis" and the Structuring of Resident Life

Grace College began in 1948 as "The Collegiate Division of Grace Theological Seminary," and the structure for managing the student body at Grace followed the patterns of the day, which included employing a Dean of Men and a Dean of Women. The primary role of these positions was the handling of problems that their respective gender might face in the transition to college. Historically, individuals who filled these roles were selected because of their natural affinity for working with students.[6] At Grace College this was also the case and it was only appropriate for men to mentor men and women to mentor women.

For the men, George Cone, Jr. served as the college's first Dean of Men, although he was quickly succeeded, in 1950, by R. Wayne

Snider, who oversaw the men living at McKee Courts and what is now Westminster Hall.[7] Snider would serve in this position until 1953, after which he assumed a full time faculty position teaching history. Not surprisingly, the administration of dorm life was not very formal during those early years; however Snider helped to tighten the structure. This continued after 1953 as the duties were divided among several men including Arnold Kriegbaum, who was appointed Dean of Students in the fall of 1961 and later was a faculty member as well.[8] As for the women, Fern Sandy and Eva Godfrey were the first to serve in the position of Dean of Women, or as "dorm mothers" as they were affectionately known. It was under Ava Schnittjer (later, Beard), however, that the position came into its own. Schnittjer cared for Grace's female students in Westminster Hall from 1955 to 1963. She was a graduate of Cornell University, and prior to coming to Grace taught 19 years in the Iowa school systems. Along with her role as Dean of Women, Schnittjer was also a professor of English and Communication, offering lectures to students and directing many of the institution's early plays and musicals.

These deans had tremendous influence in their respective dorms, much of which was directly connected to ensuring that students followed expectations for community life.

Historically, Christian colleges, especially those that are conservative, have been stricter than secular institutions[9] in their policies of lifestyle standards for students. Like the vast majority of Christian colleges in its day, Grace began with biblical/theological studies as part of its general education requirement. The school has maintained a requirement that students give evidence of a commitment to Christian faith—something that served to bind the community together and to lay a foundation for community standards. In this, Grace was not unlike any number of church-related Christian colleges during the same period.[10] In these early years, student affairs operated basically along the lines of *in loco parentis* (literally, "in place of the parent"), which meant placing a strong emphasis on maintaining lifestyle and behavioral expectations. The 1950 college catalog underscored the importance of these behavioral standards on campus in its opening pages. "Lest we forget," it declared, that Grace College and Seminary was first and foremost a community; and for those who enrolled, there was a clear set of rules and regulations.[11] Community standards of conduct were laid out in a student handbook, which was known informally as the "book of rules." The 1961 Student Handbook reminded students of the following:

> Each student shall become thoroughly acquainted with the purposes, ideals, doctrinal position and spiritual emphasis of the school as outlined in the catalog. If at any time the student's personal conduct or beliefs are not in accord with the interpretation of Bible ethics as set forth by the school, it shall become the student's duty to acquiesce or to withdraw from the school.[12]

Though an emphasis on rules and regulations may seem antiquated today, these standards were set in place to ensure the development of the whole student and his or her character and leadership. Although varying from college to college, standards for regulating student activity and decorum on and off campus were commonplace. Some of these policies were based on what were interpreted as clear biblical absolutes. Others, however, were simply cultural standards set in place for the spiritual benefit of the whole. Grace College has had an evolving set of standards over the years that have defined what a Grace College student should look like, and these standards were seen as essential for creating a strong, healthy environment for learning and Christian living.

Often consisting of simply a long list of policies, the rules sometimes made it difficult for the deans—who were frequently viewed as little more than enforcers—to build authentic relationships with students. This was a difficult, even painful, yet common experience at many Christian colleges and universities where deans were sometimes hired specifically to serve in a disciplinarian role.[13] In an interview about his responsibilities as Dean of Men, R. Wayne Snider stated, "There were always rules ... at that time we had sheets of rules, dating etiquette, eating etiquette, and things that were important to the in-and-out of class experience."[14] In acting "in place of the parent," dorm supervisors applied regulations with the best intentions—to limit potentially destructive or harmful behavior. Rules were considered necessary in fostering Christian values such as truthfulness, honor, forbearance, and self-control.

Administrators and deans recognized that college was a prime opportunity to find a mate. A 1956 "Dormitory Supplement for

Women," for example, explained that, "Grace College is in favor of the normal and natural relationships between men and women that are vital in preparation for Christian leadership and service."[15] Students were discouraged, however, from marrying too young or in the course of their matriculation. "No student will marry during the academic school year," the 1952 student handbook specified, "and if you as a student are expecting to marry during the summer, you must secure permission from the faculty (in writing). If you are under the age of 21, your parents must approve in writing your intent to marry."[16]

For most students, dating policies were more relevant than those regulating marriage. A good many early social standards were focused on limiting opportunities for intimate interaction between students of the opposite sex. "Your conduct at all times should be above reproach," students were told, "particularly in regard to public expressions of affection, which are always in bad taste."[17] Policies about library etiquette, for example, would not allow unmarried couples to sit on the same side of the table while studying and even recommended that male and female students sit at separate tables altogether.[18] Couples were not allowed to schedule dates on week nights without special permission from the dean of men or women. When dates were arranged on weekends, a chaperone was required to accompany the couple, and deans kept a list of suggested individuals who were approved to accompany dating couples. Speaking to female students, the 1951 Handbook put it this way:

> College women must secure special permission from the Dean to date men who are not enrolled in Grace Seminary or College. College women, except seniors and those over twenty-one, traveling in cars with men shall be chaperoned. The Dean will be glad to recommend chaperones on request. The ones dating will be responsible for caring for the expense of the chaperone. The escort shall assume joint responsibility with the girl when the regulations are violated.[19]

Un-chaperoned students were forbidden from entering dormitory rooms or apartments occupied exclusively by members of the opposite sex. Other policies pertained to off-campus situations. No dates were to occur while a student was babysitting, for example, and a "regular couple who are dating" were not to conduct evangelism together or serve on the same work team without special permission. Not surprisingly, couples were not allowed to sit in parked cars together either on or off campus.[20] Freshmen were not permitted to date the same person on successive Friday and Saturday nights.

Along with polices concerning intimacy and mate selection, the institution was concerned with appearance and dress. Policies were designed to emphasize that professionalism and modesty should be reflected in one's appearance. And it was important to project respect for the professor and confidence in oneself in the classroom. Clothing was therefore viewed as a "reflection" of one's "personality and standards."[21] In short, students needed to honor the Lord by appearing conservative and modest. It was expected that men would wear dress shirts and ties in the classroom; they were to maintain short hair styles and to resist the styles and fads of the day. Beards were not allowed in the early years and moustaches were expected to be maintained and neatly trimmed. For the ladies, skirts needed to cover the knees and hats were expected in church. As explained in 1956,

> You are expected to wear a hat to church on Sunday morning. While this is not particularly the popular practice among girls, it is the conventional standard for women of good taste. If a particular duty at church requires you not to wear a hat then you may leave the hat off after leaving a note in the dean of women's box explaining the situation. The note will prevent her from having to speak to you about the omission and thus will make you both feel better.[22]

Campus Life

As undergraduate programs grew, opportunities for more campus activities and programs developed. They included early programs designed to develop spiritual growth in students, the start of a formal athletic program, and the fine arts.

Spiritual Growth

Grace College has historically required its students to attend church. For many years the enforcement of this requirement fell upon the resident assistants (hall leadership) who would check every dorm room each Sunday morning. The rule was originally a requirement with the hope of instilling in students the importance of the local church and their involvement in it. (While Grace still encourages involvement in the local church, this policy was officially dropped in 1995.)

As for on-campus spiritual development, the chapel program began as one of the most important parts of campus life. Chapel was held five days each week and attendance was required for all. Both students and faculty had assigned seats, in fact, so that attendance records could be kept more easily. In addition, Spiritual Emphasis week, fall and spring Days of Prayer, as well as a Conference on Mission led in the development of the student's spiritual life. Prior to 1955, when chapel services were created specifically for undergraduates, college and seminary students attended chapel together. Chapel programs could receive mixed reviews in the early years, as they do today. For some, chapels were not planned well enough in advance. "Even though most chapel programs are well-planned and inspiring," one student complained in 1959, others evidenced a "lack of planning" that made some students refer to chapel as "surprise hour."

Regardless of the occasional complaint, chapel allowed students to set aside their academic schedule to focus on opportunities for growth and spiritual challenge. In 1970 the college employed Lee Jenkins as its first full-time chaplain. By this time the seminary's increasing reputation in evangelical circles enhanced opportunities to secure well-known speakers and Christian authors. In addition to popular Grace insiders such as Alva J. McClain, Herman Hoyt, Homer Kent, John Whitcomb, Ron Manahan, Don DeYoung, Larry Crabb, and John Davis, chapel programs included Corrie Ten Boom, Herbert Lockyer, Charles Ryrie, J. Vernon McGee, Howard Hendricks, Jay Adams, and John White (speaking on communist brainwashing techniques).

Students were also required to participate in "Christian Service" as part of their spiritual development. Begun in 1957 under the leadership of John Whitcomb, the program included any number of ministry experiences but often involved little more than going off-campus to hand out evangelistic tracts. However deep the experiences, participation in ministry provided opportunities for students to put into practice their Christian faith.[23] Students were required to fill out formal monthly reports, which were turned in to the "Christian Life Committee." The reports would then be organized by class and given to the Dean of Students who might even pass them along to the board of trustees. In 1963, Ralph Gilbert took over the role of Director of Christian Service, and was followed by Lloyd A. Woolman, who served until 1966. Donald Ogden, Ward A. Kriegbaum, Mel Friesen, and Jerry Classen also shared in the leadership responsibility between 1966 and 1970.

Student affairs also facilitated the formation of Grace Ministries in Action (GMA), which was started in 1969 as a new branch of government within Student Council. This student-led organization was charged with coordinating and leading ministry opportunities that went beyond Christian Service requirements or handing out tracts. Since its inception, GMA has sent ministry teams to local organizations such as Warsaw's Riverwood Ranch (a home for boys) as well as local Grace Brethren churches. GMA teams also served in Chicago (Inner City Impact), worked with children, and ministered in regional prison facilities, to name a few examples. Grace Ministries in Action expanded to lead two on-campus ministries that have been embraced by the Winona Lake community. The first was a unique ministry called Halloween Funfest, which was first organized by Jennifer Anderson, a GMA officer, in 1989. The event was designed as a Halloween alternative with games and candy for young children, a creative solution for dealing with the fact that the Grace campus was divided over the question of whether it was appropriate for Christians to celebrate Halloween. The 1989 event was held in the McClain Hall basement, but the attendance was so overwhelming, it was moved to the Lancer Gym for the second year. An instant success, Funfest has continued to grow and often hosts over 2,500 children for the one-night event.

Another of the more prominent GMA ministries was an event hosted around the Christmas season called Heart of the Holidays. The event began about the same time as Funfest and served to connect underprivileged families with the campus and student body. The event made use of puppet teams, dramas, and several evangelistic ministries that were organized to provide outreach to parents and children in the community. The three-hour evening included tree decorating and presents for children while parents could benefit from donated clothing and food. Heart of the Holidays continues to bring out the "heart" of the student body and its desire to bring about hope and change in families, and a desire to share the gospel with the community. These ministries have become lasting traditions at Grace College.[24]

Student Services

The decade of the 70s brought a new American Motors automobile called the Gremlin, an end to black and white television, and the beginning of TV series like *Happy Days, All in the Family, Mash*, and *Saturday Night Live*. The seventies also saw mood rings, pet rocks, the Watergate scandal, and an end to the Vietnam War. "Contemporary Christian Music" gained new momentum and artists like Phil Keaggy, Petra, Sweet Comfort Band, Brian Duncan, the Imperials, Glad, and Wayne Watson performed at Grace College. The era also brought a new kind of student to campus: the "Baby Boomers."[25]

Students now came to campus with a different level of confidence—perhaps even arrogance or swagger. With a stronger spirit of activism than earlier generations of Grace students, they were more vocal about the political scene, as can be seen in the pages of *The Sounding Board*. While many students supported the war in Vietnam, some challenged the campus toward a nonviolent ethic consistent with the Brethren tradition of the school, and called for a strong stand in support of non-combatant alternative service. (The majority of college students at the time would have received automatic draft deferment because of their student status.) A 1970 article in the student newspaper expressed support for Nixon's program for "Vietnamization," and another challenged students to support environmental efforts and the introduction of Earth Day.[26]

Students were also vocal about campus concerns, such as some of the facilities, which were starting to show their age. "Woe is McKee Courts," declared an article in *The Sounding Board*, which criticized the administration for neglecting the condition of the dormitory and the regular flooding that occurred. The administration should provide "hip boots" for residents, the article proposed sarcastically. In addition to flooding, spider colonies and potholes in the parking lot were a routine part of daily life in McKee. Student complaints were likely part of the administration's decision to remodel the dormitory in the fall of 1970.[27] That same fall, *The Sounding Board* instituted a regular "Whine In" column, which was designed as a means for students to put their complaints in print rather than waste time talking about them to other students who could do nothing about them.[28] Students used the column to "whine" about the dress code, parking policies, freshman initiation, chapel attendance policies, the grading system, movie policies, cafeteria food, the dancing policy, summer enforcement of the community standards, and the ineffectiveness of the Student Activities Board (SAB).

The end of the 1960s brought not only a new student mentality, but also new trends in the student affairs profession—trends that placed greater emphasis on student retention and improvements in graduation rates. Prior to 1970, student success was primarily left up to the faculty; but research increasingly linked student departure with factors related to morale and the campus environment.[29] In response, Grace College, like many institutions, felt a greater responsibility to meet students' moral, social, vocational, as well as health needs. Deans and other administrators began to see the necessity for educational structures that fostered more than intellectual growth, but extended to the development of the "whole student."[30]

Two of the first initiatives toward this end were the on-campus Health Center and a campus safety office. The Health Center was operational for the fall of 1970 and was staffed by a local doctor and two nurses. It provided allergy shots, flu shots, and medical information for parents as well as providing triage care for students. Four years later, in 1974, the institution introduced its first uniformed campus safety guard, John Fretz, who was responsible for managing overcrowded parking lots and instituting an "observe, report, and document" philosophy. Fretz's efforts would eventually lead to a full-fledged campus safety program in later years. Some of the most significant developments in student affairs, however, took place under Deans Daniel Snively and Miriam Uphouse.

Moving Beyond In Loco Parentis:
Dan Snively and Miriam Uphouse

Known affectionately as "Mrs. M," Miriam Uphouse (later, Chris-tensen) served as Associate Dean of Students for twenty years, be-ginning when she was 45. She was known as a very humble, loving and talented "pursuer and mentor of women" on campus, and her legacy at Grace College has been far reaching. Uphouse completed a BA from Grace College in 1963 and would later receive her MA in Guidance and Counseling from St. Francis College (now Univer-sity). This allowed her to teach Introduction to Counseling at Grace, a course she loved.[31]

Beyond the legacy she left for staff and students at Grace, Up-house's influence extended to the larger student affairs profession during a time that included advances in gender equality. Uphouse served as the president of the Christian Association of Deans of Women (CADW) for the 1969-70 academic year and again from 1978 to 1980. Between her two terms as president, the U.S. Con-gress passed the landmark 1972 Title IX legislation, which prohib-ited any form of gender discrimination at colleges and universities receiving federal financial assistance. In the wake of Title IX, CADW worked increasingly with the Association of Christian Deans and Advisors of Men (ACDAM) and in the progressive spirit of these national trends, the two organizations moved toward merging. Up-house was an active leader in this effort. During her second tenure as president of CADW, she helped facilitate the merger that eventually materialized in June, 1980. Uphouse was thus the final president of CADW as the new Association for Christians in Student Develop-ment (ACSD) was born. Today ACSD is a primary training ground for student development/affairs professionals in Christian higher ed-ucation. It serves professionals with its Journal *Growth* and an annual conference. As a leader of great vision and passion, Miriam Uphouse was a pioneer for all women who have pursued a career in the student development/affairs discipline.

Like Miriam Uphouse, Dan Snively was a leader who brought a new vision to student affairs at a time when the student body needed strong and creative leadership. He directed student life in new and innovative directions and realized the importance of student service

Global Affairs and Cold War Fears
Jared S. Burkholder

Not surprisingly, perspectives on global issues during the Cold War era reflected both the nation's fears and a desire to make sense of current events through theological understanding and biblical interpretation. Russia figured prominently in end-times scenarios for Premillennialists. L. S. Bauman began writing and preaching on Russia's role in eschatology as early as the 1930s.[1] Similarly, Charles Feinberg identified godless Russia as the "rapacious beast of the north" in his lectures at Grace in 1964.[2] The spring 1963 issue of the Grace Journal offered praise for recently published rebuttals to Communism through reviews by Grace Seminary graduate, Robert Delnay, professor at Central Conservative Baptist Seminary, and Richard McIntosh, also a Grace graduate and Dean of Students and Bible professor at Cedarville College.[3]

Although professors and campus leaders rarely made explicit political application from eschatological positions, there is little question that premillennial pessimism meshed well with concerns about the spread of Communism.[4] In 1975, for example, President Hoyt distributed copies of a federal judiciary subcommittee interview with Frederick Schwarz, founder of the Christian anti-Communist Crusade, making them available to all faculty, administration, and students. The pamphlet featured the kidnapping of Berkeley student Patty Hearst, heiress of the Hearst family fortune, by the Symbionese Liberation Army, a small leftist group of self-proclaimed "urban guerillas." Brainwashed into becoming a willing accomplice in the group's militant and violent activity, the beautiful and innocent Hearst had been defiled by godless radical thugs—proof positive for many that the dangers of communism and liberal agitators posed a grave threat to traditional American society.[5]

departments and their critical nature in helping students succeed and remain motivated to complete their education. Just as significant, Snively also understood the importance of restoration and the reality that when students make poor choices, they often need a second chance or someone to come alongside them and hold them accountable. Snively served for sixteen years[32] and moved the institution forward in student services, restoration, and in the delicate arena of discernment. Under Snively and Uphouse, student affairs at Grace made strides toward greater levels of professionalism.

These efforts included the formation of a training and counseling course for resident assistants entitled "Theory and Counseling in Practice," which was implemented in 1977. The course covered content in both leadership development and basic counseling skills, which would enable resident assistants to be more effective leaders in the dorms. Without a full-time counselor for students, more formal counseling was offered through chaplains, deans, or faculty. Roger Peugh, for example, became known as an especially capable and compassionate counselor for students.

New initiatives introduced during the 1970s also included the Student Academic Advising Center (SAAC), which focused on providing greater student satisfaction specifically for incoming freshman. Designed to increase retention rates, SAAC developed a groundbreaking peer advising program as well as a mandatory course for freshman. "College Life 101" was created with the goal of helping students in their transition from high school to college. Other targeted programs were developed to reach out to sophomores as well as students who had difficulty deciding on a field of study—a factor that historically placed a student at high risk for departure prior to graduation. The SAAC also worked with the college faculty to think of academic advising as a means of fostering student success and development rather than simply choosing classes. The new emphasis was rooted in a developmental approach to advising, which would identify and offer resources for students who were struggling academically. These new initiatives were continually refined throughout the 1980s, and in 1989 Grace's SAAC was selected the Outstanding Institutional Advising Program in the country for church-related colleges.[33]

As mentioned above, Snively implemented a paradigm shift in dealing with disciplinary issues—a shift that hinged on a restorative

In response to the times, history classes at Grace could include strong doses of Cold War doctrine on American foreign policy, and assignments included anti-Communist readings.[6] Such international concerns and the domestic upheaval that accompanied them could also fuel patriotic feelings about the home country. Frustrated with leftist agitation on other college campuses across the country, long-time history professor, R. Wayne Snider began holding an annual event on the Grace campus he called "Americans for America Week." The week-long event was designed to stimulate patriotic feelings and support for American involvement in Vietnam. Each year these weeks featured pageants, musical ditties with titles like "Stop, Hear the Freedom Bells Ring," and prayer meetings at the campus flagpole.[7] Thus, while a growing international impulse served to foster an interest in providing cross-cultural experiences and more diverse learning environments for students, at times the Grace campus found the global scene threatening and looked for ways to reinforce pro-American sentiments.

1   See Bauman's *God and Gog: or, The Coming Meet Between Judah's Lion and Russia's Bear* (1934) and *Russian Events in the Light of Bible Prophecy* (New York: Revell, 1942).

2   Charles L. Feinberg, "God's Message to Man through the Prophets" *Grace Journal* 5:2 (Spring 1964), 20.

3   Robert Delnay, "Review," Lester Dekoster, *Communism and Christian Faith*, *Grace Journal* 4:2 (Spring, 1963), 37; Richard T. McIntosh, "Review," James D. Bales, *Communism, its Faith and Fallacies: An Exposition and Criticism*, *Grace Journal* 4:2 (Spring, 1963), 43.

4   See Hankins, *American Evangelicals*, 90-96, 139-141.

5   Pamphlet in Hoyt papers, Grace Archives.

6   Steve Grill, interview by author. An example would be John A. Stormer's, *None Dare Call it Treason* (Florissant, MO: Liberty Bell Press, 1964). Stormer, a right-wing politician turned pastor and Christian school administrator, argued America's political elites were spreading "treason" through their concessions with leftist groups and communist infiltrators. Aptly published in 1964, during Barry Goldwater's campaign for president, *None Dare Call it Treason* was followed in 1968 by *The Death of a Nation*, in which Stormer made ties between the spread of communism and premillennial eschatology explicit.

7   Steve Grill interview.

model that placed less emphasis on conforming to the rules in the student handbook. *In loco parentis* was giving way to relationship-building, and the policies would change accordingly. One of the first was in the area of male grooming. Traditionally, beards were viewed as signs of rebellion and unbecoming of a Grace student, but by 1980, beards had become permissible as long as they were kept short and neatly trimmed.[34] Another rule change involved playing cards, which were long associated with gambling. But in 1988, the board of trustees voted to allow playing cards on campus. According to a report in *The Sounding Board*, the change involved three years of research, dialogue, and discussion with the board.[35]

Although the debate over playing cards was a major issue, it was not as contentious as the question of movies. Through the 1980s, the policy was clear:

> Insomuch as most of the commercial movies violate Biblical standards of morality and are detrimental to spiritual growth, Grace Schools disapproves of attendance at theaters by members of the Grace family. Therefore the following is the Grace Schools commercial movie theatre policy for students: All students are to refrain from attending commercial motion picture theaters while enrolled in courses at Grace Schools. This statement does not imply that during vacations or summers students may indiscriminately attend the theatre. The general moral quality of most commercial pictures is in direct conflict with clearly revealed Biblical standards. Movies that advocate or glorify sin are obviously immoral. Techniques and content included in motion pictures, such as profanity, nudity, violence, etc. (even though not advocating them either explicitly or implicitly) may produce immoral thoughts or actions in viewers.[36]

Some students resented this policy because the campus would at times show movies for campus activities or faculty members might include films as part of their classes. In addition, the increasingly ubiquitous video cassette recorder made viewing films in off-campus settings easy. Thus in the minds of some, the administration did not trust students enough to use discernment about their personal choice of films. "If we attend a movie away from campus we violate our Christian commitment," one student declared in *The Sounding Board*, "but if we attend one on campus we are helping to support a club or being provided with a social life on the weekends. This seems hypocritical, doesn't it?"[37] In response to increasing pressure, Snively held an open forum in mid-November of 1984 to discuss movies. He defended the prohibition against movie theater attendance during the school year. In response to a question about the difference between watching films on television and visiting the theater, Snively said that one could easily change a TV channel to avoid viewing sinful material, but one would be unlikely to walk out of a theater if they had paid for a ticket. He did agree to loosen the policy, however, giving students permission to view movies during the summers, assuming they would use discernment.[38] To address policies on media consumption, Snively also formed a "discernment committee" of other administrators, which continued to evaluate the film issue. In 1990, they introduced a "discernment policy," which allowed students to attend PG-rated movies at theaters regardless of whether or not classes were in session. Students were split in their response to the new policy. Although some were pleased, others were not, believing that a strict policy of abstinence had been more appropriate. Although he was no doubt responding to changing social and technological contexts, Snively's overarching goal was to treat students as adults and help them develop personal standards for moral and biblical decision-making.[39]

Between 1990 and 1994, there were frequent changes in student affairs leadership. Bruce Barlow, who previously worked under Snively as Associate Dean of Students, stepped into the Dean's position in 1990. Barlow continued the emphasis on developing discernment. As a means of facilitating student reflection on decisions about media consumption, for example, Barlow implemented a week of media fasting. A way of prompting students to ask themselves what they should and should not be watching, the media fast was also a means of assuring constituents and parents that the institution has not "dropped the movie rule."[40] Under Barlow, the discernment committee continued to meet and included faculty and student representatives. Rather than functioning merely to review policy, the committee's desire was to assess how successfully the campus was contributing to the moral development of students. Although Barlow served as Dean of Students for just one year, he was admired by students for his shepherding heart and passion for leadership development.

Ken Taylor replaced Barlow, serving as Dean of Students for the 1992-1993 academic year. Taylor continued the process of adapting the campus rules, bringing greater flexibility to the curfew policy, expectations for chapel attendance, and the dress code. Taylor also adjusted expectations for participation in peer groups (then called "CPR groups"), which met in the dorms to facilitate spiritual growth. Previously mandatory, these groups would become less structured and optional, though encouraged, for upperclassman. These peer groups continue on the Grace campus as "Growth Groups."

Athletics

Not surprisingly, athletics also developed as a significant part of the Grace campus experience. Athletic opportunities began informally with intramural sports and physical education programs, which made use of the small gymnasium at nearby East Wayne School (now Jefferson Elementary School). Intramurals offered students, faculty, and staff the opportunity to participate in sports on a competitive and a recreational level. This program opened the door for students at all skill levels to enjoy sports. Early sports offered were football, volleyball, table tennis, basketball, and the traditional fall retreat faculty vs. students softball game.

The program began to change, however, when Richard Messner enrolled in the seminary in 1952. With his leadership, the college began to organize intercollegiate competition. Because of the school's small size, teams, originally called "Grace Ambassadors," consisted of players from both the college and seminary. His wife, Vonnie, coached the first women's basketball teams. In 1955 Messner was appointed the first Director of Athletics and led the men's basketball team on its first road trip to the East Coast. Thus began the rich tradition of Grace basketball.[41] Messner also instituted the college's first cheerleading squad the same year. Three years later, in 1958, athletics at Grace garnered more momentum with the construction of the school's first gymnasium.

That same year, Grace held an open-school contest to decide on an improved mascot name, presumably to allow athletes to enter the court or field under a title that was more aggressive than "ambassadors." After considering several nicknames, "Lancers" was selected and announced as the team mascot in November of 1958. The decision was not without controversy, however, since the idea of an armored knight flew in the face of Brethren commitments to non-resistance. The colors red and white were then chosen to distinguish the college from the gold and white of the seminary uniforms.[42]

In 1959, Grace College became a charter member of the Mid-Central Conference (Tri-State [Trine], Concordia, Huntington, Indiana Tech and Grace). Organized basketball, baseball, and tennis teams were required to join the conference. A golf team played at nearby Rozella Golf Course, and the tennis team played on courts behind the gymnasium; both teams officially started play in the fall of 1960. Baseball played its first "official" game April 23, 1960. Track and field would follow shortly after and experienced early success, winning its first MCC Track Title in the spring of 1962 and continuing its winning ways with MCC titles in 64, 65, and 66. Cross country and men's soccer debuted in 1965 with Men's soccer (1966) and men's golf (1969) becoming official varsity sports. The men's basketball team won its first MCC title in 1969.

In 1967, Messner moved to the Advancement Office and Glen "Chet" Kammerer took over as head basketball coach. Messner had recruited Kammerer from nearby Leesburg High School to play both basketball and baseball. Although growing up in a Christian family, Kammerer was converted while a student at Grace. Graduating in 1964, he was a standout athlete and Messner groomed Kammerer to take his place. After completing an MA at Ball State, Kammerer, who still holds the all-time scoring record at Grace, served as Athletic Director and Head Basketball coach at Grace until 1975 when he took a position at Westmont College and Phil Hoskins replaced him. Kammerer would later work for the Los Angeles Lakers and the Miami Heat, professional basketball teams. In 1977, Jim Kessler, who played under Kammerer and served as assistant coach under Hoskins, became head basketball coach, a position he has held for over three decades.[43]

Noticeably missing in the early years of the institution, women's sports began in 1957. "The biggest feature of the 1957-58 sports program is the Women's Recreation Association," *The Sounding Board* announced, "Although they will not play intramurals, the WRA will have organized games among themselves and will occasionally play other colleges such as Wheaton or Goshen."[44] It would not be until November, 1960, however, that there would be an official meeting of the varsity women's basketball program, and in February of 1961, the Lady Lancers played and won their first game. Women's sports at Grace had officially begun. In the early 1970s the Lady Lancers would enjoy playing such teams as Purdue, Ball State, and Butler, and the Lady Lancer basketball team beat Butler February 5, 1972. In the wake of Title IX, which highlighted the need for more gender equality at schools like Grace, the college added women's varsity sports in track and field, cross country, softball, and soccer.

Grace College basketball enjoyed 22 years of tradition with its Turkey Tournament, an eight-team tournament held on campus over the Thanksgiving break. This tournament continues today as part of the men's schedule as the Kosciusko (Optimist) Cancer Care Fund. Those years were successful for other sports teams as well. In 1974-75, the men's tennis team won its second MCC championship. The men's soccer team was victorious over Notre Dame, and women's basketball and softball had outstanding seasons with records of 13-3 and 9-1 respectively. The decade of the 70s was an excellent time for men's soccer as they won four conference championships in six years.

On February 27, 1975, tragedy struck the campus when one of the most loved members of the Grace community, Rev. H. Leslie Moore, suffered a fatal heart attack while watching the season's final home men's basketball game. "There 'tis" he would shout as a free throw slipped through the net, an echo readily heard in the Lancer gym during home games. Mr. Moore began working with Grace Schools in June 1966 as the Director of Housing and held that position until his death. Some would say he was the Lancers most committed fan and was known for his excitement, enthusiasm, and loyalty to the team even when they lost.[45]

Boosting campus morale, the 1980s brought out the best in women's volleyball as they opened the decade with a 23-10 record in 1980. Men's basketball would continue its incredible run of winning seasons in the 80s, winning seven straight MCC championships and ultimately winning a game at the 1988 national tournament.[46] However, there will always be a debate as to whether the men's basketball team of 1982-83 with a 32-5 record was Grace's best team. This great team would ultimately lose a heartbreaker to Tennessee Temple (59-57) and fall short of a national championship. Then the 1992 team brought home Grace's one and only NAIA (National Association of Intercollegiate Athletics) national championship. The team would march to a 32-5 record as well, but finished the ultimate task with an 85-79 OT victory over the Northwestern Red Raiders of Iowa. This team's success would bring national prominence to Grace College and its athletic programs.

The early nineties would also be great for the women's softball team as they won three National Christian College Athletic Association (NCCAA) district titles. The women's volleyball team also won a national championship in the fall of 1995. In short, both men's and women's athletic programs would help unite the institution in realizing the value of athletics and how they help to develop the "whole student."

Performing Arts

The arts have also been an integral part of learning at Grace College. Music groups were vital to early ministries and recruitment. In 1954 when the college became a four-year degree-granting institution, classes were added to develop a major in music. In many ways the music groups of these early years defined the institution's success in developing leaders for Christian ministry. Performance groups eventually included Concert Choir, the Hand Bell Choir, Dimensions in Brass, The King's Brass, and Sound Investment. They traveled extensively, routinely providing students with quality opportunities to develop and use their musical talents.

In 1955, Grace College offered its first drama production on campus, *"Father of the Bride,"* which was directed by Ava Schnittjer, who at the time was a professor of English and Speech along with her role as Dean of Women. When Philathea Hall, the original college building, was completed in 1959, it included the "Little Theatre." Here students have been able to practice and develop their theatre skills and have entertained thousands of faculty, staff, students, and community members over the years. Later, Rodeheaver Auditorium was acquired and enhanced with lights and sound, which has allowed the institution's drama and music programs to perform and incorporate community members and alumni into larger theatre productions.

First-Person Reflections

A year after Ken Taylor left the position of Dean of Students, Roger Peugh, who filled-in as interim, surveyed the students to find out what they wanted in a new dean. Their feedback included a desire to find someone who would commit to providing long-term student affairs leadership. The students no doubt echoed what many faculty and administrators believed as well—that there was a need for more consistency and continuity in the student affairs office. I was employed in 1994 with this in mind and I was also coming from outside the Grace College and Seminary orbit, which was in line with student recommendations taken from the results of the student survey.[47] My initiation to Grace College included a lesson both in the tensions that always surround adjustments in student policies, as well as the tensions that can exist between the faculty side and the student affairs side of campus.

In the months prior to moving to campus, I was asked to weigh-in on an issue which had prompted discussion across campus: should the dress code be changed to allow students to wear shorts to class. Traditionally, the faculty had their own policies for classroom attire. The issue needed to be resolved quickly since the student handbook had a printing deadline, and I agreed to change the policy, which would allow students to wear non-athletic shorts in any classroom during any time and month of the school year. After arriving on campus, however, I realized some of the faculty thought I had overstepped my bounds. I was invited to a faculty retreat in which I was asked to field questions about my philosophy as a first-year dean. Agreeing to offer my thoughts, I was put in a chair front-and-center while the faculty asked rather pointed questions. Several used the opportunity to communicate to me that changing student policies that affected the classroom environment, such as a prohibition against wearing shorts to class, was not to be the prerogative of the student affairs office. It became clear to me that the majority of the faculty believed that student life decisions should be secondary to the faculty's own interests. (We subsequently amended the policy to return to the faculty the authority to dictate dress codes in their classroom.)

As I attempted to navigate this, as well as other cultural tensions on campus, Student affairs sought to address the needs of newer generations of students. Every new cohort of students brings with it the push for institutional change. This idea is always met with a combination of fear and excitement. Throughout the 1990s, this included the students of "Generation X" (born between the years 1965 and 1983), which cultural critics have characterized as pessimistic about the value of education. [48] Perhaps, as some have indicated, "Gen-Xers" have felt underappreciated while living in the shadow of the baby boomers. "We're kind of an afterthought generation," according to one Gen Xer, "The spotlight is on the Boomers and old people. We're basically ignored."[49] Generation X was also a more tolerant cohort than their predecessors, adopting greater latitude regarding individual beliefs, truth-claims, and lifestyle choices, for which they have been criticized.[50] Regardless of the degree to which Grace students reflected the cultural norms of their generation, these attributes signaled for us the need to be a more relational department—accepting of students' efforts, not just their accomplishments and appreciating their worth in order to help them feel secure within the college environment.[51] Tensions over community lifestyle standards also continued, as Gen-Xers found themselves within a campus culture that continued to be conservative and laden with policies, despite the loosening of rules since the 1980s.

It seemed clear to us in student affairs that Grace College was asking students to live under policies that were non-developmental and based on antiquated social expectations. This became even more apparent with the arrival of the "Millennial" generation (born 1984-2004). A large cohort nationally (close to 100 million), Millennials are also "highly relational" although they seem to older generations to be permanently attached to smart-phones, social media, and ear-buds.[52] (While students of the 1970s were thrilled with the installation of phone lines to individual dorm rooms, land-lines are no longer dormitory amenities.) The shift from rules to relationships continues to be apparent within student affairs at Grace. And this has meant more adjustments to lifestyle standards. Rules such as the "three-person rule," which prohibited couples from being alone in an off campus home, were adjusted, and more changes came to curfew, dancing, and music policies. The film policy, which caused so much discussion in the late 1980s was modified yet again before the turn of the new millennium. In the last decade and a half, the student alcohol policy has become more flexible and standards on body-piercings have also loosened. The changes were made in part to connect better with a generation that wanted to focus more on relationships than rules. As one writer on evangelical youth culture has observed, the new millennium brought a new correlation between relationships and positive change:

"Rules – Relationship = Rebellion
Rules + Relationship = Positive Response."[53]

In other words, we came to believe that Grace needed to learn to pursue students differently. The campus was beginning to understand that students needed to know that they, as individuals, were more important to staff and faculty than the rules themselves.

We have much to learn from our "Millennial" students. They have challenged us to care deeply about political and social issues both nationally and globally. This is in part because they have seen and witnessed tremendous tragedy in events such as 9/11, campus shootings, tsunamis, and hurricanes. I have loved watching this cohort of students respond to serious challenges that face this world through their desire to make a difference. As a response, Grace has sent groups to several different needs over the years, driven and led by the student body and their desire to make an impact: Hurricane Katrina, Haiti, child slavery, and tsunami relief in Japan, to name a few.

Yet challenges continue. At this writing, Grace College students are more stressed and anxious than previous generations. Research indicates that the majority of incoming students feel frequently overwhelmed as well as harboring high expectations for success.[54] They also expect their college or university of choice to provide high levels of academic and personal support services. This has added pressure on the Grace Campus, as well as campuses across the nation, as we have grown and developed in our capacity to provide student services to meet the greater service demands and expectation of this generation.

Partly in response to the needs of this generation, I have sought to put "proactive" programs in place with the goal of "whole person" development as well as making personnel changes. In the fall of 2005, Deb Musser was hired as dean of students. At the time, Deb held the highest ranking administrative position of any female in the history of the.institution. Musser's hiring was in part linked with a desire to remove the antiquated models of dean of men and dean of women. Musser, along with her team, would bring an intentional developmental approach to the residence halls, utilizing hall programming and a focus on developing integrity, identity, and healthy relationships.

Perhaps the most far-reaching recent development in student affairs has been the implantation, in 2007, of a more centralized model under the direction of Provost Bill Katip. While hall and dormitory programming would remain a vital part of the student affairs office, this new model brought greater integration of academic and student services under one administrator. Among other personnel changes, this brought Jacqueline Schram to the student affairs side of campus as an associate dean who would supervise the academic service programs of the college's "Core" curriculum (general education) as well as a sequence of courses we know as the "First Year Experience." This model also placed the library and registrar's office, which naturally have strong connections to the academic sector of campus, under the student affairs umbrella.

In 1994, as I sat on the "hot-seat" at my first faculty retreat, the disconnect between the academic (faculty) and student affairs sectors of campus was all too tangible. Yet in the last decade, the sense of unity has grown considerably, particularly with the innovative changes in 2007. Collaborative efforts between academic affairs and student affairs were both fortunate and inevitable and have come in the form of opportunities to teach in the core curriculum, develop comprehensive assessment plans that hold programs accountable, and assist services like the library in a time of great change in technology. Such collaboration is consistent with calls within the literature for enhancing student learning while creating innovative solutions and programs to meet the ever-changing needs of students.[55] "If undergraduate education is to be enhanced," Ernest Pascarella and Patrick Terenzini have argued, faculty members, joined by academic and student affairs administrators, must devise ways to deliver undergraduate education that are as comprehensive and integrated in ways that students actually learn … A whole new mindset is needed to capitalize on the interrelatedness of the in-and-out of the classroom influences on student learning and the functional interconnectedness of academic and student affairs divisions.[56]

In short, our recent strides toward a seamless learning environment are rooted in professional standards of excellence as well as the goals and desires of Grace College administrators since our founding. Models have changed to be sure— student affairs professionals are no longer simply policy enforcers or social directors. Cultural norms and generations of students have evolved as well. But the student affairs team at Grace College has always been intentional in recognizing that intellectual growth and spiritual growth are equally important in developing the "whole person," and herein lies an abundance of opportunities.

Notes

1. "The Student Personnel Point of View: A Report of a Conference on the Philosophy and Development of Student Personnel work in College and University," (*American Council on Education Studies* 1:3, June 1937), 3.

2. Ibid. For more on the impact of this report, see N. J. Evans, D. S. Guido, L. D. Renn, and K. A. Renn, *Student Development in College: Theory, Research, and Practice* (San Francisco, CA: Jossey Bass Publishing 2010).

3. John R Thelin. *A History of American Higher Education*, 2nd ed. (Baltimore: Johns Hopkins University Press, 2004), 260-316.

4. William C. Ringenberg, *The Christian college: A history of Protestant Higher Education in America* (St. Paul, MN: Baker Academic, 2006), 155-182.

5. Terry White and R. Wayne Snider, *25 Years of God's Grace: 1948-1973* (Winona Lake, IN: Grace College and Seminary, 1973).

6. R. A. Schwartz, "The Disappearing Deans of Men—Where they Went and Why: A Historical Perspective" (Paper presented at the annual meeting of the American Educational Research Association, Seattle, WA, April 10-14, 2010).

7. Both of these dormitory spaces were buildings that were rented from the Winona Assembly. McKee Courts was on McDonald Island, and Westminster Hall was owned at the time by Homer Rodeheaver and was used as a dorm and the student cafeteria.

8. R. Wayne Snider, interview by author, June 13, 2012; Miriam Uphouse, interview by author, June 13, 2012.

9. See Thom S. Rainer and Jess W. Rainer, *The Millennials: Connecting to America's Largest Generation* (Nashville: B&H Publishing Group, 2011).

10. Ibid.

11. Grace College Catalogue, 1950.

12. Grace College Student Handbook, 1961, 8.

13. James R. Appleton, Channing M. Briggs and James J. Rhatigan, *Pieces of Eight: The Rites, Roles and Styles of the Dean* (Portland, OR: NASPA Institute of Research and Development, 1978), 99-104.

14. Snider interview.

15. Grace College Women's Dormitory Supplement, 1956, 11.

16. Grace College Student Handbook, 1952, 8. In the years after a dean of students was hired, the dean would give such permission.

17. Women's Dormitory Supplement, 1956, 11.

18. Student Handbook, 1952, 8.

19. Student Handbook, 1951, 6.

20. Student Handbook, 1969, 13.

21. Student Handbook, 1956, 6.

22. Ibid.

23. White and Snider, *25 Years of God's Grace.*

24. Ibid.

25. On the Baby Boomer generation, see William Strauss and Neil Howe, *Generations: The History of America's Future, 1584 to 2069* (New York: William Morrow and Co., 1991), 299-316.

26. *The Sounding Board*, May 1, 1970, 2.

27. *The Sounding Board*, October 30, 1970, 4.

28. *The Sounding Board*, November 13, 1970, 2.

29. See W. G. Spady, "Dropouts from higher education: An interdisciplinary review and synthesis," *Interchange* 1:1 (1970), 64-85.

30. For a helpful history of campus culture in America, consult Helen Lefkowitz Horowitz, *Campus Life: Undergraduate Cultures from the End of the Eighteenth Century to the Present* (Chicago: University of Chicago Press, 1987); on Christian perspectives specifically, see David S. Guthrie, ed., *Student Affairs Reconsidered: A Christian View of the Profession and its Contexts* (New York: Calvin Center Series and University Press of America, 1997).

31. Miriam Uphouse, interview by author, June 13, 2012.

32. Ibid.

33. Ibid.

34. Student Handbook, 1951, 6.

35. Teresa Palmitessa, *The Sounding Board*, May 5, 1988.

36. Grace College and Seminary Student Handbook, 1987, 29.

37. Jerry Filger, *The Sounding Board*, November 11, 1982.

38. *The Sounding Board*, Nov.15, 1984, 1.

39. Dan Snively, interview by author, June 13, 2012.

40. Ibid.

41. Ibid.

42. Ibid.

43. Jim Kessler, Interview by author, June 30, 2014.

44. *The Sounding Board*, October 11, 1957, 4.

45. *The Sounding Board*, March 5, 1975, 3.

46. *Grace Magazine*, 1998.

47. Ibid.

48. On this cohort of students ("Generation X," "Baby Busters," or the "Thirteenth Generation") see George Barna, *Baby Busters: The Disillusioned Generation* (Chicago: Northfield Publishing, 1992) and Strauss and Howe, 317-334.

49. Barna, 19.

50. For an example of evangelical reaction to attitudes about toleration, consult Josh McDowell and Bob Hostetler, *The New Tolerance: How a cultural movement threatens to destroy you, your faith, and your children* (Wheaton, IL: Tyndale House Publishers, 1998).

51. Josh McDowell, *The Disconnected Generation: Saving our Youth from Self Destruction* (Nashville: Word Publishing, 2000), 25-43.

52. On Millennials, including "Generation iY", see Tim Elmore, *Generation iY: Our Last Chance to Save their Future* (Atlanta: Post Gardener Publishing, 2010); William Strauss and Neil Howe, *The Fourth Turning: What the Cycles of History Tell us about America's Next Rendezvous with Destiny* (New York: Broadway, 1997), 239-251; Rainer and Rainer, *The Millennials*; and Larry Rosen, *iDisorder: Understanding our Obsession with Technology and Overcoming its hold on us* (New York: Palgrave Macmillan, 2012).

53. McDowell, *Disconnected Generation*, 30.

54. Grace College and Theological Seminary Student Affairs Office (This data can be found in the results of the Cooperative Institutional Research Program (CIRP), which Grace College has used as a research tool given to freshman on an annual basis.)

55. Student needs that have prompted the organizational adjustments at Grace under Musser as well as more recent changes in student affairs, including the move toward more collaboration, are discussed throughout the work of Rainer and Rainer, Rosen, Elmore and McDowell. Other pertinent studies would include those in Margaret J. Barr, Mary K. Desler, and Associates, *The Handbook of Student Affairs Administration* (San Francisco, Jossey-Bass, 2000); N. J. Evans et al, *Student Development in College*; and Adrianna J. Kezar and Jaime Lester, *Organizing Higher Education for Collaboration: a Guide for Campus Leaders* (San Francisco: Jossey-Bass, 2009).

56. Quoted in John H. Schuh and Elizabeth J. Whitt, eds., *Creating Successful Partnerships between Academic and Student Affairs* (San Francisco: Jossey-Bass, 1999), 6.

Chapter 7

Community
An Expanding Horizon

M. M. Norris

A STRONG SENSE OF COMMUNITY HAS BEEN INTEGRAL TO THE ANA-baptist and Pietist heritage of the Brethren movement. Indeed, as cultural outsiders, the Brethren fostered close-knit congregations that became the conduits for discipleship. Perhaps this is one reason the Grace community is sometimes referred to as a family with a highly relational atmosphere. Among the faculty and staff, this sense of community has been intentionally fostered throughout the decades, largely through celebrations, retreats, and on-campus organizations. These efforts continue and have been enhanced by forums that offer outlets for faculty scholarship, team building opportunities for first-year faculty members, and service-oriented initiatives. While this internal sense of community is vital, the focus of this chapter is on efforts to expand this sense of community beyond the horizons of the Winona Lake campus. This chapter focuses heavily on the innovative spirit of the Manahan administration and explores the development of an increasing desire for community engagement that has only recently been more fully developed.

Initial Challenges

Although the founders of Grace were progressive enough to embrace something new, there still developed something of a separatist mindset. Though they did not foster the kind of separatism preserved by Old Order traditionalists, genuine engagement with the community

149

was sometimes limited to door-to-door evangelism. As depicted in the 1962 yearbook, this was fostered as part of students' required "Christian service." A two-page spread highlighted four photographs, the first of which depicts a clean-shaven male Grace student with closely cropped hair and wearing an argyle sweater, sitting at his desk diligently studying. The caption reads: "PRAYER PREPARATION and thorough study is necessary before one sets out to witness." The next picture is of the same young man wearing a long black coat as he knocks on the door of a house, a Bible and other resources in hand. The caption reads: "ONE MUST depend on the Holy Spirit both to prepare the way before him and to guide him in the way." The third picture in the series shows the young man opening the door. "AN INVITATION to enter provides the opportunity to witness" reads this caption. The final picture is of the same young man sitting on a stool, still wearing his coat, reading the Bible to an elderly woman. The caption reads: "THE SHARING of God's words and truth with others brings joy and thrill to one's heart."[1]

The "separated life" was an important part of the campus' early identity. Perhaps reacting to the fact that Ashland's President Anspach was perceived as soft on his stance against worldliness, McClain sought to codify a stricter principle of separatism.[2] Contributing to this, is the fact that after the Grace/Ashland divorce, both sides felt betrayed. For its part, Grace Seminary was founded with a defensive mindset, and as former President Homer Kent, Jr. has noted, it took time for the young institution to set down roots and to have a mature community outlook.[3] By the late 1960s, however, the institution began to foster a more robust notion of community service and involvement. Thus this is really a story of the growth of an expanding horizon, which has produced new opportunities for Grace to move forward as its regional influence continues.

The Winona Lake Connection

One of the most significant opportunities for community involvement for Grace College and Seminary was the Bible Conference grounds on the shores of Winona Lake. In 1968 Grace Schools acquired the Winona Christian Assembly and its twenty-five acres, worth in excess of one million dollars.[4] Herman Hoyt was soon elected president of the Winona Assembly as well as chairman of the board. Additionally, Grace began using the facilities in numerous capacities. Rodeheaver Auditorium and the Billy Sunday Tabernacle became the sites for combined seminary/college chapel services and campus concerts. (One of the first new uses of the Rodeheaver Auditorium was the memorial service of Alva J. McClain who died in November of 1968.) The Winona Hotel was transformed into housing for students, and the Eskimo Inn, renamed "The Lamp," became Grace's first (and thus far only) student center.[5]

Though Grace benefitted from the acquisition of the Assembly grounds, there were also liabilities. The Winona Christian Assembly had had several cycles of financial trouble and the Bible Conference fervor was waning, partly owing to the rise of better and faster transportation to more exciting tourist destinations. (During one such downturn the previous decade, the Assembly had nearly been purchased by the Billy Graham Association.) Some of the buildings were in disrepair, and Grace Schools assumed the Assembly's debt of nearly seven hundred thousand dollars. Over the next two decades, however, President Hoyt was able to increase revenue streams by continuing to rent out some of the facilities to evangelical organizations and conferences, and he made an aggressive attempt to raise funds toward the final years of solvency. Still, the summer Bible Conferences were soon reduced to four weeks and then, in 1970, to three. Lack of interest and deteriorating facilities could not be overcome.[6] In 1988, continued financial difficulties forced Grace to discontinue the Bible Conference venue altogether.[7]

An additional factor may have been the fundamentalist separatism that came to characterize the later years of the Winona Lake Christian Assembly. Under its founder, Solomon Dickey, as well as later leaders, the Winona programs attracted evangelicals from a broad range of backgrounds, and the culture clearly came from a broader degree of denominational cooperation. By the 1960s, however, including under Hoyt's administration, Grace and the Assembly were decidedly narrower.[8] Speakers, such as Bob Jones Jr., who was much more of a fundamentalist than his father, were frequently on the program, and even Ian Paisley of Northern Ireland spoke in the 1970s—a representative of the muscular far right of British Fundamentalism.[9] Thus, the base of support may have been limited accordingly. At any rate, in the early 1990s, amid disappointment for many in the community, the dilapidated, though by now iconic, Billy Sunday Tabernacle was torn down. To many in Kosciusko County and beyond, nothing more symbolized the end of an era.

A more positive outcome came in the form of the college's participation in Concerned Organizations for a Better Winona Lake (COBWL). Founded in 1971 by local resident Lester E. Pifer, who had served on the town board for eight years and as executive secretary for Brethren Home Missions, COBWL oversaw fundraising and other initiatives meant to address the needs of the town. Winona Lake's lack of revenue stemmed from a unique problem. Over half of its property was owned by not-for-profit, tax-exempt organizations—all within a small geographical area; and, as Pifer realized, funding problems in the township were insurmountable.[10] Grace was a significant part of the solution and a strong participant in COBWL, donating roughly $4,000 annually.[11] Herman Hoyt served as a trustee and later as president of COBWL. Homer Kent, Jr. would then serve in Hoyt's place and Wayne Snider, long-time professor of history, eventually served as vice-president.[12]

COBWL asked the Winona Lake not-for-profit companies to consider contributing 20 percent of what would be a normal tax bill. Its mailing list included Grace College and Seminary, the Brethren Home Missions Council, The Brethren Foreign Missionary Society, The First Presbyterian Church, the Winona School of Professional Photography, the Free Methodist Publishing House, the Brethren Investment Foundation, the Free Methodist Headquarters, the Winona Lake Christian Assembly, the Chapel Crusaders, the Chicago Boys Club, Winona Lake Grace Brethren Church, and the Winona Lake Free Methodist Church.[13] At times, the Town of Winona Lake submitted a project list and from it COBWL members chose those they could fund.[14] Indeed, in addition to raising money for the town—nearly 100,000 dollars by the 1980s—COBWL provided gifts, including a 1984 Plymouth Gran Fury police car.[15] These efforts benefitted the infrastructure of the town and its employees, "who often times," said John Trier, former Winona Lake town marshall, "would find it impossible to properly carry out their duties, without these items."[16]

Presidential Patterns: Hoyt, Kent, and Davis

Community involvement often depended on the vision and gifts of individual presidents. Hoyt travelled extensively as part of his fundraising efforts and was often gone three weeks out of the month. Therefore, he just was not in the Winona Lake/Warsaw communities much, which limited his effectiveness at community building. Still, Hoyt attempted to model community service. He was an active member of the Kiwanis club and attended the group when he was in town. As mentioned in a previous chapter, Hoyt also served for a time as president of the Winona Lake Christian Assembly and a member of the Winona Lake town board. He was also a respected preacher in the community and, as we have seen above, active in the leadership of COBWL. What is more, in June of 1974, Hoyt's advisory committee passed a motion for Grace to subsidize administrative and faculty dues at service clubs. The president and the public relations director were to have the entire cost of membership, and up to six other faculty members were to have half of their dues paid.

Hoyt also supported a new initiative for training Christian School administrators, which would foster future connections across the country. The effort was spearheaded by William Male, who served in various capacities at Grace, and Roy Lowrie, an influential leader in the growing Christian School Movement.[17] Male and Lowrie began a one-week summer institute for Christian school administrators on the Grace campus, which led to the founding of the Institute of Christian School Administration (ICSA) in 1971. Though Male had facilitated earlier efforts soon after he was hired, his efforts with Lowrie in the 1970s and 1980s were much more fruitful. This was not merely owing to the networking abilities of Lowrie, but also because of the growing culture wars that surrounded public education during those decades. Contentious concerns included the issue of organized prayer in schools, debates over teachings about human origins, and sex education. Some also reacted in fear against efforts to desegregate public schools. For all of these reasons, private education became, for some, a welcome refuge and helped to fuel the Christian School Movement. Attendance at the ICSA peaked in 1978 with an enrollment of 344 administrators.[18] That year a meeting was held in McClain Hall which led to the incorporation of the Association of

Christian Schools International (ACSI) after which it was decided
to locate the organization's headquarters in La Habra, California.
Soon, however, it relocated to Colorado Springs, a future hotbed of
American Evangelicalism. In addition to the ICSA, Grace Seminary
launched an MA program in Christian School Administration under
the direction of Lowrie. This lasted from 1986 to 1993, when Lowrie's health began to fail.[19]

Hoyt's successor, Homer Kent, Jr., brought a far different personality to the president's office in 1976. He was thoughtful, irenic,
and valued consensus. Kent also made specific attempts to improve
Grace's image in the community by introducing community leaders
to the institution. He invited civic and business leaders to periodic
lunches in the Dining Commons Alumni Room, informing them of
the events and programs of the school and encouraging their involvement.[20] In addition, under his administration, various disciplines in
the liberal arts continued to expand and, according to historian Ron
Clutter, one of Kent's goals was to develop "a climate where the pursuit of a spiritual life and biblical lifestyle" was a natural expression
of the campus culture and did not need to be "regimented." [21] Serving for many years as dean of the seminary under Hoyt, Kent chose
to move away from his predecessor's top-down leadership style. He
made immediate senior level changes, forming a multilateral "administrative council," which differed from Hoyt's council that was
merely advisory in nature. Kent's leadership style, which perhaps
represented the Pietist spirit of cooperation, served the institution
well and enrollment grew from 1168 to 1378 during his ten-year
presidency.

The Business Department, which has created some of the most
substantial avenues for participation in the community, was also established during Kent's tenure. Bill Gordon, the first chair of the
department has noted that when the department was created, there
was a concerted effort to reach out to local businesses and fine-tune
the department to meet the needs of the community. "We set up
an executive advisory board," Gordon recounted, "used local leaders
in our classes, presented student research findings about the local
economy." Some of the initial business classes were even offered on-
site at Zimmer, a local giant in the orthopaedic industry.[22] Because
of this industry, Warsaw was increasingly becoming an area to which

much money and talent flowed, and Grace's Business Department wanted to engage in this industry for the benefit of its students and for the institution as a whole. Beginning in 1980, these connections turned into opportunities for internships with various orthopaedic companies. Later initiatives, such as the Orthopaedic Scholar Institute and the Institute for Enterprise Development were direct results of these foundational efforts to engage local industry.[23] (Thirty years after Bill Gordon began the first Grace internships, these and other efforts culminated in the Ron and Barbara Manahan Orthopaedic Capital Center—something that provides an idea about the scale of time it can take to develop a climate of community involvement at an academic institution.) In spite of these advances, however, Kent was only partially successful in changing the campus culture.

Davis, as all presidents before him, was a reluctant president, preferring an archaeology dig and the classroom to presidential administration. He was the institution's "Indiana Jones" and has excavated an impressive 113 tombs dating back to ancient Israel and Jordan. Davis, who continued to teach for Grace Seminary full-time after he retired from the president's office, strove for a visible community presence. He wrote a regular column that appeared in the *Warsaw Times Union,* and members of the community would often find him socializing at the lunch counter at Breadings Cigar Store, a historic gathering place in Warsaw.[24] In a real sense, Davis helped define a cultural identity that would be present long after he retired—one that was less concerned with the outward markers of traditionalism yet retained a strong concern for "conservative" doctrine.[25]

Growth of Undergraduate Programs

In many ways, the desire for outreach and the expanding horizons of the Grace campus were enhanced by the growth of the institution's undergraduate programs. No doubt every department and/or program has made significant contributions to Grace College's legacy through the years. Highlights, however, would include the science program, which was one of the original programs of study. Established by Jesse Humberd, it was first housed within the college building (Philathea Hall) and then in 1978, owing to Humberd's leadership, a new Science Center was dedicated.[26] In 1984 and

Education for Society's Good and the Prisoner's Redemption: Reflections on Grace College's Prison Program

Frank Benyousky

Grace College's Prison Extension Program started simply enough. During the 1980s, Ken Taylor, professor of sociology at Grace College, had for some time been working among male prisoners at the Indiana State Prison (ISP), the maximum security facility at Michigan City, conducting seminars and occasional Bible studies under the auspices of Charles Colson's Prison Fellowship. As he taught and counseled the inmates, he learned of their desire for more extensive training in biblical studies and related areas. They even asked if he might arrange to have Grace College courses available to them inside the prison. While others might have found little potential in these future students, Taylor placed great value in them and refused to believe that people lost all worth to society the minute they walked through a prison gate.

Taylor began a feverish campaign to gain permission from prison officials and Grace administrators to launch a formal educational program in the prison. His plan was to begin small—holding classes in New Testament and Old Testament within the facility each semester. When approvals finally came through in 1986, Taylor and ten interested students at ISP were more than ready to get to work. Taylor was joined by Old Testament professor Ted Hildebrandt and New Testament professor Skip Forbes. They would usually drive in pairs to save on transportation costs, making the 90-minute drive from the campus to the prison one day each week. There, they took turns teaching a three-hour class period, each also waiting while the other conducted

1985 Deborah Cooley, who was instrumental in starting the nursing program in the 1970s, gifted funds to help pay off the building's mortgage. The building was then renamed, in 1985, in honor of her husband, Chester E. Cooley. With the new building, and the addition of mathematics to the curriculum, the program matured under the direction of long time professors Rich Jeffreys, Dick Dilling, and Marcia Lee, who also oversaw the growth of the medical pre-professional program. Jeffrey's pre-medical curriculum consistently placed graduates in medical schools across the country. Owing to the influence of John Whitcomb, flood geology and young earth creationism have been strong themes within the curriculum of the Science Department, especially through Don DeYoung, who carried the young earth mantel after John Whitcomb left the school. Like Whitcomb, DeYoung has become something of a celebrity within young earth circles, in part because of his prolific writing career. Yet DeYoung has cultivated connections in circles that would have been anathema to Whitcomb. He has consistently supported Au Sable, for example, a Reformed retreat and discovery center run by Christian environmentalists, many of whom hold to theistic evolution.[27] Thus this emphasis, and DeYoung's irenic personality, have yielded significant connections among evangelicals.

More recently, the sciences have seen a shift toward fresh avenues of community involvement through an emphasis on environmental stewardship. Beginning in 2009, new programs in environmental science were created, alongside the newly formed organization, Kosciusko Lakes and Streams (now Center for Lakes and Streams), which was supported directly by President Manahan. Spearheaded by Grace Professor Nathan Bosch, the Center for Lakes and Streams has organized community events that draw thousands from the surrounding regions and facilitate research that engages broader circles within the sciences than would have been possible in the past.[28]

One also thinks of the significant contributions of the Department of Music, which established a musical tradition through individuals such as nationally known trumpet player and department chair, Jerry Franks, and especially his successor, Tim Zimmerman, who also specialized in the trumpet. Frank's brass band, Dimension in Brass, as well as Zimmerman's The Kings Brass, became well known in the region and beyond.[29] The department was later reorga-

his class with a break for a meal in between. The tired drive back to campus was often made in the dark.

In 1989, under this writer, the program was expanded in order to transform the stand-alone courses into a formal associate degree program in biblical studies. In addition to adding courses and lining up more professors, enlarging the program also meant that courses would have to be offered throughout the week to accommodate prison schedules. The new format worked well, resulting in greater enrollment. Intent on proving the judgments of others wrong, many of these students were quite serious about their work and wanted to be assured that the courses taught at ISP were every bit as rigorous as courses taught on campus. Once the associate's degree had proven popular and sustainable, a full bachelor's degree program was established. Biblical Studies was kept as the minor, but organizational management became the degree major. With this degree the men completed a distinctly faith-oriented curriculum, but they also took courses that could help them find a career once they were released from prison.

From the beginning the Michigan City students found ways to put course experiences to work in their daily prison life. One man developed a tutorial program that helped others cope with deficiencies in English, math, and general study-skills. Another man pastored a prison-run church that promoted serious discipleship and positioned itself as a complement to the existing prison chapel. A number of the men used what they learned in biblical and counseling courses to encourage and challenge fellow inmates. Thus the prison extension at Michigan City grew and prospered over time.

It was so successful, in fact, that Grace began to seek permission to duplicate the program at another Indiana maximum security facility located in Wabash Valley, about thirty minutes from Terre Haute. Here Grace used a number of Indiana State University professors who were Christians to introduce the program, and then slowly built a cadre of professors in the area who could strengthen and enrich the course work.

nized as the School of Music under the direction of Patrick Kavana-ugh. Kavanaugh's vision for high caliber music performance and his connections in professional circles were also critical to establishing the summertime educational and performance venues of the Master-works Festival.[30] Although there was no formal connection with Wi-nona's Chautauqua heritage, Masterworks programs, which brought top-tier musicians to the Grace campus, harkened back to that edu-cational and musical heritage, as well as that of Homer Rodeheaver's summertime School of Sacred Music. Just as these earlier programs became part and parcel of community life in Winona Lake, Mas-terworks has become an integral part of the region's cultural events.

Just as important are contributions from other sectors of the campus. What is now the School of Behavioral Science has fostered community connections largely through its faculty members. Profes-sor of Sociology Ken Taylor established the educational programs in regional prisons that would become the prison extension program, for example. More recent faculty members, such as Kevin Roberts, have built bridges with local counseling facilities and fostered sig-nificant research initiatives on healthcare reform. Community en-gagement also grew in the area of teacher education. Shara Curry developed an increasingly professional program that moved the cam-pus beyond an emphasis on Christian school education. Embracing the local public school system, Curry's department not only fostered professional connections but placed hundreds of student teachers in regional schools. Continuing under Laurie Owen, teacher education continues to maintain strong networks throughout the Midwest. The earlier impulse to separate from area school systems, in other words, gave way to genuine and vibrant engagement. Many other depart-ments, including English, mathematics, and history, routinely take students to undergraduate discipline-specific conferences, which also enhance the horizons of Grace faculty and students.

The communication program has been one of the strongest av-enues of community involvement, particularly through the legacy of Steve Grill. Although Grill did not begin the Department of Com-munication, he was instrumental in building the theater program which has continued and flourished under Michael Yocum, who has continued to maintain an on-going relationship with Warsaw's nearby Wagon Wheel Theatre. Founded in 1956, the Wagon Wheel

At Wabash Valley, Grace had a wonderful supporter in the person of Karen Richards who worked in the prison's education unit and did all she could to provide support. Also, Grace was fortunate to have two of the men who served as superintendents (wardens) of the facility teach in the program and vigorously support it.

Wabash Valley offered opportunities to try two new approaches within the prison educational experience. Unlike Michigan City, Wabash Valley had multiple security levels (that is, the men were rated numerically according to the seriousness of their crimes), so the program began simultaneously to offer courses on parallel tracks to two separate sets of inmates. Second, the program installed new transmission equipment at the prison and on the Grace campus that allowed courses to be taught, with audio and visual connections, at one site and transmitted to another. Thus, new technology helped maximize resources while bringing diverse groups of students together.

In time, the program added another site at Miami Correctional Prison, a medium security facility in Miami County (Indiana). The prison was only one hour from the main campus at Winona Lake and situated next door to Grissom Air Base. Miami Correctional expanded its own facilities and the program expanded with it. Miami became an exciting place to teach because the men there, having committed lesser crimes, had a much shorter time to serve and therefore were much nearer their release dates. As a result, professors knew that material taught in the courses could soon help these men re-acclimate to the real world upon their release. Clearly, classroom work could have a serious impact on recidivism.

The final facility added to the Grace Prison Extension was the mixed security level facility in Pendleton, Indiana. At Pendleton, Grace was able to draw professors from the Indianapolis, Noblesville, and Anderson areas. Students at this facility tended to be older, more worldly-wise, and more serious about completing their work with the college. In 2006, John

is a professional and regionally recognized venue for major productions. Yocum's students have often performed at the local theatre, as does Yocum himself. Some have gone on to work with national tours and entertainment companies. Grill continues to serve as a respected civic leader and has mentored others, such as Allyn Decker, a communication alumnus, who followed Grill as chair of the department and now, in his role in the School of Adult and Community Education, builds bridges with local schools, the orthopaedic industry, and local organizations such as the Kosciusko Leadership Academy.

With his leadership and public relations skills, Grill was a logical choice to spearhead an on-campus museum dedicated to Winona Lake's heritage, particularly since he had always had a fascination with the region's local history and its religious background. In 2000, The Reneker Museum of Winona History (now the Winona History Center) opened in the west wing of the newly renovated Westminster Hall, and Grill was assisted by Carol Forbes, wife of Bible faculty member, Skip Forbes, as well as art faculty member, Tim Young.[31] The museum was directly related to Manahan's efforts to improve local community relations. In tandem with this, Grill was instrumental in establishing the Winona Lake Historical Society, the Lyceum Lecture Series, which brought popular speakers to Winona Lake, as well as other community initiatives.

Grace faculty, staff, and students would also find avenues of community involvement in various non-academic sectors of the campus as well. Prime examples are the youth athletic camps, which began with Lancer Basketball Camp in 1968 under the direction of Chet Kammerer. Kammerer, who would go on to a career as a vice president with the Miami Heat professional basketball team, was instrumental in bringing Grace athletics into larger networks of Christian colleges and universities and was himself involved in various organizations. He served as district chairman for the National Association of Intercollegiate Athletics district 21 (state of Indiana) as well as president of the National Christian College Athletic Association while athletic director and head basketball coach at Grace.[32] Kammerer's legacy has continued as thousands of young people have attended Lancer athletic camps, including the 24 camps Grace sponsored at the time of this writing.[33]

Teevan took over the management of the prison program and directed its course during its final several years. Enrollment grew to 356 during the last year of the program (2011). Over the years Grace prison graduates completed 640 A.S. degrees and 444 B.S. degrees. Time cuts earned by graduates of the prison program totaled 1,528 years. Nevertheless, the State of Indiana cut funding to all college prison programs in 2011, and Grace College was forced to discontinue its program. Teevan, who had been promoted as executive director of all of Grace extension efforts, continued to work with the state to find alternatives for prisoners, which they did.

In 2013, Grace re-established their educational efforts within the prison system with a new focus on GED and Career Tech programs. As of this writing, under the oversight of Denny Duncan, Grace College continues to offer classes to hundreds of students in the Miami, Westville, and CIF (Correctional Industrial Facility) prison.

The Manahan Era

President Manahan is a study in contrasts. As president, he was quiet and humble, yet he was able to effect great changes at Grace, raise more capital than any other president, and double the campus facilities. He came in as a president who vowed that there would be a more open spirit at Grace and at the same time did not hesitate to make top-down decisions. He was broad-minded and tolerant, but greatly concerned about orthodox belief and practice. Manahan believed in the simple truths of the Scripture, but is without a doubt the most philosophical senior administrator Grace has had. He is perhaps the president with the fewest personal connections with the Brethren tradition, but arguably the most successful of any president in bringing the spirit of practical Brethren piety to the campus. He has been one of the most influential people in Kosciusko County yet also extremely personable and humble.

This president with his unique blend of gifts was born in February of 1943 to parents who had lived through abject poverty and, like the four presidents before him, he was shaped by his many experiences. Manahan's academic background, for example, gave him an appreciation both for the value of seminary training as well as for a liberal arts environment. He attended Grand Rapids School of Bible and Music where he received a diploma in 1964. He received his BA at Shelton College in 1967, then an MDiv (1970), and a ThM (1977) from Grace Seminary.

As an undergraduate, Manahan grappled with the question of whether to pursue a PhD or seminary work. His undergraduate advisor, C. Thomas McIntire, suggested that he attend the University of Pennsylvania, but he chose instead to study and then teach full-time at Grace. At Grace, he chaired its undergraduate division of religion and philosophy until 1977, and worked on a ThD, which he completed at Grace in 1982. From 1985-87 he was assistant academic dean and coordinator of general education. He was vice president for academic affairs from 1987-1990 where he led the faculty to a revision of its education core. He also held faculty workshops and led the institution through a deeper understanding of its educational values and mission. From 1990 to 1993 he was provost of the college and seminary where he continued to help the institution focus on its mission. It is astonishing that he led the first full scale seminary curricular revision since its founding in 1937, updating what had been largely the work of McClain, frozen in time for nearly sixty years.

By this time, he was responsible for the day to day running of the institution, so it was probably no surprise that on Davis' retirement from the presidency in 1993, Manahan was appointed as acting president, a position that was made permanent in 1994. In 1993 the enrollment of the institution was 886. (Though it had earlier reached 1087 in 1987—the highest during the Davis administration). By spring 2013, after twenty years of Manahan at the helm, head count was over 1,900.[34] Like Davis, he was an Old Testament scholar and focused more on biblical theology rather than on systematic theology. He also came to his presidency with strong administrative credentials. In all, he was the type of administrator who led in a rethinking of the philosophy and curriculum of his department, of the seminary, of general education, and then of the mission of the institution itself. Under Manahan, the institution's mission statement became: "Grace College is an evangelical Christian community of higher education which applies biblical values in strengthening character, sharpening competence, and preparing for service."[35]

Like J. Allen Miller at Ashland many decades before, Manahan had a vision for the community. In many ways, in fact, it could be argued that under Manahan, Grace has reestablished these roots. Having benefited from the hard choices of Davis, Manahan was able to move Grace out of a separatist mindset and forge a new future for the college.[36] He laid out the core of this vision at his inauguration, at which Marilyn Quayle, wife of then Vice President Dan Quayle, spoke. In responding to Quayle, Manahan began with his typical self-deprecating wit: "These inaugural events are very humbling to me ... I am so glad that all of you could come to my public humbling." Manahan also quipped: "One of the saving graces of new presidents is that they can't possibly know ahead of time how well they will do in some cases ... and how magnificently they will bomb in others!"[37]

The substance of his address, however, included not just an emphasis on remaining faithful to the theological commitments of the school, but also included a strong admonition toward service, promoting wholeness, as well as social justice and increasing diversity within the Grace community.[38] In this regard, Manahan described the way he was influenced by the writings of Dutch Reformed philosopher, Herman Dooyeweerd, whose writings he had studied as an undergraduate student. Because of the fall, Dooyeweerd taught, people often lose site of the fact that, within God's sovereignty, there is an interconnected wholeness to the created order and human society.[39] People should remember that "there's a whole world to explore," Manahan said, "and it's interconnected and it's nuanced and layered together and we need to be aware of that."[40] That tied in directly with the final emphasis in his inaugural address—the quality of "largeness." According to Manahan, "Christian institutions ought to be characterized by nurturing consideration of big issues—matters that transport the student beyond campus perimeters to global issues."[41]

At the outset of the new administration, Manahan and the board of trustees sought the advice of the former president of Greenville College, Dr. Richard Stevens. Manahan recalls that Stevens advised him to focus on the broad mission of the institution and on being a leader who sets a vision for where the campus needs to go. This, Stevens encouraged, was the job of the president.[42] Stevens also recommended establishing a baseline evaluation for both Manahan as well as the board and took a broad survey of Grace constituents. When Stevens reported to the board in the fall of 1994, he said very bluntly that the reputation of Grace "stunk" in the community and that something needed to be done about it. Manahan took Steven's counsel to heart, including the task of improving relations with the surrounding community. He led the board in making deliberate efforts to reach out. The board itself met with faculty and students on campus and with area leaders, and Manahan began planning how to make the campus more outwardly focused.[43] He also worked to slowly adjust the way the board worked with the institution. Board minutes indicate that in the past, trustees tended to be involved in more day-to-day affairs of the seminary and college, and they were all Brethren. Manahan oversaw changes that focused on more macro-level goals and his broader vision for the institution. More work was given to subcommittees who helped encourage various aspects of the campus, for example. He also slowly and deliberately moved the membership of the board to reflect evangelicals in the community rather than a preponderance of FGBC pastors. By 2013, though all members still needed to be evangelical, now just over half had to be Grace Brethren.

Manahan's first major interaction with the community developed during one of Professor Bill Gordon's community and business functions. Soon after coming to Grace as a faculty member, Manahan met Dane Miller, founder of Biomet, one of the three international orthopaedic corporations located in Warsaw. Miller had always had an interest in the community. Very early in the 1990s, Grace hosted a panel discussion that consisted of business students and several business leaders, including Miller. This was Manahan's first interaction with Miller as it related to the campus. Soon thereafter, Jean Northenor, a mutual friend of Miller and Manahan, arranged for a meeting between them and another community leader. From that time on, Manahan remained in contact with Miller.[44]

Much of the collaboration with him and other community leaders was in relation to campus facilities, such as what is now Westminster Hall, then called The International Friendship House. Owned by the Free Methodist Foundation, it had become available for purchase in 1993, but the owners could not find a buyer. A newly formed Westminster Steering Committee, which included Miller, was formed to seek funds for the purchase of the building. Half of the funds raised by the committee were from the community, which was important for strengthening the relationship between Grace and the local community. Grace purchased Westminster outright in 1994, and Miller agreed to help with the cost of restoring the historic Chautauqua-era building.

The following year, 1995, Grace sold the lake front property that it had acquired decades earlier from the Winona Lake Christian Assembly. Then, in 1998 the Free Methodist Headquarters building (Mount Memorial) was also added to the campus after an extensive renovation, and Dane and Mary Louise Miller gave funding for the project.[45]

The next key phase of the Manahan/Miller relationship resulted in a closer link both between Grace and the orthopaedic industry as well as among the various companies within the industry itself. At a professional gathering in downtown Warsaw, the hypothetical question was raised as to what would happen if the orthopaedic firms were not given sufficient incentive to remain in Warsaw. Manahan recognized the importance of the industry for the ongoing economic success of Northeast Indiana. "I started thinking, 'what if the orthopaedics industry left Warsaw? What would happen to our community?' It would be a real loss."[46] Then, while attending a conference in Indianapolis, Manahan talked with one of the presenters about his concerns. "Well, what are you going to do about it?" the presenter asked, sparking an "ah-hah moment" that challenged Manahan.[47] What ensued was a complex process of relationship-building and meetings, the result of which was a seven million dollar grant from the Lilly Foundation that established OrthoWorx—a new initiative designed specifically to help keep the orthopaedic industry in Warsaw. OrthoWorx has helped fund organizations in the community as well as research initiatives such as a Cambridge study of the Warsaw schools, which implemented progressive reform in the school district.[48]

Manahan also learned that the orthopaedic companies were faced with increasing local, state, and national regulations and that there was a great lack of understanding in that area. That led to the founding at Grace of the graduate certificate program in Orthopaedic Regulatory and Clinical Affairs (ORCA), which was also funded through OrthoWorx. These efforts were largely the reason Manahan received the Warsaw/Kosciusko County Chamber of Commerce Man of the Year award for 2010.[49] David Johnson of Bio Crossroads noted to Manahan of his involvement: "Without you as strategist, visionary, and peacemaker in the Warsaw community, our orthopaedic companies would never have been prepared to come together as OrthoWorx."[50]

One of the final challenges of Manahan's presidency was leading the institution as it navigated the rough waters of the Great Recession, which began near the end of 2007. Seeing the recession as an opportunity to cast new vision for the institution, Manahan, along with Bill Katip, then provost, orchestrated some significant changes. Katip had a long history with Grace College, coming to Winona Lake first as a student and then later working at Grace in 1974. After rising to administrative positions at several other Christian colleges, Katip was elected to the Grace Board of Trustees in 2005 and then appointed as provost in 2007. He then succeeded Manahan as president in the spring of 2013.

Though a leader of conviction, Katip is also a pragmatist who complemented the vision of Manahan, and they worked together to respond to the recession. Immediately when he arrived, Katip convened an *ad hoc* faculty committee, which examined all academic programs and looked at their financial vitality. The greatest fallout from the results of this committee was the controversial decision to close the School of Music. The social work program was also a casualty of the downturn, and a few individual majors were cut as well, including physical education and German language. As mentioned in a previous chapter, the undergraduate religious studies program was also cut and biblical studies classes were taken on by the seminary faculty. The loss of faculty members within these programs was particularly painful, of course.

The Manahan/Katip vision went beyond these cuts, however, and included aggressive and innovative efforts to refine and grow the institution. Another of Katip's earliest moves as provost was to facilitate review of the general education curriculum for the institution. Through faculty committee work, the result was a leaner "Grace Core" built around four key student relationships: with God, self, others, and finally, the world and the environment. Katip also sought to promote learning communities as well as collaboration between faculty and student affairs—a relationship that can often prove challenging. Katip has endorsed faculty-led efforts to build a stronger sense of community within the on-campus academic sector as well. This has included support for the development of the Office of Faith, Learning, and Scholarship, which has welcomed involvement from a number of faculty members and has sponsored, among other initiatives, forums on faculty scholarship.

Perhaps the most significant effort has been the "reimagine" campaign. Manahan had come to believe that the traditional model of financing higher education was, in effect, broken, and small colleges and universities needed to adjust if they were going to survive. In response, Katip gathered campus leaders for a brainstorming session that produced what was later called the "reimagine campaign." Here was a bold new initiative to implement an applied-learning requirement of twelve credits for all Grace undergraduate students. Free online courses were to be offered during the summer, as well as a three-year option for all majors. It included an aggressive advertising campaign carried out by Brandpoet, the firm that had recently been hired to improve marketing. The result was a surge in applications.[51] A new dorm was soon built and opened in time for fall 2013 and another new dorm opened the following year. These initiatives have also been augmented by increased online course offerings. (Manahan regretted that Grace did not embrace online education when it first emerged.) Other initiatives included the Henry and Francis Weber School, a multi-campus venture funded by Weber, as well as the very successful GOAL (degree completion) program established by Steve Grill. The Grace community has finally released itself from its geographical boundaries. Since the hard decisions of 2007, full time enrollment has increased significantly.

It is ironic that the kind of robust community engagement that matured under Manahan's administration was not unlike what existed at

Ashland College and Seminary in the 1930s, before the schism. For example, John Allen Miller, dean of the seminary and president, modeled community involvement and urged all faculty members to be active in serving the community.[52] Martin Shively, bursar of Ashland College, noted of Miller, "The entire city of Ashland was his neighborhood, and all its citizens were his neighbors."[53] Admittedly, accounts of Miller were often flattering, but there is historic basis to this mythology.[54] An emphasis on the broader community was not limited to Miller. President Anspach also fostered community involvement through internships and other forms of service. We could also point to L. S. Bauman, whose service to the Ashland College and Seminary Board of Trustees was that of fundraiser and unofficial public relations officer to members of Brethren Churches and to larger evangelical networks.[55] It would seem that the upheaval of the split, the efforts to begin a new institution, and the separatist tendencies of some were all factors that amounted to lost momentum in regard to community interaction. The efforts that began at Ashland in this area were not sustained at Grace, at least at first. As we have seen above, the community around Grace was, early on, viewed simply as something to be converted.

But with time, efforts to build deep connections with the local community became more tangible. The transplanted Ohio seminary did, eventually, extend its influence and service in Winona Lake as it took over the Assembly and as it became involved with Concerned Organizations for a Better Winona Lake. Attempts were made to bridge into the greater Warsaw area by earlier presidents but with mixed results. President Kent tried with some success to change the tenor of the campus community, and his laid-back and collaborative style allowed for innovation. While Davis was faced with making hard decisions during a time of fractured community, Manahan strengthened community both internally and externally. He successfully achieved the more inviting, nonthreatening, and gracious campus spirit that Kent had aspired to. In addition, Manahan transformed Grace into an institution that saw itself as one that was to be a channel for God's grace to the community. Benefiting from earlier work established by Kent and the Business Department, he was able to bring the giant orthopaedic companies together for the good of the community. More recently, Bill Katip reorganized Grace during the recession to become an institutional leader with its applied-learning emphasis, its new communal and collaborative liberal arts identity, its innovative across the board three-year degrees, and its aggressive online and non-traditional education. Katip entered his presidency with hope of tapping new academic opportunities now from a much more confident, nurturing, and mature Grace College and Theological Seminary.

Notes

1. *Grace Yearbook*, 1962, 20, 21.

2. Culver noted in June 2013 at the Winona Lake Grace Brethren Church that one of the more prominent characteristics of the future Grace Group was an emphasis on the "separated life." A variety of sources and letters indicate that this included a distain of bobbed hair for women, dancing in any form, an eventual dislike of the "moving pictures," and a total ban on smoking and playing cards. Membership in Masonic lodges was considered cultic, especially given the traditional Brethren proscription of the swearing of oaths. Since the Masons gave secret oaths, this became especially egregious for traditional and evangelical brethren. Oddly enough, alcohol does not surface much in the sources, but the progressive Brethren were strong proponents of the temperance movement.

3. Homer Kent, Jr. Interview by author and Scott Moore, October 22, 2007. Transcription by Hillary Burgardt.

4. Terry White, *Winona at 100*.

5. Ibid., 204.

6. Ibid., 3, 76, 152.

7. Ibid., 152.

8. See Mark Sidwell, "The History of Winona Lake Bible Conference," Ph.D. dissertation, Bob Jones University, 1988. It contains a wealth of important and insightful information on the Winona Lake Bible Conference. He notes in some detail the shift from a more orthodox evangelicalism to a militant fundamentalism.

9. Concerned Organizations for a Better Winona Lake (COBWL) Collection, Grace College and Theological Seminary Archives and Special Collections (Hereafter Grace Archives). Paisley was a strident fundamentalist who practiced strict separation and was known for his strong anti-Catholic and anti-homosexual sentiments. He was also heavily involved in politics in Northern Ireland. Historian John Mitzko, chairperson of the Division of Social Sciences at Bob Jones University, and who is currently writing a biography of Bob Jones Sr., has speculated that had Winona Lake taken The Billy Graham Association's 1959 offer, the Winona Christian Assembly may not have taken this strongly fundamentalist turn.

10. Grace Brethren Annual, 1978, 92; Lester E. Pifer to W. Clement Stone, July 26, 1977; Lester E. Pifer to Donna S. Bradshow, president, W. Clement & Jessie V. Stone Foundation, September 9, 1974. COBWL Collection, Grace Archives.

11. Receipts 1971-1975. Also, Lester Pifer to Homer A. Kent Jr., September 22, 197,7 COBWL Collection, Grace Archives.

12. COBWL Minutes, August 24, 1976. "A motion was presented that Dr. Kent succeed Dr. Hoyt as a director. The motion carried." COBWL Collection, Grace Archives.

13. COBWL mailing list, November 5, 1979. COBWL Collection, Grace Archives.

14. COBWL Project List for 1983. COBWL Collection, Grace Archives.

15. State of Indiana Office of the Secretary of State, Certificate of Incorporation, no. 364, January 12, 1972; See the minutes of Tax Exempt Organizations in the Town of Winona Lake, Rev. Lester Pifer, 7 Sept. 1971 and application for Recognition of Exemption Under Section 501(c)(3) of the Internal Revenue Code, February 4, 1976 and stamped March 3, 1976. However, this was not formally approved until later – see Herman Hoyt to Leister Pifer, November 24, 1971. A picture was taken of the presentation of the keys of the car by town board president Dave Wolkins to town Marshall John Trier with representatives of the board looking on. This is in front of the Billy Sunday Tabernacle. COBWL Collection, Grace Archives.

16. John T. Trier to COBWL, April 23, 1984. COBWL Collection, Grace Archives.

17. William Male, interview by author and Hillary Burgardt, July 18, 2012. Transcription by Hillary Burgardt.

18. White, 180; Male, interview.

19. White, 180-182. After Lowrie's death these degrees were then moved to Columbia International University in Columbia, South Carolina.

20. Thanks to Jesse Deloe, who attended many of these meetings, for providing insights on Kent's efforts in the community.

21. Ron Clutter, "History of Grace Theological Seminary," unpublished manuscript (Winona Lake: Grace College and Theological Seminary, 1987), 38.

22. An orthopaedic presence in Northeast Indiana emerged with Revra DePuy who began his company in Warsaw in 1895. In 1927 DePuy employee J.O. Zimmer started a rival company, which was followed by Biomet, founded by Dane Miller in 1977. At the time of this writing, Warsaw's orthopedic companies account for almost one third of the thirty-eight billion dollars generated by all orthopedic companies worldwide. The industry generates about forty-five percent of employment in Kosciusko County. For more on this subject, see http://orthoworxindiana.com/about-us/the-orthopaedic-capital-of-the-world/.

23. Bill Gordon, interview by author, June 15, 2013.

24. John Davis, interview by M. M Norris and Jared S. Burkholder, June 11, 2012. Transcription by Hillary Burgardt.

25. Ibid. Davis also hired the Grace Brethren pastor and well known leader David Plaster who was moderator of the FGBC when it went through the turmoil of the Whitcomb controversy and ensuing fights over baptismal membership that led to the Conservative Grace Brethren/Grace Brethren split. Plaster was best known for the students he mentored. He served as a tireless professor and academic dean though his love was in the classroom. He also served as a shepherd of the college and Fellowship as relationships, families, and churches were ruptured. Plaster continued to serve under President Ronald Manahan, and they and other leaders worked to heal wounds and bring the school's mission into the 21st century.

26. Jesse Humberd, interview by author, Scott Moore, and Andy Clark. August 8, 2009. Transciption by Hillary Burgardt.

27. http://ausable.org/

28. http://lakes.grace.edu/

29. http://trumpetherald.com/forum/viewtopic.php?t=39903&sid=5a98d8fb3 7ebffca77edd26402cf651b; Zimmerman, who now resides in Pennsylvania, continues to lead The King's Brass. See http://www.kingsbrass.org/.

30. http://www.masterworksfestival.org/index.php.

31. http://www.winonahistorycenter.com.

32. Jim Kessler, interview with Jared Burkholder, June 30, 2014.

33. http://www.grace.edu/athletics/sports-camps

34. Enrollment figures obtained from Carrie Yocum in the Office of Academic Affairs.

35. Ron Manahan, interview by author and Hillary Burgardt, January 18, 2013. Transcription by Hillary Burgardt.

36. See chapter 3 in the present volume.

37. Ronald E. Manahan, Presidential Inauguration Response, October 6, 1994.

38. Ibid.

39. On Dooyeweerd, see James Skillen, "Herman Dooyeweerd's Contribution to the Philosophy of the Social Sciences," *Journal of the American Scientific Affiliation* (March 1979), 20-24. An English translation of portions of Dooyeweerd's, *De Wijsbegeerte der Wetsidee* (*The Philosophy of the Law Idea*) by J. Glenn Friesen can be found at: http://www.members.shaw.ca/jgfriesen/Mainheadings/Prolegomena1.html.

40. Manahan, interview.

41. Manahan, Presidential Inauguration Response.

42. Manahan, interview.

43. Ibid.

44. Ibid.

45. Manahan, interview.

46. Lilly Endowment Annual Report, 2010, 18. David Johnson, Bio Crossroads to Ron Manahan April 12, 2013, in author's possession. The emphasis is Johnson's.

47. Manahan, interview.

48. Ibid.

49. He had received the Winona Lake Bill Reneker Memorial Community Service Award in 2000.

50. David Johnson to Ron Manahan.

51. William Katip, interview by author and Hillary Burgardt, spring 2013. Transcription by Hillary Burgardt.

52. Martin Shively, *The Brethren Evangelist,* Number XXXVIII "Some Brethren Church Leaders of Yesterday as I Know Them, J. Allen Miler," 5, 6; *the Brethren Encyclopedia*, Vol. 2, 839.

53. Ibid.

54. Miller sat on committees for the town of Ashland, including one that created the town's form of government. He served on a civil-service commission, was

active in and eventually president of Ashland's Rotary Club, and a member of the Ohio Philosophical Association. He also served on many important boards of the Brethren denomination including the foreign mission board. See "A Faithful Christian's Journey: To the Memory of Dr. J. Allen Miller by The Students and Faculty who loved him As a Teacher and as a Christian Gentleman," *Ashland College Bulletin* VIII (May 7, 1935).

55. L. S. Bauman's son Paul would later be appointed public relations officer at the new Grace seminary.

Part II
Contexts

Chapter 8

The Winona Lake Context
Finding a Home in the Center of the Bible Conference Movement

Terry White

SEVENTY-FIVE YEARS AGO, AS GRACE THEOLOGICAL SEMINARY WAS starting classes in the Ellet neighborhood of Akron, Ohio, the town of Winona Lake was already a well-known community in Northeast Indiana, and to a lesser extent, across the country. Given the fame of the quaint but bustling Chautauqua village, it seems likely, from the vantage point of the 21st century, that the new location of the seminary may have been a key to its success. Though Grace College and Seminary was not founded with a formal connection to the Bible conference grounds, Winona Lake's Chautauqua and Bible conference heritage served as a functional, if unofficial, ally and offered a geographical setting that was already saturated with religious culture. What is more, both the town and the campus became instrumental within the growing fundamentalist subculture in America, and Winona Lake would come to play a leading role at the center of the Bible Conference Movement.

Origins of Winona's Religious Culture

Founded by John Heyl Vincent and Lewis Miller in 1874, the original Chautauqua site in western New York (named for Chautauqua Lake) offered summertime venues of cultured entertainment, education, and leisure that reflected the reforming impulses of Progressive Era America. Other programs, which followed Vincent and Miller's model, sprang up all over the Midwest and so, like other Chautau-

177

qua sites, Winona Lake's history began in the final decades of the 19th century. The town's founding fathers were the Beyer brothers.[1] J. F. Beyer came to neighboring Warsaw, Indiana, in February of 1877, where he conceived the idea of establishing "an educational and pleasure park" on the shores of Eagle Lake (later Winona Lake).[2] To this end he purchased extensive tracts of land along the eastern shore of the lake, and in 1888, with his brothers, founded Spring Fountain Park as a summer resort. Soon they began to clear out the underbrush, prepare fish ponds, build fountains, and make numerous other improvements. Construction projects included an early roller coaster, military parade grounds, a race track, as well as hotels and even a Cyclorama with a 15,000 square foot canvas.[3]

Although the Beyer Brothers gave their resort grounds a religious flavor through a Sunday school operated by the church of which the Beyer family were members, its reputation as a Christian resort town came from Solomon (Sol) Dickey. Dickey, a Presbyterian minister as well as the superintendent of home missions for the Presbyterian Church of Indiana, had earlier proposed that the Presbyterian synod establish a "religious Chautauqua" at some location "where ministers and church workers would assemble for Bible study and the discussion of church problems."[4] Dickey's desire for a Chautauqua site was not unique. Indeed, according to historian Michael Kazin, "By 1900, over a hundred independent Chautauqua assemblies had sprung up in localities from southern California to New Hampshire. Most were scattered in such midsized, Midwestern communities as Marinette, Wisconsin, and Crete, Nebraska."[5] Getting approval for the idea, Dickey initially looked at a location on Bass Lake in Starke County, Indiana. This location fell through, so Dickey negotiated the purchase of Spring Fountain Park after meeting one of the Beyer brothers on a train in 1894.

With the Presbyterian synod providing the capital for the purchase, Dickey renamed the lake "Winona Lake," and the Winona Assembly and Summer School was incorporated the following year. The printed program for the 1896 edition of the Winona Assembly and Summer School describes the facilities in this way:

> The Association has purchased 160 acres of land that stretches for a mile and a half along the eastern shore of the lake.

The grounds include what has heretofore been known as Spring Fountain Park. They have been beautified with small lakelets, arbors, flower-plots and winding walks, making it very attractive . . . Some fifteen acres, on a point extending out into the lake, have been prepared for athletic grounds. No better field for bicycling, running matches, base-ball, and other outdoor sports can be found. It is overlooked by an amphitheater capable of seating 2,500 people. Athletics will be a prominent feature of the Assembly this year.[6]

Dickey was intent on imbuing his new Chautauqua programs with a distinctly Christian flavor. Sundays were strictly observed, for example, and the 1897 program declared,

In keeping with the rules which obtain at all well-regulated Chautauquas, Sunday is strictly observed at Winona as a day set apart for worship and rest. Only those holding season tickets are admitted to the grounds [on Sundays]. A fully organized Sunday school meets at 9:30 a.m., followed by church services at which some prominent minister will preach each Sunday. The crowning event of the Sabbath is the hillside service when, as twilight approaches, all gather in the open air for a service of song and prayer. In these informal meetings led by experienced workers, an opportunity for participation by all is given.[7]

The town's Bible conferences added to the distinctly Christian feel. The Bible Conference Movement in America was comprised of a number of large nondenominational conferences that were begun in the latter part of the nineteenth century. With the goal of combining relaxing vacations for families along with inspiring Bible teaching and music, a number of such conferences were founded in the late 1800s and early 1900s. The two conferences, which historians generally agree started the movement, were D. L. Moody's Northfield Conference, founded in 1893 in Moody's hometown in Massachusetts, and the Niagara Bible Conference. The Niagara Conference began as the "Believers' Meeting for Bible Study" in 1876 in Massachusetts, but eventually settled on annual meetings located at Niagara-on-the-Lake, Ontario, Canada.[8] Conferences at Winona began in August, 1896—the first summer after the Winona Assembly was created.[9]

In Winona, Dickey secured J. Wilbur Chapman to lead the Bible conferences, which he did until 1908. Dickey had met Chapman, a Presbyterian pastor who would soon become known worldwide as an evangelist, in 1894 at the Denison Hotel in Indianapolis. Dickey later recalled, "I told him of my hope and plan to start Winona. Dr. Chapman evinced real interest and asked me to keep him posted in the development of the plan." Through the urging of Moody, Dickey re-connected with Chapman later and convinced him to accept the leadership of the Winona Bible Conference.[10]

Dickey's programming included a diverse range of luminaries and world-class performers. William Jennings Bryan, for example, regularly gave speeches at Winona, and later served a term as president of the assembly. Other lectures and performances were given by the New York Symphony Orchestra, former president Benjamin Harrison, polar explorer Admiral Richard E. Byrd, Jr., aviator Glenn H. Curtiss, author Helen Keller, humorist Will Rogers, bandleader John Philip Sousa, writer and poet James Whitcomb Riley, violinist Efrem Zimbalist, Sr., and Metropolitan Opera contralto Ernestine Schumann-Heink, to name a few.[11]

The Winona Assembly boasted a large auditorium, "where the lectures and entertainments are given with its opera chairs, its pipe organ and its perfect acoustic properties, often declared to be one of the best summer auditoriums in the United States."[12] Although various amusements such as boating and cruising on the lake continued, attention was also given to education and culture. Wealthy businessmen, including Thomas Kane, John Studebaker, John Wanamaker, H. J. Heinz, and John D. Rockefeller, invested their wealth in developing the town and at times lent their administrative skills to its leadership. Kane, Studebaker, and Heinz, for example, served terms as presidents of the Assembly.[13]

The many cultural, spiritual, and natural attractions at Winona eventually drew an average of 250,000 visitors each summer during the "golden years."[14] By 1915, however, the association was experiencing financial problems and the rising popularity of radios and automobiles eventually contributed to the Chautauqua's decline. The Winona Lake gates were dismantled in 1930. But by this time, the Bible conferences and evangelical revival services had begun to eclipse the Chautauqua attractions thanks in part to famed evangelist

Billy Sunday, who had made Winona Lake his home and headquarters since 1911.[15]

With the presence of this evangelical superstar, Winona become a major center for conservative American Protestantism and thus continued to draw massive crowds of evangelical vacationers. Reporting on events in August, 1915, for example, the *Indianapolis Star* led with the headline, "Sunday Record Day at Winona." Second and third-deck headlines screamed "Billy Sunday, Bryan, and Schumann-Heink Main Attractions at Exercises Attended by Crowd of 20,000 Persons," "1,500 Autos Bring Visitors," and "Huge Overflow Meetings Held in Morning and Afternoon—Prof. E. O. Excell Leads Chorus of 600 Voices."[16] The article reported that with Sunday, Bryan, and Schumann-Heink as the main attractions, the Winona Bible Conference experienced the greatest day in its twenty years of existence. At least 7,500 of the 20,000 attendees came in automobiles from cities and towns within a radius of 100 miles. Actual counting showed more than 1,500 automobiles parked along the driveways.[17] Bryan was the morning speaker in the auditorium, speaking to an audience of 6,000. Sunday addressed the overflow in one of the greatest outdoor meetings ever held at Winona. In the afternoon, Bryan introduced Sunday in the auditorium, then went to the hillside to assist evangelist Robert "Bob" Jones and other speakers in addressing the crowd that could not be accommodated inside. Meetings also were conducted at Indian Mound by the Rev. W. E. Biederwolf and at another point by Sunday's wife, Helen (Nell), and noted vocalist, Virginia Asher.[18]

In 1920, construction began on a new 7,500 seat tabernacle, which was at the time the largest auditorium of its kind in Northeast Indiana and would become the central venue for the Bible conferences and Billy Sunday revivals.[19] Two years later, in 1922, William E. Biederwolf became the director of the Bible conferences, overseeing some of the greatest conferences before his death in 1939. As a teenager, Biederwolf had been converted under Solomon Dickey's preaching and eventually became an evangelist in his own right, first appearing on the Winona platform in 1902. Biederwolf had a strong fundamentalist orientation and guided Winona Lake in this direction, cementing ties with well-known fundamentalists such as Bob Jones and his son, Bob, Jr. who were regular speakers at Winona for many years.[20]

Homer Rodeheaver, the campaign song leader for Biederwolf and then Billy Sunday, also moved to Winona and directed his annual Sacred Music Conference which always climaxed in the huge Billy Sunday Tabernacle with his famous Sacred Music Festival. Hundreds of choir directors, evangelistic song leaders, soloists and others in the religious music field came for training each summer.[21] Living at Winona, in a home he called "Rainbow Point," Rodeheaver's charismatic but down-home presence only added to the religious mystique of Winona.[22]

Grace College and Seminary's place in Winona's Religious History

Brethren groups used the Winona grounds for their annual conferences beginning in 1890. In 1900, the first Brethren foreign missionary society was founded during one of these meetings. Jacob C. Cassel, a prominent elder in the church, presented a controversial paper at the 1900 conference on the subject, "Are We Ready to Enter the Foreign Missionary Field?" When the issue of organizing a foreign mission society was brought to the conference, it met with no enthusiasm. The missionary enthusiasts were informed that there was plenty of room "out under the trees" where they could go to begin their organization, and that is exactly what they did, retiring to a small knoll nearby.[23] The Brethren Church continued to meet in Winona and in 1921-1922 donated $10,000 for the construction of the Billy Sunday Tabernacle.[24]

In 1937, the same year of the schism at Ashland College and Seminary (see chapter 2), the national conference for the Brethren Church was held at Winona Lake. McClain's group found a supportive base. An unofficial rally was held in the Winona Lake Presbyterian Church with a crowd of more than 500 present. There was singing, testimony, prayer, and an announcement concerning the plans for the opening of Grace Theological Seminary. Several financial gifts were given, including $1,000 from Estella Myers, pioneer missionary to Africa. Biederwolf was impressed with the proceedings and the spirit of the gathering and, seeing an opportunity, Biederwolf invited McClain to locate the seminary in Winona Lake.[25]

Winona, in fact, had a long history as something of an educational center in Northeast Indiana that extended back to its Chautauqua days. Between 1901 and 1908, nearly one new educational enterprise was begun each year, including a normal school for women, a technical institute, an agricultural institute, and a school for underprivileged boys.[26] The Winona Lake School of Theology, one of the most prominent Winona schools, was established in 1920 amid the Bible conference frenzy. It was created by G. Campbell Morgan, a well-known English pastor, whose courses were so popular they were held twice daily and could attract as many as 600 ministers. Morgan led the school in 1920 and 1921, and he was succeeded in 1922 by George W. Taft, president of Northern Baptist Seminary in Illinois. In 1923, Biederwolf became head of the school.[27] Although Biederwolf held the title of president of the school until his death in 1939, in reality the school was shaped and organized by Jasper Huffman, who would later become one of the founding members of the National Association of Evangelicals and founding editor of the organization's publication, the *United Evangelical Action Magazine*.[28]

This presence of the School of Theology offered perhaps the biggest draw for the new seminary since Biederwolf made the school's library available for use by the early students of Grace Seminary. After McClain agreed to move the seminary to Winona Lake, early classes were held on the top floor of the Free Methodist Publishing Company headquarters, (now the Mount Memorial building). The central rooms were used as classrooms, the south wing was used as the library, and the north wing was used for chapel services. Later, the design of the McClain Hall seminary building, completed in 1951, reflected this same layout with the library at one end and a chapel (later named Ashman Chapel) at the other.[29]

Grace Seminary continued to grow and expand with the acquisition of acreage east of Kings Highway and south of Wooster Road. The school first acquired "a beautiful tract of land comprising about three and one-half acres within the precincts of Winona Lake and adjacent to the Free Methodist building on the south."[30] Leadership soon realized the site would not be large enough for full-scale development of a school, so the seminary board purchased from Leo Polman more than 30 acres east of Kings Highway, just outside the town limits.[31]

The new campus had other close connections with the Winona Lake grounds. By the time Grace moved to Winona Lake, Billy Sunday had died, but Homer Rodeheaver's fame continued to spread.

By 1941, Rodeheaver's publishing company and recording label had relocated to the Westminster Hotel, and it became one of the leading producers of gospel music literature and recordings in America during the period.[32] N. Bruce Howe, Jr., the Rodeheaver Music Company's CEO, lived upstairs in the hotel as did Grace students who used the hotel as a dormitory. According to one of these students, in quiet moments, students might hear the strains of B. D. Ackley arranging music. On other occasions, Jim and Ruth Rodeheaver Thomas would leave their Rainbow Point home and join the students for Sunday dinner, with Ruth sometimes singing. It was not uncommon for visiting Christian recording artists—affiliated with the Rodeheaver Company—to give short after-dinner concerts for Grace students in the Westminster dining room.[33]

After assuming control of the assets and liabilities of the Winona Christian Assembly in 1968, Grace utilized more Assembly properties. The Westminster, McKee Courts, the Winona Hotel, and many smaller buildings became housing for Grace's growing student body. The Eskimo Inn became a student union. Existing dwellings were converted for use by the Art and Music Departments. Many of the facilities offered student employment opportunities, as well. Other former Winona Lake Christian Assembly facilities used at one time by the college included Delta (Park Ave. and Administration Blvd.) Grace Courts, Lakeside (both on Park Ave. on opposite sides of the post office) and the Winona Hotel. Epsilon (Wooster Road) and Kappa (Kings Highway) were purchased and converted from private residences to dormitories.[34]

Locating the seminary in Winona Lake held denominational significance as well. For the Brethren churches that aligned with the "Grace group," Winona Lake became the de facto headquarters for the new "fellowship," and until 1973 nearly all Grace Brethren national conferences were held there with five exceptions.[35] Additionally, after its start on the small knoll near the swan pond in Winona Lake, the (Grace) Brethren missionary society, now named Encompass World Partners, has come to have a presence in more than 35 nations of the world. Approximately 90 percent of all Grace Brethren worshipers worldwide, in fact, meet in churches that were begun or planted by Brethren missionaries. Grace Brethren churches abroad are especially strong in Argentina, Brazil, Central African Republic, and a number of countries throughout Asia and Europe.[36]

In addition, the Brethren Missionary Herald Company (BMH) was formed in 1940 as the communications unit for Grace Brethren churches. BMH published a magazine and assisted the growing group of churches with communication functions and became the unofficial publisher for Grace Seminary professors. BMH also published *The Brethren Missionary Herald*, which was founded by Leo Polman (1901-1979), a traveling evangelist and pastor who had been converted under the ministry of Billy Sunday. The magazine often included articles by Grace Seminary professors. Since then a cluster of Grace Brethren-related organizations have headquartered in Winona Lake, performing functions for Grace Brethren churches in the areas of church planting, architectural design and building construction, facility financing, youth and Sunday School programming and curriculum, retirement facilities, and more.

The narrowing fundamentalist direction established by Biederwolf served to flavor the Bible conferences in the decades after the Grace campus was established in Winona. Bob Jones, Jr. served as a member of the board of directors between 1940 and 1960. Other prominent preachers of the period included Charles Feinberg, longtime dean of Talbot Seminary; Will Houghton, president of Moody Bible Institute; and Harry A. Ironsides, pastor at the Moody Memorial Church.[37] Helen Sunday, who lived at Winona until her death in 1957, maintained connections with Bob Jones University, Youth for Christ, HCJB, and other persons and institutions in the growing fundamentalist networks.[38]

The Youth for Christ organization was founded at Winona Lake in 1944 by Dr. Torrey Johnson, and for many decades thousands of teens and their leaders convened at Winona every summer for YFC national and international conventions.[39] One could argue that the career of evangelist Billy Graham was launched from an all-night prayer meeting conducted by Armin Gesswein in the Rainbow Room (named for Rodeheaver's recording label, Rainbow Records) of the Westminster Hotel just prior to Graham's leaving for California to preach his great 1949 Los Angeles crusade. It was during that crusade that publisher William Randolph Hearst found and promoted Graham, and Graham's remarkable evangelistic ministry was catapulted into the public eye.[40]

After putting down its roots at Winona, Grace Seminary, and later the college, would continue to move toward the center of dispensational evangelicalism. The Winona community, having secured its place of significance within the Bible Conference Movement in America, thus served as a significant backdrop for the Grace campus, and an ally in its evangelical efforts.

Notes

1. J. F., C. C., and J. E. Beyer were wholesale dealers in dairy products and produce. The natural springs of cool water in the area offered a place where they could cool and store their milk products. Immediately, they constructed several spring houses which served as a successful and profitable cooling system.

2. From J. E. Beyer's handwritten diary, provided by his granddaughter.

3. White, *Winona at 100*. 20-22.

4. Ibid, 35.

5. Michael Kazin, *A Godly Hero: The Life of William Jennings Bryan*, (New York: Alfred A. Knopf, 2006), 135.

6. The annual programs and promotional booklets for the Winona Assembly and Summer School are available in binders at the Winona History Center in Westminster Hall in Winona Lake.

7. Ibid.

8. On the Bible Conference Movement in America, see Mark Sidwell, "Come Apart And Rest A While: The Origin Of The Bible Conference Movement In America." *Detroit Baptist Seminary Journal*, 15:0 (2010), 75.

9. Mark Sidwell, *The History of the Winona Lake Bible Conference*. Unpublished Ph.D. dissertation, Bob Jones University, Greenville, S.C., 1988, 63.

10. White, *Winona at 100*, 42.

11. See Al Disbro, *Images of America: Winona Lake* (Charleston, SC, Arcadia Publishing, 2012), 102.

12. Winona Assembly and Summer School program for summer 1900.

13. Vincent Gaddis and Jasper A. Huffman. *The Story of Winona Lake* (Winona Lake, IN; Jasper Huffman, 1960), chapter 3; also page 41.

14. The years 1896-1914 are often referred to as Winona's "Golden Years," when Winona drew an average of 250,000 visitors each summer. Although the origin of this designation is unsure, it was widely used, as in this example "Moment of Indiana History" at http://indianapublicmedia.org/ momentofindianahistory/winona-lake/.

15. Although his popularity peaked during the years 1908-1920, Sunday had a 39-year career as a platform evangelist, speaking in person to more than 100 million people. His career included at least 548 separate revival campaigns or speaking ap-

pearances that ranged over 40 states. Shortly before his death in 1935, he estimated for *Ladies Home Journal* that he had delivered nearly 20,000 sermons over his lifetime—an average of 42 per month.

16. *The Indianapolis Star*, Sunday, August 29, 1915, 1.

17. Ibid.

18. Virginia Asher's life and work are featured in three short chapters of *When Others Shuddered* by Jamie Janosz (Chicago, Moody Publishers, 2014), 114-129.

19. White, *Winona at 100*, 263.

20. Bob Jones. *Cornbread and Caviar* (Greenville, SC: Bob Jones University Press, 1985), chapter 9, "Winona Lake Bible Conference: Its Heyday".

21. Homer Rodeheaver's obituary from the Warsaw, Indiana, *Times-Union* newspaper, which contains a wealth of information about his life and career, may be found online at http://yesteryear.clunette.com/rodeheaver.html.

22. Bert Wilhoit. *Rody: Memories of Homer Rodeheaver*. (Greenville, SC: Bob Jones University Press, 2000).

23. David Plaster. *Finding Our Focus*, 83.

24. White, *Winona at 100*, 237.

25. Plaster, 114.

26. White, *Winona at 100*, 59.

27. Gaddis & Huffman, 136.

28. White, *Winona at 100*, 113.

29. Terry White & Wayne Snider. *25 Years of God's Grace: 1948-1973*. (Winona Lake, IN: Grace College & Seminary, 1973), 22.

30. Plaster, 143.

31. From personal interview with Joyce Griffith, daughter of Leo Polman.

32. Its *Old Fashioned Revival Hour* songbooks and recordings were used each week by 750 radio stations throughout the nation, and a western branch office was established in Inglewood, California, in 1948. For details see White, *Winona at 100*, 123 ff.

33. Ron Henry, interview by author.

34. Detailed explanations of Grace's use and acquisition of facilities may be found in White, *Winona at 100*, 250 ff.

35. *The Brethren Encyclopedia*, Vol. 2 (Philadelphia and Oak Brook IL: The Brethren Encyclopedia Inc., 1983), 1351.

36. Plaster, 84.

37. The collected sermons from Winona speakers were printed, bound, and distributed every year by publisher Victor Hatfield under the name *Winona Echoes*. Samples are in the Winona History Center.

38. See the Theresa E. Hart Papers in the Winona History Center.

39. White, *Winona at 100*, has an entire chapter on Youth for Christ and its worldwide influence.

40. Sherwood E. Wirt. "The Lost Prayer Meeting." *Decision Magazine*, March 1973, 4.

Chapter 9

The Denominational Context
Doctrinal Statements among
Grace Brethren Groups

Robert G. Clouse

IN PRINCIPLE, THE BRETHREN TRADITION IS NON-CREEDAL, THAT IS, it has sought to avoid unnecessary entanglements with human creeds and doctrinal formulations. In practice, however, Brethren leaders have at times felt the need to set down "statements" that helped to provide a sense of theological identity and orientation.[1] In any religious body, the evolution of faith statements sheds light on historical developments and reflects both a desire for unity and the reality of disunity. Grace College and Seminary has always existed with strong ties with the Fellowship of Grace Brethren Churches (FGBC), owing largely to the fact that the origins of the two were so closely connected. For this reason, a study of the evolution of doctrinal statements within Grace Brethren groups can be illustrative of important issues and cultural markers that have been prevalent not only in the denominational context, but at the seminary as well. ("Denomination" is used loosely in this chapter, since, as insiders are quick to point out, the FGBC is not technically a denomination, but rather a "fellowship.")

In this chapter, the texts of three doctrinal statements are offered, along with commentary and analysis that help to place the statements in historical context. While the content is not insignificant, the evolving degree of definition is striking. The first two—the 1921 "Message of the Brethren Ministry" (461 words), and the 1969 Statement of Faith of the National Fellowship of Brethren Churches

(665 words)—demonstrate an increasing desire for greater doctrinal definition among those who began the group that would become the Fellowship of Grace Brethren Churches. The third exhibit, the Statement of Faith of the Conservative Grace Brethren Churches, International (1160 words) then reflects still further definition and narrowing that took place with the creation of this new fellowship in 1992.

The Message of the Brethren Ministry (1921)

Introduction and Analysis

To understand the context of the "Message of the Brethren Ministry", it is important to begin in the nineteenth century. In this period, the Brethren would try to settle their differences at Annual Meetings, which combined the characteristics of a family reunion, a camp meeting, and a business session. All those who attended were given hospitality by the host congregation, and a tent or a large hall was erected to accommodate them. Often, a group of influential ministers or elders who comprised what the Brethren called the Standing Committee prepared the business items to be presented to the conference by combining questions, or queries, put forward by the congregations. These sessions would strive to reach agreement by unanimous consent. Great weight was given to the pronouncements of previous meetings, and although the Brethren did their best to try to work with the forces of change, year after year of arguing over progressive proposals began to strain their patience.[2]

To those who advocated more rapid changes within the church, it seemed that the reliance on the teaching of the elders and the seeming inability to adjust more rapidly to the challenges of the day meant that their ideas would never be put into practice. Much of the agitation focused on a single charismatic leader, Henry Ritz Holsinger (1833-1905). Descended from a long line of Brethren, he became a minister in 1866. The previous year he began publishing the *Christian Family Companion*. The new paper was printed weekly and had an air of freedom about it. As Holsinger characterized it:

A free rostrum was announced for the discussion of all subjects pertaining to the welfare of the church. Any person who was able to communicate an idea to the comprehension of the editor was sure to appear in the paper. No matter how scrawling the handwriting, or how stammering his words, the article would be put into good shape...Another peculiarity of the paper was that every contributor was required to write under his own signature. In this way authors were brought face to face with each other, and required to meet the issue of their individual productions.[3]

As with most publications, however, the policy of the editor tended to direct the "free discussion," and Holsinger became the leader of a growing group that argued for changes in the church. Rather than looking to the past, these progressives were optimistic, forward-looking individuals who felt the need to abandon many of the traditional practices of the church. In addition to discontinuing certain customs, Holsinger encouraged new methods and ideas. His paper advocated a series of reforms including a paid ministry, personal choice in dress, a new approach to missions, an interest in education, and evangelistic meetings. The *Companion* was very successful and caused a conflict to develop between Holsinger and the leadership of the church.[4]

The struggle between Holsinger and the Annual Meeting continued year after year, centering on one matter of the progressive agenda after another. By 1873 the pressure was so great that Holsinger sold the *Companion* to Elder James Quinter. The following year Holsinger moved to Berlin, Pennsylvania, where he became a preacher and endeavored to raise money to establish a Brethren college. Many people urged him to resume his publication, so in 1878 he began to publish *The Progressive Christian*.[5]

Conservatives were angered by Holsinger's continued criticism of their policies, and they called for a committee of elders to visit him in his home church in Berlin, Pennsylvania, to investigate his views to determine if he should be disciplined. The committee recommended to the 1882 Annual Meeting that he be barred from fellowship, and despite last minute attempts at reconsideration, the report was adopted. Alienated by Holsinger's treatment, his supporters held a series of meetings which eventually led to the establishment of a new denomination, the Brethren Church, at Dayton, Ohio, in 1883.[6]

Freed from what they considered to be the dead hand of the past, the Brethren proceeded to put into practice the various items of the Progressive agenda by setting standards for a paid ministry, establishing a publishing house, and organizing state and district conferences. They also made plans to support Ashland College, sponsor evangelistic meetings, begin Sunday schools, and allow their members to dress in a more stylish manner. The traditional Dunker concept of antagonism to the world was replaced by an acceptance of many facets of modern society. The work of spreading the Gospel went on rapidly for several decades after the division of 1883, but as is true with many splinter groups, the Progressives showed considerable agreement in what they opposed, but were less united in what they wished to create.

Tensions developed over the control of denominational organizations that centered at Ashland, Ohio. Even Ashland College, at first a unifying point for the church, became a center of controversy when arguments arose over the direction of the college. "The Message of the Brethren Ministry" is rooted in these tensions and was the result of a 1921 committee that was gathered by the Brethren Church's National Ministerial Association with the goal to bring greater definition to Brethren beliefs. (An earlier General Conference committee, which was chaired by Louis S. Bauman and included Alva J. McClain, had begun this process.) The twenty-five person committee was chaired by McClain, who was at this time becoming an influential figure.[7]

The statement that emerged from this committee's work reflected McClain's desire for greater doctrinal precision, one of the factors that led to his divorce from Ashland seminary. Although this statement was adopted before the FGBC existed, McClain's leadership in its creation (along with J. Allen Miller) makes it significant to the early formation of Grace Theological Seminary and the fellowship that emerged from it. This statement is also significant because its adoption means that the real victory over liberalism took place in 1921—more than a decade before the creation of Grace Seminary in 1937.[8]

Text[9]

The Message which Brethren Ministers accept as a divine entrustment to be heralded to a lost world, finds its sole source and authority in the Bible. This message is one of hope for a lost world and speaks with finality and authority. Fidelity to the apostolic injunction to preach the Word demands our utmost endeavor of mind and heart. We, the members of the National Ministerial Association of the Brethren Church, hold that the essential and constituent elements of our message shall continue to be the following declarations:

1.   *Our motto: The Bible, the whole Bible and nothing but the Bible.*

2.   *The authority and integrity of the Holy Scriptures.*
     The ministry of The Brethren Church desires to bear testimony to the belief that God's supreme revelation has been made through Jesus Christ, a complete and authentic record of which revelation is the New Testament and, to the belief that the Holy Scripture of the Old and New Testaments, as originally given, are the infallible record of the perfect, final and authoritative revelation of God's will, altogether sufficient in themselves as a rule of faith and practice.

3. *We understand the basic content of our doctrinal preaching to be:*

   (1) The Pre-Existence. Deity and Incarnation by Virgin Birth of Jesus Christ, the Son of God;

   (2) The Fall of Man, his consequent spiritual death and utter sinfulness, and the necessity of his New Birth;

   (3) The Vicarious Atonement of the Lord Jesus Christ through the shedding of His own blood;

   (4) The Resurrection of the Lord Jesus Christ in the body in which He suffered and died, and His subsequent glorification at the right hand of God;

   (5) Justification by personal faith in the Lord Jesus Christ, of which obedience to the will of God, and works of righteousness, are the evidence and result; the resurrection of the dead, the judgment of the world, and the life everlasting of the just;

   (6) The Personality and Deity of the Holy Spirit, Who indwells the Christian and is his Comforter and Guide;

(7) *The personal and visible return of our Lord Jesus Christ from Heaven as King of kings and Lord of lords, the glorious goal for which we are taught to watch, wait and pray;*

(8) *The Christian should "be not conformed to this world, but be transformed by the renewing of the mind"; should not engage in carnal strife, and should "swear not at all";*

(9) *The Christian should observe, as his duty and privilege, the ordinances of our Lord Jesus Christ, among which are: (a) Baptism of Believers by Triune Immersion; (b) Confirmation; (c) the Lord's Supper; (d) The Communion of the Bread and Wine; (e) the Washing of the Saints' Feet; and (f) the Anointing of the Sick with Oil.*

Statement of Faith of the National Fellowship of Brethren Churches (1969)

Introduction and Analysis

The founding of a separate seminary by the "Grace group" led to the division of the church in 1939 and later, the founding of the National Fellowship of Brethren Churches.[10] (In 1976, the official name was changed to the Fellowship of Grace Brethren Churches.) Members of the new denomination believed they were continuing the traditions of the Brethren Church. This view was expressed by one of their early leaders, Louis S. Bauman, who found many similarities between the problems encountered by the Grace group and those faced by the Progressive Brethren of the nineteenth century. These included the struggle to maintain congregational church government and to keep the Bible central to the Christian life.[11]

After the struggle with the Ashland faction was over, the leaders of the Grace Brethren could devote their considerable talents and zeal to the cause of missions, evangelism, and church growth. The division had left them with about one half or 15,000 members of the Brethren Church in 70 congregations. They also controlled the Foreign Missionary Society, and had attracted younger seminary graduates who would in time found and serve home mission points. In addition to annual conferences, the Grace Brethren organized district conferences that functioned along the same lines as the national meetings. Because of their fear of centralization, they established separate but cooperating corporations, including the Foreign Missionary Society of the Brethren Church (now Encompass World Partners), the Brethren Home Missions Council, Grace Theological Seminary and Grace College, the Brethren Missionary Herald Company (now GraceConnect), the National Fellowship of Grace Brethren Ministers (now the Association of Grace Brethren Ministers), the Women's Missionary Council (now Women of Grace USA), and the National Brethren Retirement Homes (now Grace Village Retirement Community).

There were further developments in the belief and practices of the FGBC that can be illustrated through a comparison of the "Message of the Brethren Ministry" of 1921 with the "Statement of Faith of the National Fellowship of Brethren Churches" adopted by the Annual Conference in August, 1969. Between the formulations of these two statements, however, Grace College and Seminary adopted, in 1937, a separate Covenant of Faith, which was essentially a doctrinal statement for the institution (see Appendix B). Not surprisingly, it too reflected the Grace group's desire for increased definition. The 1969 statement for the National Fellowship of Brethren Churches is essentially an amalgamation of the 1921 "Message of the Brethren Ministry" and the Seminary's Covenant. When compared with the 1921 statement, the 1969 declaration is presented in a more scholastic form; its statements are supported by proof texts from the Scriptures and certain sections such as those dealing with the Bible, the church, the Christian life, and eschatology are expanded. The more recent statement supports baptism by triune immersion and the threefold communion consisting of feetwashing, the love feast, and partaking of the bread and the cup. Other distinctive Brethren practices are placed in the section on the Christian life, which is described as one of separation "from the evil ways of the world."

Perhaps the statements in the 1969 document that elaborate on eschatology represent the most notable divergence between the two documents. The 1921 statement, with its general comments on the Second Coming, is augmented with articles on Satan and the "Future Life." The devil is described as a personal being who is doomed but, in the meantime, has the ability to oppose God's people. Christ's return is explained as visible, personal, and imminent. The Second

Coming is to be in two stages; the first, to "remove" the church from earth before the tribulation period and the second, to descend with the church to establish the thousand-year kingdom of God on earth. Details of the future life include the conscious existence of the dead, the resurrection of the body, the reward of believers with eternal life, and the condemnation of unbelievers to eternal punishment. Throughout the document (below) there is an obvious stress on the Bible as "verbally inspired in all parts, and therefore wholly without error as originally given by God." An explanation of the background for these changes will help to characterize the outlook of the Grace Brethren.

The adoption of the statement of faith represents to a great extent the impact of Alva J. McClain on the fellowship through his role as professor of theology at Grace Seminary. He has often been described as a Calvinist, and to a certain extent that is true. However, if his dispensational eschatology were taken into account, he would be more accurately classed as a modified Calvinist. His emphasis on the Sovereignty of God, the eternal security of the believer, and salvation by faith alone would place him among Reformed theologians. He frequently reminded his students that God controlled everything from the fall of a sparrow to the fall of an empire. Typical of many Grace Brethren, he had studied in places where dispensational fundamentalism was taught. His works, including *Law and Grace* and *The Greatness of the Kingdom*, present a form of dispensationalism which distinguished between law and grace in such a way as to deemphasize the role of The Ten Commandments in the life of the believer during the Age of Grace.[12] He also taught that there is a universal kingdom of God which never ceases to exist that contrasts with the mediatorial kingdom. The latter kingdom was offered to the Jews at the time of Christ but they rejected it. Consequently Israel has been replaced by the church during the present age, but will be restored to God's favor when Christ returns. McClain's views were accepted by many non-Brethren fundamentalists, and he was made a member of the committee to revise the *Scofield Reference Bible*. Most of the ministers in the FGBC at that time had either studied under him or were influenced by him and preached dispensational theology from their pulpits. The major innovations in the 1969 statement result from the influence of McClain's theology.

Text[13]

We of the National Fellowship of Brethren Churches, in harmony with our historic position, believing the Bible, the whole Bible, and nothing but the Bible to be our infallible rule of faith and of practice, and feeling our responsibility to make known the divine message of the Bible, present the following articles as a statement of those basic truths taught in the Bible which are common to our Christian faith and practice:

THE BIBLE: the Word of God, the sixty-six Books of the Old and New Testaments, verbally inspired in all parts, and therefore wholly without error as originally given of God (II Tim. 3:16; II Peter 1:21).

THE ONE TRUE GOD: existing eternally as three persons-the Father, the Son, and the Holy Spirit (Luke 3:22; Matt. 28:19; II Cor. 13:14).

THE LORD JESUS CHRIST: His preexistence and deity (John 1:1-3), incarnation by virgin birth (John 1:14; Matt. 1:18-23) sinless life (Heb. 4:15), substitutionary death (II Cor. 5:21), bodily resurrection (Luke 24:36-43), ascension into heaven and present ministry (Heb. 4:14-16), and coming again (Acts 1:11).

THE HOLY SPIRIT: His personality (John 16:7-15); and deity (Acts 5:3-4); and His work in each believer; baptism and indwelling at the moment of regeneration (I Cor. 12:13; Rom. 8:9); and filling (Eph. 5:18) to empower for Christian life and service (Eph. 3:16; Acts 1:8; Gal. 5:22-23).

MAN: his direct creation in the image of God (Gen. 1:26-28), his subsequent fall into sin resulting in spiritual death (Gen. 3:1-24; Rom. 5:12), and the necessity of the new birth for his salvation (John 3:3-5).

SALVATION: a complete and eternal salvation by God's grace alone, received as the gift of God through personal faith in the Lord Jesus Christ and His finished work (Eph. 2:8-9; Titus 3:5-7; I Peter 1:18-19).

THE CHURCH: one true Church, the body and bride of Christ (Eph. 1:22-23; 5:25-32), composed of all true believers of the present age (I Cor. 12:12-13); and the organization of its members in local churches for worship, for edification of believers, and for world-wide gospel witness, each local church being autonomous but cooperating in fellowship and work (Eph. 4:11-16).

CHRISTIAN LIFE: *a life of righteousness, good works, and separation unto God from the evil ways of the world (Rom. 12:1-2), manifested by speaking the truth (James 5:12), maintaining the sanctity of the home (Eph. 5:22-6:4), settling differences between Christians in accordance with the Word of God (I Cor. 6:1-8), not engaging in carnal strife but showing a Christ-like attitude toward all men (Rom. 12:17-21), exhibiting the fruit of the Spirit (Gal. 5:22-23), and maintaining a life of prayer (Eph. 6:18; Phil. 4:6), including the privilege, when sick, of calling for the elders of the church to pray and to anoint with oil in the name of the Lord (James 5:13-18).*

ORDINANCES: *the Christian should observe the ordinances of our Lord Jesus Christ, which are (1) baptism of believers by triune immersion (Matt. 28:19) and (2) the threefold communion service, consisting of the washing of the saints' feet (John 13:1-17), the Lord's Supper (I Cor. 11:20-22, 33-34; Jude 12), and the communion of the bread and the cup (I Cor. 11:23-26).*

SATAN: *his existence and personality as the great adversary of God and His people (Rev. 12:1-10), his judgment (John 12:31), and final doom (Rev. 20:10).*

SECOND COMING: *the personal, visible, and imminent return of Christ to remove His Church from the earth (I Thess. 4:16-17) before the tribulation (I Thess. 1:10; Rev. 3:10), and afterward to descend with the Church to establish His millennial kingdom upon the earth (Rev. 19:11-20:6).*

FUTURE LIFE: *the conscious existence of the dead (Phil. 1:21-23; Luke 16:19-31), the resurrection of the body (John 5:28-29), the judgment and reward of believers (Rom. 14:10-12; II Cor. 5:10), the judgment and condemnation of unbelievers (Rev. 20:11-15), the external life of the saved (John 3:16), and the eternal punishment of the lost (Matt. 25:46; Rev. 20:15).*

Statement of Faith of the Conservative Grace Brethren Churches, International

Introduction and Analysis

With the retirement of McClain and many of the other leaders who had provided guidance for the Grace Brethren since the 1930s, there were new challenges to face. One of these was caused by the success of the church in winning members from other evangelical traditions. A major problem with which the new generation of leadership was forced to struggle was what to do when individuals from non-Brethren groups who were satisfied with their own form of baptism and content with their observance of communion wished to join a Grace Brethren Church. The solution was found in a revised method of accepting individuals into church membership. Passed at the National Conference in 1964, it indicated that all Brethren Churches should continue to baptize by triune immersion but that: "Churches which receive members without triune immersion shall have their delegates seated in national conference with voting privileges on all matters except those involving the subject of water baptism in relation to church membership."[14] Although there was continuing discussion about this decision, it was not until the 1980s that the subject was reopened with particular vigor. By 1989 an attempt was made to rescind the action of the 1964 annual meeting, but it was defeated. By then there were two major positions advocated within the fellowship. One of them, referred to as the "open" position, supported the 1964 decision and the other, the "closed" view, wished to exclude non-triune immersed believers from membership.

The schism in the church would not have come, however, if it had not been for the leadership of some older Brethren, especially John C. Whitcomb, Jr.[15] During the same year that he was dismissed from the Seminary, the Conservative Grace Brethren Association was formed. The group included several influential pastors and seminary leaders such as James Boyer and especially former Grace College and Seminary president, Herman Hoyt, who threw his support behind the new Conservative fellowship. Hoyt, in fact, seems to have been praying for a split, claiming in a letter that Whitcomb had been fired from the seminary as a result of his "stand for the faith." At last, Hoyt said to

Whitcomb, "the lines are clearly drawn" and he predicted there would be a new [Grace Brethren] conference by the end of summer. "Nothing like this," Hoyt declared, "will serve so well to launch the new conference." "The Lord has used you," Hoyt affirmed, "for the initiation of another great, great venture for Christ."[16] He wrote to Whitcomb,

> It [a new fellowship] will crystallize and give clear evidence of the need to do what the Lord wants to do. It will help hundreds of Brethren to realize the seriousness of the crisis in the Brethren church and help them to know that there are many who stand for the Bible and the authority of Christ. Don't let any doubts creep into your thinking. You may start small, but you'll grow faster than you think.[17]

Two years after the dissenters had organized the Conservative Grace Brethren Association, when the 1992 National Conference (held at Winona Lake, Indiana) voted to reaffirm the open church membership policy, the conservatives stood up in the midst of the conference delegates and Whitcomb dramatically led them out the door. Almost immediately they announced a meeting at the Winona Lake Presbyterian Church to formally create a new fellowship.

While baptism was the immediate concern, the new group stated that the issues dividing them from the main body went deeper than the baptism/membership controversy. They included the tendencies towards denominationalism as expressed by a Fellowship council of representatives of the church that met more frequently than the annual conference. They also condemned the toleration of open membership churches by both Foreign and Home Missions offices. Developments at Grace Schools also troubled them—especially the acceptance of those on the faculty and board who did not insist on triune immersion. However, their most serious accusation against the Brethren was "a new way of interpreting Scripture . . . (which) looks at truth with a subjective eye and seeks to divide God's Word into levels of certainty or clarity."[18]

Forging a new path was the only option, given Whitcomb's separatist convictions.[19] True to this spirit, the "conservatives" set up a dissenting organization, elected several committees, and agreed to a three-year transition period during which they could belong to both the FGBC and the new Conservative Grace Brethren group. They needed time to complete their organization and to convince their churches to leave the Winona Lake group. They also expressed problems over finances and the debt owed by many churches to the Grace Brethren Investment Foundation.[20] The conservatives have continued their existence in a loose association of churches that functions through a series of "protocols." There is a president, vice-president, and a conference coordinator. In common with other Brethren groups, they have annual conferences. In addition to the offices there are unincorporated bodies including a College of Pastors, a Foreign Mission Association, and a USA Home Mission Society.[21] After just over two decades, the CGBCI remains small with most congregations concentrated in the Midwest and Pennsylvania. In 2007, some momentum was lost through yet another split of sorts when a dispute occurred over the discipline of a pastor in Mansfield, Ohio, resulting in the withdrawal of several congregations.[22]

Yet Whitcomb's legacy continues to serve as a strong sense of identity. Without the resources to support a traditional seminary, Whitcomb, who, recorded almost every class he ever taught, established The Christian Workman Schools of Theology using a correspondence curriculum that has enabled local congregations around the world to develop church leaders and church planters. With recorded lectures and syllabi prepared by recognized pastors and theologians and a suggested curriculum of courses leading to diplomas or degrees, these widely-used materials have found their way into seminaries, mission schools, local churches, and home schools.[23]

Naturally, strong feelings were evident on both sides of this new schism. Some believed Whitcomb was guilty of slander and held him personally responsible for nearly destroying Grace Seminary and then compounding matters by leading a split in the fellowship.[24] Those in the Conservative Fellowship, however, believed the separation of their churches carried on the legacy of the generation that began the "Grace group" in 1937. This sense of legitimacy was bolstered by the fact that late in his life, McClain had expressed suspicion over the direction of neo-evangelicalism, and they were convinced that McClain would have supported the conservative split had he still been alive.

Following the precedent of the earlier Grace Brethren, the Conservatives issued a statement of faith (below), which is based on the 1969 declaration of the Grace Brethren and is understood to be a clarification of the earlier statement. The additions emphasize the absolute authority of the Bible and dismiss the charismatic movement by claiming "Apostolic sign-gifts and miracles . . . ended with the apostolic era." They also insist on a dogmatic interpretation of human origins and society by explaining that there was a "recent, direct creation of the heavens, the earth, and all their hosts in six literal 24-hour days" and that there is a "distinct function of men and women in the home and the church."

Another statement insists on the requirement of triune immersion for church membership by claiming that it "may not be circumvented except for medical reasons of a physical nature." Conservative Grace Brethren are reminded of the need for nonresistance (to evil) although this was not to be equated with pacifism. Another statement maintains "that only triune immersion and only threefold communion meet the biblical mandates of our Lord Jesus Christ concerning ordinances." The dispensationalism of the 1969 statement is made more explicit by insisting that the church will be "raptured" before the seven year tribulation period and that the millennium "will include the literal fulfillment of God's covenant promises to ethnic Israel." To be certain that their doctrinal trumpet makes no uncertain sound, each of these statements is buttressed with Scripture references which are more specific and numerous than those found in both the 1921 "Message of the Brethren Ministry" (which had none) and the original 1969 document.

This declaration of faith reflects the influence of Whitcomb who was its major author. In fact, most of the leaders of the new movement were his students and accepted his interpretation of the Christian faith. For Whitcomb, creeds were necessary, but could never take the place of a strong leader for safeguarding doctrinal purity. "A written creed is indeed essential," he wrote,

> but it is also completely insufficient to maintain doctrinal unity; for the human mind is notoriously adept at interpreting the specifics of a creed as well as God's own Word in such a way as to destroy unity. The key factor in God's plan is therefore not simply a doctrinal statement, but a Christian leader who determines in his own conscience before the Lord what is not acceptable in interpreting the given pattern

of doctrinal commitment. He then must gather around him a team of fellow workers who share with him in these guidelines and goals and who have a large degree of confidence in his God-given leadership.[25]

The drift toward compromise and "neo-evangelicalism" that Whitcomb and those in his circle believed could be found in the Grace Brethren ranks was condemned by the new document.[26] Over a century of division prepared many members to accept the idea of a new denomination, assuming that divisions were a necessary means to stave off apostasy.

Text[27]

We, the Conservative Grace Brethren Churches, International, in harmony with our historic Grace Brethren position, believing the Bible, the whole Bible, and nothing but the Bible to be our infallible rule of faith and practice, and understanding our responsibility to make known the divine message of the Bible, present the following articles as a statement of those basic truths taught in the Bible, and which every member church of the Conservative Grace Brethren Churches, International believes, holds as its conviction, and practices.

1. *THE BIBLE: We believe the Word of God, the sixty-six Books of the Old and New Testaments, verbally inspired in all parts, and therefore wholly without error as originally given of God (2 Tim. 3:16; 2 Peter 1:21). This record is final, authoritative, and unchanging! We believe the Bible to be the all-sufficient rule for faith and conduct (apart from integration with any other discipline) through the power of the Holy Spirit to regenerate, sanctify, and equip the believer for life and service (John 17:17; Heb. 4:12; James 1:18-27.)*

2. *THE ONE TRUE GOD: We believe in the One True God (Deut. 6:4, Isa. 44:6) existing eternally as three persons—the Father, the Son, and the Holy Spirit (Luke 3:22; Matt. 28:19, 2 Cor. 13:14). This tri-unity is clearly set forth in the form and formula of Christian baptism (Matt. 28:19-20).*

3. *THE LORD JESUS CHRIST: We believe in the Lord Jesus Christ, His pre-existence and deity (John 1:1-3), incarnation by virgin birth (John 1:14; Matt. 1:18-23), sinless life (Heb. 4:15), substitutionary*

death (2 Cor. 5:21), bodily resurrection (Luke 24:36-43), ascension into heaven and present ministry (Heb. 4:14-16), and coming again (Acts 1:11). Further scriptural evidence of His pre-existence as God the Son is found in John 8:58; His deity, John 20:28 & 1 John 5:20; and His coming again, John 14:3.

4. THE HOLY SPIRIT: We believe in the Holy Spirit, in His personality (John. 16:7-15); and deity (Acts 5:3-4); and His work in each believer: baptism and indwelling at the moment of regeneration (1 Cor. 12:13; Rom. 8:9); and filling (Eph. 5:18) to empower for Christian life and service (Eph. 3:16; Acts 1:8, Gal. 5:22-23). We believe that the Holy Spirit provides to each believer one or more spiritual gifts "for serving one another" (1 Peter 4:10); and gifted men to the Church for perfecting (Eph. 4:11-13). However, apostolic sign-gifts and miracles, even in the early Church, were not for all believers (1 Cor. 12:28-30) and ended with the apostolic era (I Cor. 13:8; 2 Cor. 12: 12; Heb. 2:3-4). We also believe that Spirit baptism is a once for all action, at the moment of regeneration (Eph. 4:5; 1 Cor. 12:13).

5. MAN: We believe in man's direct creation in the image of God (Gen. 1:26-28), his subsequent fall into sin resulting in spiritual death (Gen. 3:1-24; Rom. 5:12), and the necessity of the new birth for his salvation (John 3:3-5). We believe in the recent, direct creation of the heavens, the earth, and all their hosts, without pre-existing material in six literal 24-hour days (Gen. 1:1-2, 25; Exod. 20:11; John 1:3; Col. 1:16; Heb. 11:3). We believe in the sanctity of human life (Gen. 9:6; Ps. 139: 13-16) and in the distinct function of men and women in the home and the church (Eph. 5:22-33; 1 Tim. 2:8-15).

6. SALVATION: We believe in a complete and eternal salvation by God's grace alone, received as the gift of God through personal faith in the Lord Jesus Christ and His finished work (Eph. 2:8-9; Titus 3:5-7; 1 Peter 1:18-19).

7. THE CHURCH: We believe in the one true Church, the body and bride of Christ (Eph. 1:22-23; 5:25-32), composed of all true believers of the present age (1 Cor. 12:12-13); and the organization of its members in local churches for worship, for edification of believers, and for world-wide gospel witness, each local church being autonomous but cooperating in fellowship and work (Eph. 4:11-16). We be-

lieve confession of faith and triune immersion to be the two essential scriptural requirements for membership in the local church (Matt. 28:16-20; Acts 2:38). Each local church shall determine its own additional membership requirements (Acts 2:42-47), and the discipline of its own members (1 Cor. 5:3-5). Triune immersion may not be circumvented except for medical reasons of a physical nature.

8. *CHRISTIAN LIFE: We believe the Christian Life consists of a life of righteousness, good works, and separation unto God from the evil ways of the world (Rom. 12:1-2), manifested by speaking the truth (James 5:12), maintaining the sanctity of the home (Eph. 5:22-6:4), settling differences between Christians in accordance with the Word of God (1 Cor. 6:1-8), not engaging in carnal strife but showing a Christ-like attitude toward all men (Rom. 12:17-21), exhibiting the fruit of the Spirit (Gal. 5:22-23), and maintaining a life of prayer (Eph. 6:18; Phil. 4:6), including the privilege, when sick, of calling for the elders of the church to pray and to anoint with oil in the name of the Lord (James 5:13-18). Not engaging in carnal strife is understood to include not only war but also church and personal relationships. This is to reaffirm the biblical teaching on non-resistance (not to be equated with pacifism) in war and peace (Matt. 5:39-41; Luke 6:27-29; John 18:36).*

9. *ORDINANCES: We believe the Christian should observe the ordinances of our Lord Jesus Christ, which are (1) baptism of believers by triune immersion (Matt. 28:19) and (2) the threefold communion service, consisting of the washing of the saints' feet (John 13:1-17), the Lord's Supper (1 Cor. 11:20; 33-34; Jude 12), and the communion of the bread and the cup (1 Cor. 11-23-26). We believe that only triune immersion and only threefold communion meet the biblical mandates of our Lord Jesus Christ concerning ordinances (Matt. 28:20; John 13:13-17].*

10. *SATAN: We believe his existence and personality as the great adversary of God and His people (Rev. 12:1-10), his judgment (John 12:31), and final doom (Rev. 20:10).*

11. *SECOND COMING: We believe in the personal, visible, and imminent return of Christ to remove His Church from the earth (1 Thess. 4:16-17) before the tribulation (1 Thess. 1:10; Rev. 3:10), and af-*

terward to descend with the Church to establish His millennial king-dom upon the earth (Rev. 19:11-20:6). [We believe the tribulation will be a seven-year period (Dan. 9:24-27) following the rapture of the Church; and we believe the thousand-year kingdom will include the literal fulfillment of God's covenant promises to ethnic Israel (Jer. 33:14-26; Ezek. 36:25-28; 40-48; Rom. 11:23-32).

12. *FUTURE LIFE: We believe in the conscious existence of the dead (Phil 1:21-23; Luke 16:19-31), the resurrection of the body (John 5:28-29), the judgment and reward of believers (Rom. 14:10-12; 2 Cor. 5:10), the judgment and condemnation of unbelievers (Rev. 20:11-15), the eternal life of the saved (John 3:16), and the eternal punishment of the lost (Matt. 25:46; Rev. 20:15). We understand eternal punishment to be a conscious state (Rev. 14:11).*

The question of whether or not the heightened sense of theological precision and narrowness found in the Conservative Fellowship best reflects Grace Brethren identity or that of American Fundamental-ism is a matter of interpretation. Taken together, however, the state-ments of faith spotlighted in this chapter illustrate, for good or for ill, a striking trajectory toward greater degrees of theological defini-tion. Although these statements are technically situated only within the denominational context of these Grace Brethren groups, they provide an illustrative perspective on the setting in which Grace Col-lege and Seminary has developed and the theological issues that have been part of its history.

Notes

1. "Non-creedalism," in *The Brethren Encyclopedia*. See also Dale Stoffer, "The Brethren, Creeds, and the Heidelberg Catechism," *Old Order Notes* 22 (Fall-Winter 2000): 7-20.

2. For the troubles of the Brethren in the 19th Century, see the relevant sections of Carl F. Bowman, *Brethren Society* and Donald F. Durnbaugh, *Fruit of the Vine, A History of the Brethren 1708-1995.* (Elgin, IL: 1997). Note also the helpful treat-ment of the growth of the Brethren movement in Dale R. Stoffer, *Background and Development of Brethren Doctrines,* chaps. 14-15.

3. Henry R. Holsinger, *Holsinger's History of the Tunkers and the Brethren Church.* (Oakland, Calif.: for the Author, 1901), 472.

4. "Henry R. Holsinger" and "Christian Family Companion" in *The Brethren Encyclopedia*.

5. "The Progressive Christian," in *The Brethren Encyclopedia*

6. "The Brethren Church," in *The Brethren Encyclopedia*.

7. There is no adequate biography of either Bauman or McClain, but on McClain see Norman Rohrer, *A Saint in Glory Stands*. Consult as well M. M. Norris, "A Cord of Many Strands" in *The Activist Impulse*, 171, and Martin, "Law and Grace," 81.

8. Norris, "Cord of Many Strands" in *The Activist Impulse*, 171.

9. Kent Sr., *Conquering Frontiers*, 132-134.

10. See the articles by Dennis Martin, "Ashland College Versus Ashland Seminary," 37-50 and "What Has Divided the Brethren Church?" (Spring 1976), 107-119.

11. Louis S. Bauman, "Address to the Brethren National Conference, Sept. 1, 1942, at Winona Lake, Ind., *Brethren Missionary Herald* 4 (Dec. 26, 1942), 3-10.

12. Alva J. McClain, *The Greatness of the Kingdom*. (Grand Rapids, Mich.: Zondervan, 1959).

13. Kent Sr., *Conquering Frontiers*, 223-225.

14. Quoted in Homer A. Kent, Sr., *Conquering Frontiers*, 221.

15. For a congratulatory sketch of Whitcomb's life, see Paul J. "A Biographical Tribute," 443. For Whitcomb's significance to the development of Flood Geology, consult Ronald L. Numbers, *The Creationists*.

16. Hoyt to Whitcomb February 6, 1990. Photocopy provided to Jared Burkholder by John Whitcomb.

17. Hoyt to Whitcomb April 30, 1990. Photocopy provided to Jared Burkholder by John Whitcomb.

18. Gary Crandall, *1993 Grace Brethren Annual*. (Winona Lake, Ind.: The Brethren Missionary Herald Co., 1992), 21.

19. John C. Whitcomb, "God's Truth Circles." See also chapter three in this volume.

20. This group was organized by the Brethren Home Missions Council to finance churches which experienced difficulty obtaining commercial loans. If such churches left the Brotherhood before they had paid their loans, they would be in default on their loans and could lose their buildings. At the time of the division there were about 46 churches and 78 Pastors in the Conservative Grace Brethren group.

21. http://www.cgbci.org/.

22. This small schism led to the founding of the Reformed Brethren Church in 2007. The new fellowship rejected the "purpose driven movement" as a model for church growth. They also condemned the "Free Grace Theology," dispensationalism, and "cultural relativism" of the Grace Brethren. The Reformed Brethren accepted Threefold Communion, nonresistance and other "historic" Brethren positions. Despite the use of the word "reformed" the new Church does not teach Calvinist or Covenant Theology. The use of the term "reformed" in a way that seems strange to most church historians is another example of how the Brethren because of their

distinctive church ordinances are always forced to swim in a current slightly aside from mainstream evangelicalism.

23. http://www.whitcombministries.org/christian-workman-studies-in-theology.html.

24. For the charges that Whitcomb leveled against the seminary, see chapter 3 in this volume.

25. John C. Whitcomb, "Doctrinal Unity and Diversity," Unpublished mimeographed paper n.d.

26. For evangelicalism in general and its many recent divisions, see George Marsden, *Reforming Fundamentalism,* and *Evangelicalism and Modern America* (Grand Rapids, Mich.: Wm. B. Eerdmans, 1984). Joel A. Carpenter, *Revive us Again* and Douglas A. Sweeney, *The American Evangelical Story.* An older book of essays that gives different views of the movement is *The Evangelicals: What They Believe, Who They Are, Where They Are Changing,* Eds. D. F. Wells, and J. Woodbridge (Nashville: Abingdon Press, 1975). For an explanation of the extreme separation views of the Fundamentalists, see Ronald H. Nash, *Evangelicals in America: Who They Are, What They Believe.* (Nashville: Abingdon Press, 1987), 72-75; and for a more complicated attempt to categorize the bewildering number of groups that are termed evangelical, see *The Variety of American Evangelicalism,* Eds. D. W. Dayton and R. K. Johnson (Knoxville: University of Tennessee Press, 1991). For an explanation of the major theological issues that divide Evangelicals see Gregory A. Boyd and Paul R. Gody, *Across the Spectrum, Understanding Issues in Evangelical Theory* Second Edition. (Grand Rapids: Baker Academic, 2009).

27. www.cgbci.org/statement-of-faith.html.

Part III
Responses

Chapter 10

Critical Reflections

Steven M. Nolt, Goshen College*

IT'S AN HONOR FOR ME TO BE WITH YOU THIS EVENING AND TO celebrate this 75th anniversary with you. I was first on this campus when I was a senior at Goshen College and one of my religion professors brought a group of students to attend a lecture in Rodeheaver Auditorium. And last spring I was pleased to bring several students to the Chicagoland Christian College History Symposium that Professors Norris and Burkholder hosted here.

We've heard three stimulating talks this evening, covering the seminary and college history. There is much that I learned and much that I could affirm. But tonight I will make three observations, one of which is something of a question. We have larger than life personalities: Louis Bauman, Alva McClain, Herman Hoyt, and John Whitcomb. We have remarkable if not miraculous developments: the launching of a new seminary in the midst of the Great Depression and institutional growth and enrollment that placed this institution at the center of twentieth-century evangelicalism. Indeed, I was surprised to learn of the wide range of interchurch connections of some of the founding figures, such as L. S. Bauman, or the role that nationally known figures, such as Larry Crabb, played in Grace's history.

---

* Nolt was the invited commentator for the first of three "Heritage Forums" held on October 9, 2012, which included oral presentations of chapters by M. M. Norris, Jared Burkholder, and Christy M. Hill.

But there are also stories of conflict and pain. And here I commend the institution for not shying away from those stories of conflict and the subplots of discord. Here we face head-on the conflicts at Ashland, friendships fractured, character flaws in college administrators, conflicts among seminary colleagues, and painful schism in the 1990s. Attention to conflict is important for several reasons, and one of them is that it shows us what people cared passionately about—where there is conflict, something important is at stake. That may be easier to affirm when one is not directly involved. But it is true, I think, that we have here a story that mattered to people – people on campus and people in the pew and people who read *Grace Journal* and so on. How disheartening it would be if the conflicts of the past 75 years had only been intra-campus disputes that mattered to no one else. That pastors, alumni, and conference delegates cared deeply about what was being taught here suggests that what is taught here matters. And that is worth noting, even if we might wish that the way conflicts were handled might have been, in some cases, different. I think it is also a tribute to this school's maturity as an institution that stories of conflict can be addressed frankly. An anniversary year is a time for many things, and sometimes it is taken to be a time to avoid any painful reckoning of the past. I take it that the story here, like the biblical narrative, includes both the positive and the negative. Indeed, without the stories of pain and failure, there would be no need for grace.

My second observation is also a question and is prompted by all three papers. It has to do with how we think about the larger story that all three scholars tell. One way to hear the story—and I'm not suggesting that our speakers said this, but simply that it is one way many us may hear their stories and frame the story—is as a story of *outside influences* persistently shaping and remaking the Brethren/Grace Brethren/Grace Seminary narrative. When we hear the story that way, we are tempted to begin with an original "core" of beliefs, dispositions, and practices that are subsequently reshaped by outside influences, whether those be BIOLA or dispensationalism, or psychological counseling. Outside influences do not have to be negative, but hearing the story framed in such a way can leave us with a defensive institutional narrative. We follow along and the core is either preserved or eroded as outside influences buffet and dilute it—and then we wonder if, 75 years later, there is any connection to where we started.

But another way of hearing the story is not as a narrative of outside influences on Grace, but of Grace's being a leavening agent in all sorts of new settings, and in that way persistently acting in concert with its heritage. Pietism is a key piece of the Brethren heritage, and Pietism was a renewal movement to leaven churches of all sorts. Pietists were less in the business of shoring up their own institutions than they were in infiltrating and renewing others. So rather than a story of outside influences diluting Brethrenism, should we hear Grace's story as a decidedly Pietist story of leavening? If so, then the story might not be one of diluted Brethrenism, but of consistent Pietism leavening others—a persistent continuity amid all the change. As I read these essays I was struck by the fact that for every "outside influence" on Grace, there was also a Herman Hoyt lecturing at Talbot Seminary or serving as president of the Christian League for the Handicapped, a Jack Whitcomb or a Larry Crabb influencing a larger evangelical world, an Alva McClain theological statement still being taught at Ashland after 1937, and so on. So, that is my second observation, or maybe a question: How do we think about the many interactions and developments that these 75 years represent? Are we charting outside influences or the outworking of influence? (No doubt it is some of both.)

My final observation comes from the dynamic combination of progressive Brethren and a declension of premillennialism that we have in the stories presented by Dr. Norris and Dr. Burkholder. This is a rich story and, as a historian, what struck me as fascinating was this combination of progressive sensibilities and a theology that assumed declension. When one sees that combination, you know you are going to be in for something interesting. "Progressivism" as a cultural movement in the late 1800s and early 1900s, was not synonymous with liberalism. Rather, in the hands of Louis Bauman and others, it was a conviction that traditional Dunker separatism was misguided, not because it seemed outmoded, but because progressives contended that Brethren values, such as freedom of conscience and separation of church and state, were essentially *American* values, as well. Thus, the progressives believed faithful Brethren did not stand in tension with American culture, but were fundamentally aligned with it. Progressive Brethren embraced the style, refinement, and good taste that progressives believed characterized modern American society, and did not instinctively fear acculturation.

Progressivism provided the confidence to launch periodicals, mission boards, and schools along American models. It also opened progressives to newly popular premillennial eschatology that rejected progressive assumptions and assumed a declension theory of history. In this view, America and the rest of the world were inevitably moving in the wrong direction. Things were not getting better, but worse. So let's review: progressive Brethren believed that their values were consonant with American values, but America was running downhill, prompting pessimism and an impulse to withdraw on the part of people whose identity had hinged on happy engagement. Combine premillennial progressives and engaged declension, and is there any wonder there was so much creative tension in the story of Bauman's reforming Brethrenism or in President Hoyt's *Grace Journal* columns that encouraged both praise and excoriated Cold War America? There are a number of helpful interpretations of Grace College and Seminary that these papers suggest, from geographic factors to personality conflicts to nuanced theological developments. I would add the inherent and potentially creative tension between progress and declension.

I think it's fair to say that historians are instinctively suspicious of progressive claims. The idea that things are getting better and better strikes us as misguided. Historians, including most Christian historians, are also suspicious of models of declension. We also don't see decline as the only pattern in the past. (Well, maybe in terms of dress – dress standards may have declined since the days of Alva McClain raking leaves in a coat and tie!) Instead, we tend to see the human experience as the interplay between continuity and change. And casting a light on that interplay is a gift of these presentations tonight.

Here, I think of the short parable at the end of Matthew 13. After a day of teaching, Jesus concluded by telling his disciples that "Every scribe who has been trained for the kingdom of heaven is like the master of a household who brings out of his treasure what is new and what is old." Bringing forth both old and new: there is a tension there, too, at least potentially, between old and new, in our individual lives and in our collective and institutional lives. The tensions may appear between Anabaptism *and* Pietism, Brethrenism *and* premillennialism, Nora Springs, Iowa *and* Long Beach, California, Ashland, Ohio *and* Winona Lake, Indiana, *The Message of the Brethren Ministry and* the *Scofield Reference Bible*, fundamentalism *and* neo-evangelicalism, Nouthetic counseling *and* Psychological Christian counseling, didactic lecture *and* Studies in Spiritual Formation.

The ministry of the historian—and we have seen it here tonight—is to bring from the storehouse of the past something old and something new, not as ends in themselves, but as the work of stewards seeking the Kingdom of heaven in a wonderfully delightful yet painfully broken world. May that also be the value of this anniversary year, to bring forth old and new as a testimony to God's grace and to a place called Grace.

Chapter 11

Critical Reflections

Timothy Paul Erdel, Bethel College*

It is a great privilege to share in this 75th Anniversary Heritage Forum, and I am indebted to Professors Mark Norris and Jared Burkholder for their gracious invitation to do so. Both men have kindly shared their wisdom and research in public lectures at Bethel College in Mishawaka, Indiana, over the past school year.

Believe it or not, some 40 years ago this March my college basketball career came to an end here on the Grace College campus in an NCCAA district championship game, when the Fort Wayne Bible College Falcons were skewered by the Lancers. The game was played on 3 March 1973 in the old Lancer Gym. Grace crushed FWBC 83-65, though I scored the final basket to conclude a bizarre sequence of events during the last seconds of the game—a story for another time. Somewhat ironically, my competition against collegiate players began at Grace as well, when a little over six years before (December 1966), as a high school sophomore, I was the starting point guard on a hastily assembled all-star team that scrimmaged against Grace hoopsters during a Boys Brigade leadership retreat on the Grace campus. The Grace varsity pounded the all-stars as well. For what it's worth, I now work at Bethel College, where our longtime tongue-in-cheek prayer has been that God would give us Grace, Hope, and

---

* Erdel was the invited commentator for the second of three "Heritage Forums" held on February 19, 2013, which included oral presentations of chapter by Jared Burkholder, Robert Clouse, and Juan Carlos Tellez.

Huntington! The Lady Lancers and Lady Pilots are at it yet again tonight in the Crossroads League tournament as we speak. The men's teams, whose rivalry began on 25 January 1960, currently stand dead even at 60 and 60 after 120 incredible contests!

Way back then Grace already impressed me as a center marked by intimidating excellence. Whether one was referring to men's basketball, to the brass ensemble, or to the fabled faculty in the old Doctor of Theology program, Grace was a recognized force across the evangelical world. Tonight we are trying to assess some of that storied legacy, including important dimensions that were not always so visible to the broader evangelical public. While I have no serious quarrels with any of the three fine papers we have just heard, I do have a few comments. I will respond to each paper in turn, though there may be some overlap along the way.

Following Jared Burkholder's lead, I am whole-heartedly in favor of a movement that blends the best of Anabaptism, Pietism, and evangelicalism. When one looks at those denominations that have tried to do so, however, the evangelical stream almost always predominates over time. So, for example, the Evangelical Mennonite Brethren Church became the Fellowship of Evangelical Bible Churches, the Defenseless Mennonites ultimately became the Fellowship of Evangelical Churches, the Mennonite Brethren in Christ, Pennsylvania became the Bible Fellowship Church, the Mennonite Brethren in Christ ultimately became part of the Missionary Church, and the Missionary Church Association also became part of the Missionary Church. These examples could be multiplied, especially if one included parachurch organizations. But Anabaptism's most serious losses over time to evangelicalism may have been on the individual or congregational levels. Usually there is a move toward Calvinism and "Christendom," with a concomitant loss of the peace witness, among other matters. So Anabaptist historians may be tempted to proclaim a declension thesis, bemoaning the loss of Anabaptist commitments.

Whether or not a denomination such as the Fellowship of Grace Brethren Churches can genuinely recover and fully sustain its twin heritages of Anabaptism and Pietism alongside its evangelical heritage that currently prevails remains an open question. Neo-fundamentalism is a powerful tide that tends to submerge everything else. While I am encouraged by the tenor of the two anniversary forums held to date, I really have no idea how Anabaptism and Pietism will play out at Grace over the long term, nor across the Fellowship of Grace Brethren Churches as a whole. But in a universe fundamentally transformed by the Resurrection, there is always hope.

Although no less a thinker than Mark Noll charges Pietism with having a negative impact upon the life of the mind, Jared's claim that there is a solid historical precedent for a rich intellectual life within Pietism seems correct to me. It is my hope that Grace will always cling tightly both to serious, tough-minded scholarship and to sincere, tenderhearted piety. Christian higher education is desperately in need of models that earnestly and effectively conjoin head and heart. Bethel University in St. Paul, North Park University in Chicago, and nearby Bethel College in Mishawaka are among the institutions self-consciously trying to blend learning and piety. Grace College differs from them, however, in that it was also characterized by dispensational theology and by open fundamentalism to a degree that the afore-mentioned were not. (I am using the phrase "open fundamentalism" in more than one sense here. For many years both the Grace Brethren and their schools willingly and openly identified themselves with fundamentalism, given their origins in a fundamentalist break from a "liberal evangelical" body, the Brethren Church; but the Grace orbit was also open to cooperation with other Christian groups in a way that "double-separation" closed fundamentalists were not.) Since Noll also excoriates fundamentalism for undercutting serious thought, it would seem that, on Noll's analysis, Grace faces a double challenge. My own preference would be to shed fundamentalism even while deliberately reclaiming Pietism on the assumption that the genuine strengths of fundamentalism may still be found in a broader evangelicalism.

It is a great honor to even be on the same program with Professor Clouse, who was already a key figure among evangelical historians when I first joined the Conference on Faith and History in 1975. Most of my contacts over the years, though, have actually been with his long-time colleague at Indiana State University, namely, Richard V. Pierard.

Much of Clouse's paper is given over to the texts of successive doctrinal statements associated with the Grace Brethren. What is fascinating is the extent to which a church that was initially anti-creedal began to issue statements that became more particular and dogmatic, moving from simple, broad claims approaching "mere Christianity" (while also affirming Anabaptist and Pietist convictions), to precise theological stances representing the rigor of Calvinist, dispensational, and fundamentalist temperaments. There is a curious sense in which, at least for a time, the Grace Brethren may have owed more to the theological heritage of the Anglo-Irish Christian ("Plymouth") Brethren, a font of dispensationalism, than to the German (Schwarzenau) Pietism, whose streams fill the entries of *The Brethren Encyclopedia*. The influence of Alva J. McClain is noted on both the softer 1921 statement and the sharper one in 1969, which in turn mirrors the Covenant of Faith McClain crafted for Grace College and Seminary around 1938. Presumably the latter reflects his mature views, especially with respect to eschatology, though by 1969 there is also the handiwork of John C. Whitcomb, which comes to full flower in the 1992 statement for his new home, the Conservative Grace Brethren Churches.

By 1969 it is not enough for Scripture to be declared infallible; it must also now be without error. It is not enough for Jesus Christ to return again, he must do so within a specific timeline of end-time events. By 1992 it is not enough for the Holy Spirit to indwell, comfort, and guide the believer; rather Spirit baptism is linked directly and solely with regeneration at conversion, thereby excluding most Wesleyans, Pentecostals, and Charismatics. Post-apostolic miracles are repudiated, thereby denigrating the personal experiences of millions of earnest believers whose faith has been strengthened by them. Traditional Anabaptism and Pietism are downplayed, with the caveat that a warning against "carnal strife" does *not* entail pacifism. A young earth six-day, twenty-four hour creationist stance becomes the only acceptable orthodoxy, despite the fact that this is a position with a rather curious history and pedigree, rooted among early Seventh-Day Adventists, especially George McCready Price, although later taken up with a vengeance by Whitcomb and Henry M. Morris. Not least, men and women are now said to have roles clearly defined by Scripture.

In one sense, the wording changes are so dramatic they scarcely need commentary, although Professor Clouse in fact does a nice job of filling in background and pointing out the roles of key players. The formal legislation of strict beliefs and practices—especially ones formerly alien to Anabaptism and Pietism—introduces a wholly new mindset. But it is important to remember that this severe boundary-drawing belongs primarily to the Conservative Grace Brethren Churches, not to the Fellowship of Grace Brethren Churches or to Grace College and Seminary. Nor do I mean to imply that every change in wording is wrong or bad. I myself affirm the doctrine of biblical inerrancy, and do so without apology. But such an approach is a definite change from an earlier, rather different sensibility.

Our third paper is refreshing for its focus on mission, evangelism, cross-cultural ministries, global outreach, ethnic diversity, and international education. We have left behind most intra-Brethren quarrels and are doing what evangelical Pietists do best, namely, reach out to others in need of the Gospel. The percentage of graduates who went into missions from Grace during its earliest years is simply astounding, as are their subsequent lives of sacrificial service. There are many parallels in this paper with other denominations, including my own tradition, the Missionary Church, right on down to the name of the denominational mission, which is World Partners for the Missionary Church and Encompass World Partners for the Grace Brethren. (It was my father, Paul Erdel, DMiss, a career missionary to Ecuador and former mission executive, who initially suggested the name "World Partners" in the early 1980s.)

This is an inspiring story that needs to be told and re-told. Christianity is now the one truly global religion because of these sorts of initiatives, which have played out again and again in many traditions, especially over the past two centuries. One of my own theses is that mission almost inevitably changes senders as much as it does the recipients. That too has happened at Grace, as a narrowly ethnic denomination and its schools became more diverse in membership and more aware of other cultures. Inter-cultural contacts spread out in so many directions with so many good results. I am not a prophet, but it would not surprise me if the new Doctor of Missiology program proved more influential for the global church than the old Doctor of Theology ever was. The future is brimming with possibilities.

I conclude by returning to men's basketball. Morale was at a low ebb at Grace in the spring of 1992, when suddenly the campus claimed the inaugural NAIA II national championship. A sports victory is a rather slim buoy by which to keep two schools and an entire church tradition afloat, but athletic triumphs are sometimes a wonderful metaphor for God's sustaining grace in our lives.

The message that I hear in reflecting upon all three papers, as well as those in the first Heritage forum last fall, is about the surprising grace of God, which has preserved Grace College and Seminary for decades, whatever the human flaws, foibles, or failures along the way. It is a grace that touches every character in the story, even those we might at times be tempted to portray as villains, and a grace that flows across the campus to this very day. Whatever the losses and disappointments—gifted people who have left, prized programs that are no more, precious sensibilities all but forgotten, there is clearly a dynamic renewal at Grace that points to the grace of God being poured out again and again. May it ever be so, grace upon grace upon Grace.

Chapter 12

Critical Reflections

Perry Bush, Bluffton University*

I AM SURE I AM ECHOING THE OTHER RESPONDENTS TO PAPERS PRE-
sented in this Heritage Forum series when I begin by saying that it
really is an honor to serve in this capacity on an occasion such as
this. Anniversary celebrations are weighty and special occasions. One
of my Bluffton colleagues has spent a lifetime in association with
one of our sister Mennonite colleges who has really been struggling
in recent years, and he assures us that he's never worried about its
survival. Institutions like colleges, he says, are "hard to kill." I agree;
over the years they develop a kind of institutional momentum that
is difficult to derail. At the same time, I don't want to engage in any
kind of naïve historical determinism here. Many people who exam-
ine histories of institutions like colleges—a number which now, after
two previous sessions, probably includes most of you here—would
easily agree that colleges may be hard to kill but they are a lot like
cats: they maybe have eight or nine lives. Most of them have some
dicey moments and near misses. From my reading of Grace College
history, you may have 75 years in now and are going strong, but you
have had *plenty* of dicey moments and near misses. So the first thing
to say, on occasions like this, is congratulations on making it this far.
It's an honor to be here as a part of the celebration.

---

* Bush was the invited commenter for the third of three "Heritage Forums" held on
September 10, 2013, which included oral presentations of chapters by Terry White,
M. M. Norris, and James Swanson.

There is a good reason why religious colleges in particular tend to have shaky survival stories. Maybe it really comes down just to the nature of being religious. Nearly all religious bodies—especially, perhaps, conservative ones—continually wrestle with the age-old question of how much to accommodate to outside society while not surrendering basic group beliefs. Orthodox Jews, conservative Muslims, fundamentalist Buddhists, as well as Christians of many stripes, all struggle with how, in Christian parlance, to "be in the world but not of the world." As a Mennonite historian, it seems to me that Anabaptist-related groups seem to have struggled with this problem with maybe a bit more intensity than most. Memories of Anabaptist ancestors put to death in large numbers by the reigning church-states of their day reinforced a subsequent Mennonite determination to keep their distance from society. Throughout most of their history in North America, they constructed socio-economic walls that reinforced their physical and cultural separation and further reinforced these walls with a theology that branded outside cultural intrusions as "worldly" and sinful.

Beginning in the second half of the nineteenth century, however, such cultural walls began to crumble. Under the pressure of a variety of irresistible forces—changing technologies in transportation, communications, agriculture, the crusades of the national warfare state, and the blandishments of a burgeoning and increasingly attractive outside culture—Anabaptists as well as other Christians have struggled with how to manage the delicate process of acculturation. Their responses differed widely and can be arrayed on a kind of continuum. On the one end might be placed individuals who have succumbed completely to these forces, left their church communities, and fully assimilated into mainstream society. On the other end of the spectrum might be placed groups like the Amish and other Old Orders. Scholars of those traditions have outlined in detail how they have reinforced their traditional religious/cultural walls with stricter church discipline while simultaneously engaging in a delicate and creative brokering of these pressures in ways that have successfully preserved their Old Order identities.

In between those two kinds of responses, many Christian groups—especially again, conservatives—have carved out some interesting middle paths that take a page from the Amish. These involved borrowing from the outside in a manner that preserved their identities but didn't borrow too much and didn't give it all away. I am not a sociologist but, I suspect the process is still ongoing. As a historian it seems clear to me that this process of selective borrowing really intensified through much of the twentieth century when the assimilating pressures struck the churches with particular force. Some Christians attempted to resist the enticements of American society by adapting either an outside cultural/theological import called protestant fundamentalism or a softer, less hard-edged evangelicalism. Others gravitated toward a denominational expression of mainstream American progressive reform. Of course, the two divergent visions quickly came locked into inescapable conflict, and for many Christian groups the cockpit of that conflict has been their colleges. It's in the colleges, of course, where the innovators have gathered, the ambitious, the people pushing for change.

This is the analytical prism that, in my mind, can help me understand much of what's been going on here at Grace, and that particularly lends itself to interpreting these three interesting papers. Grace has been creatively borrowing from a variety of influences that it has filtered through the years: Pietism, of course, and later, dispensationalism, a harder-edged fundamentalism and a softer-edged neo-evangelicalism. Other filtering influences included new professional standards, psychological counseling, and even the initiatives and energies of the secular, liberal national government. What makes Grace's story so interesting, I think, is how it has filtered and shaped these influences, ultimately in a way to preserve and propel its mission, survive, and, at times, prosper.

Terry White, for instance, has done much with this progressive/fundamentalist split to sketch out this division that occurred in early Brethren mission efforts. We history professors ask students to parachute themselves into history from the vantage point of decades or centuries removed. When they begin to explore the foreign terrain where they have landed, of course they are mystified at what they find. As White takes us by the hand through the intersecting worlds of Brethren higher educational and missions enthusiasms, centered here at Grace, we come face to face, with some interesting questions – questions which are especially troubling to those of us from evangelical backgrounds. We wonder how Christian people could have

225

viewed evangelism and missions as up for debate and those who advocated for such efforts as radical progressives. What could possibly be so controversial about that? I appreciated very much the way Dr. White has situated early Brethren missions efforts in that contested climate of the tradition-bound Brethren church of the early twentieth century. I especially loved that interesting moment in 1900, right here in Winona, when these zealous young missionaries—clearly borrowing from the gung-ho missions enthusiasm then permeating larger Protestantism—met with such suspicion from an older generation still dedicated to the ways of their ancestors, and were told quite bluntly to take their passions out of the conference and go "out under the trees." From that exact moment and place, he tells us, came the Foreign Missionary Society of the Brethren Church. As the Brethren missionary movement evolved, he recounts, the struggle seems to have shifted from controversy over its appropriateness to a struggle over comparative and sometimes dwindling resources.

In his exploration of the relationship that Grace has fostered with its surrounding community, Mark Norris has taken up the same line of analysis and traced the struggle over these shifting resources with some care, as again they played out against the same question about the degree to which Grace would borrow from outside currents. We hear some faint echoes of the traditional town-gown split, though in Grace's case these seem to have been minimized in recent years by the adept pastoral leadership of skilled presidents like Ronald Manahan. Not that Grace's relationship with its community always went smoothly. As Norris relates, in its early years, Grace was so reflective of the morays of American Fundamentalism that its relationship with the wider community suffered. It's hard to have a cooperative relationship with the community, he notes, when you saw your neighbors only as potential targets for religious conversion. Over a half-century later, other problems emerged. There were also telling moments in 1994 when Richard Stevens of Greenville College, an outside administrator brought in for consultation, bluntly told the Grace College Trustees that Grace's reputation in the community "stunk." But Manahan seems to have adeptly healed that breach, especially in the cooperative and mutually beneficial relationships he forged between Grace and three large orthopaedic companies in the area. As Grace has continued to draw on the theology and subculture of neo-evangelicalism, Dr. Norris describes its ensuing community relations as having been a source of rejuvenation and renewal.

Finally, Jim Swanson's paper traces a similar set of dynamics that played out at Grace in the area of student affairs. He relates a rich and engaging progression of three different eras of student affairs over the past 75 years, all of which borrowed creatively from the outside. The first two phases saw Grace reflect the *in loco parentis* attitudes shared widely across American higher education. Reflective of its engagement with conservative evangelicalism, however, Grace held on to this pose considerably longer than secular and even other Christian schools, maintaining bans on card-playing, movie-going, and strict dress codes through—do I have this right?—the 1980s. Paradoxically, at the same time, student life at Grace was also deeply shaped by the dictates of a secular progressive state. Perhaps it was even enriched; one wonders if the Lady Lancers would have achieved the athletic success they did—or if there even would have been Lady Lancers at all—without the wider US feminist movement and the watershed of Title IX. Finally, Swanson relays that in the last two decades student affairs at Grace have been pushed more toward a relational view of students as learners, again reflecting larger socio-cultural developments moving through the nation with the arrival of the hi-tech Millennial generation of students.

In all these ways, what I see happening here at Grace, in this moment of taking stock at your 75th birthday, is an institution continuing to keep that delicate balance between a deep engagement with its society and a diligent fidelity to its mission. As in the history of every other human institution, it hasn't always been a smooth and flawless trajectory; there have been some bumps and bruises along the way. Yet, as I look over your history through the prism of these papers, I leave here tonight with no doubt that this balance will continue, and that you will continue to produce students who will go out from here and be fit vessels of God's Good News. All I can do, as I conclude, is to wish you Godspeed, and congratulations.

Appendix A

Covenant of Faith

WHEN THE SEMINARY BEGAN NEAR AKRON, IT WAS REGISTERED WITH the state of Ohio under the original articles of incorporation and the seminary's initial statement of faith was the 1921 Message of the Brethren Ministry. After the seminary moved to Winona Lake in 1939, new articles of incorporation were approved and filed with the state of Indian on April 29, 1940. The Indiana articles contained a new statement, or "covenant" of faith, that was consistent with the Message of the Brethren Ministry but was original to the seminary and the future college.

The Holy Scriptures

We believe in the Holy Scriptures, accepting fully the writings of the Old and New Testaments as the very Word of God, verbally inspired in all parts and therefore wholly without error as originally given of God, altogether sufficient in themselves as our only infallible rule of faith and practice (Matt. 5:18, John 10:35, 16:13, 17:17, 2 Tim, 3:16, 2 Pet. 1:21).

The One Triune God

We believe in the One Triune God, who is personal, spirit, and sovereign (Mark 12:29, John 4:24, 14:9, Psa. 135:6); perfect, infinite, and eternal in His being, holiness, love, wisdom and power (Psa. 18:30, 147:5, Deut. 33:27); absolutely separate and above the world as its Creator, yet everywhere present in the world as the upholder of all things (Gen. 1:1, Psa. 104); self-existent and self-revealing in three distinct Persons—the Father, the Son, and the Holy Spirit (John 5:26, Matt. 28:19, 2 Cor. 13:14), each of whom is to be honored and worshiped equally as true God (John 5:23, Acts 5:3-4).

The Lord Jesus Christ

We believe in the Lord Jesus Christ, who is the Second Person of the Triune God, the eternal Word and Only Begotten Son, our great God and Savior (John 1:1, 3:16, Tit. 2:13, Rom. 9:5); that, without any essential change in His divine Person (Heb. 13:8), He became man by the miracle of virgin birth (John 1:14, Matt. 1:23), thus to continue forever as both true God and true Man, one Person with two natures (Col. 2:9, Rev. 22:16); that as Man, He was in all points tempted like as we are, yet without sin (Heb.4:15, John 8:46); that as the perfect Lamb of God He gave Himself in death upon the cross, bearing there the sin of the world, and suffering its full penalty of divine wrath in our stead (Isa. 53:5-6, Matt. 20:28, Gal. 3:13, John 1:29); that He rose again from the dead and was glorified in the same body in which He suffered and died (Luke 24:36-43, John 20:25-28); that as our great High Priest He ascended into heaven, there to appear before the face of God as our Advocate and Intercessor (Heb. 4:14, 9:24, 1 John 2:1).

The Holy Spirit

We believe in the Holy Spirit, who is the Third Person of the Triune God (Matt. 28:19, Acts 5:3-4), the divine Agent in nature, revelation and redemption (Gen. 1:2, Psa. 104:30, 1 Cor. 2:10, 2 Cor. 3:18); that He convicts the world of sin (John 16:8-11), regenerates those who believe (John 3:5), and indwells, baptizes, seals, empowers, guides, teaches, and sanctifies all who become children of God through Christ (1 Cor. 6:19, 12:13, Eph. 4:30, 3:16, Rom. 8:14, John 14:26, 1 Cor. 6:11).

The Creation and Fall of Man

We believe in the creation and fall of man; that he was the direct creation of God, spirit and soul and body, not in any sense the product of an animal ancestry, but made in the divine image (Gen. 1:26-28, 2:7, 18-24, Matt. 19:4, 1 Thess. 5:23); that by personal disobedience to the revealed will of God, man became a sinful creature and the progenitor of a fallen race (Gen. 3:1-24, 5:3), who are universally sinful in both *nature and practice (Eph. 2:3, Rom. 3:23, 5:12), alienated from the life and family of God (Eph. 4:18, John 8:42-44), under the righteous judgment and wrath of God (Rom. 3:19, 1:18), and have within themselves no possible means of recovery or salvation (Mark 7:21-23, Matt. 19:26, Rom. 7:18).*

Salvation by Grace Through Faith

We believe in salvation by grace through faith; that salvation is the free gift of God (Rom. 3:24, 6:23), neither merited nor secured in part or in whole by any virtue or work of man (Tit. 3:5, Rom. 4:4-5, 11:16), but received only by personal faith in the Lord Jesus Christ (John 3:16, 6:28-29, Acts 16:30-31, Eph. 2:8-9), in whom all true believers have as a present possession the gift of eternal life, a perfect righteousness, sonship in the family of God, deliverance and security from all condemnation, every spiritual resource needed for life and godliness, and the divine guarantee that they shall never perish (1 John 5:13, Rom. 3:22, Gal. 3:26, John 5:24, Eph. 1:3, 2 Pet. 1:3, John 10:27-30); that this salvation includes the whole man, spirit and soul and body (1 Thess. 5:23-24); and apart from Christ there is no possible salvation (John 14:6, Acts 4:12).

Righteous Living and Good Works

We believe in righteous living and good works, not as the procuring cause of salvation in any sense, but as its proper evidence and fruit (1 John 3:9-11, 4:19, 5:4, Eph. 2:8-10, Tit. 2:14, Matt. 7:16-18, 1 Cor. 15:10); and therefore as Christians we should keep the Word of our Lord (John 14:23), seek the things which are above (Col. 3:1), walk as He walked (1 John 2:6), be careful to maintain good works (Tit. 3:8), and especially accept as our solemn responsibility the duty and privilege of bearing the Gospel to a lost world in order that we may bear much fruit (Acts 1:8, 2 Cor. 5:19, John 15:16); remembering that a victorious and fruitful Christian life is possible only for those who have learned they are not under law but under grace (Rom. 6:14), and who in gratitude for the infinite and undeserved mercies of God have presented themselves wholly to Him for His service (Rom. 12:1-2).

The Existence of Satan

We believe in the existence of Satan, who originally was created a holy and perfect being, but through pride and unlawful ambition rebelled against God (Ez. 28:13-17, Isa. 14:13-14, 1 Tim. 3:7); thus becoming utterly depraved in character (John 8:44), the great Adversary of God and His people (Matt. 4:1-11, Rev. 12:10), leader of all other evil agents and spirits (Matt. 12:24-26, 25:4), the deceiver and god of this present world (Rev. 12:9, 2 Cor. 4:4); that his powers are supernaturally great, but strictly limited by the permissive will of God, who overrules all his wicked devices for good (Job 1:1-22, Luke 22:31-32); that he was defeated and judged at the Cross, and therefore his final doom is certain (John 12:31-32, 16:11, Rev. 10:10); that we are able to resist and overcome him only in the armor of God and by the Blood of the Lamb (Eph. 6:12-18, Rev. 12-11).

The Second Coming of Christ

We believe in the second coming of Christ; that His return from heaven will be personal, visible and glorious—a Blessed Hope for which we should constantly watch and pray, the time being unrevealed but always imminent (Acts 1:11, Rev. 1:7, Mark 13:33-37, Tit. 2:11-13, Rev. 22:20); that when He comes He will first by resurrection and translation remove from the earth His waiting Church (1 Thess. 4:16-18), then pour out the righteous judgments of God upon the unbelieving world (Rev. 6:1-18:24), afterward descend with His Church and establish His glorious and literal kingdom over all the nations for a thousand years (Rev. 19:1-20:6, Matt. 13:41-43), at the close of which He will raise and judge the unsaved dead (Rev. 20:11-15), and finally as the Son of David deliver up His Messianic Kingdom to God the Father (1 Cor. 15:24-28), in order that as the Eternal Son He may reign forever with the Father in the New Heaven and the New Earth (Luke 1:32-33, Rev. 21:1-22:26).

Future Life, Bodily Resurrection and Eternal Judgment

We believe in future life, bodily resurrection and eternal judgment; that the spirits of the saved at death go immediately to be with Christ in heaven (Phil. 1:21-23, 2 Cor. 5:8), where they abide in joyful fellowship with Him until His second coming, when their bodies shall be raised from the grave and changed into the likeness of His own glorious body (Phil. 3:20-21, 1 Cor. 15:35-38, 1 John 3:2), at which time their works shall be brought before the Judgment Seat of Christ for the determina-

tion of rewards, a judgment which may issue in the loss of rewards but not the loss of the soul (1 Cor. 3:8-15); that the spirits of the unsaved at death descend immediately into Hades where they are kept under punishment until the final day of judgment (Luke 16:19-31, 2 Pet. 2:9 ASV), at which time their bodies shall be raised from the grave, they shall be judged according to their works and cast into the place of final and everlasting punishment (Rev. 20:11-15, 21:8, Mark 9:43-48, Jude 13).

One True Church

We believe in the One True Church, the mystical Body and Bride of the Lord Jesus (Eph. 4:4, 5:25-32), which He began to build on the day of Pentecost (Matt. 16:18, Acts 2:47) and will complete at His second coming (1 Thess. 4:16-17), and into which all true believers of the present age are baptized immediately by the Holy Spirit (1 Cor. 12:12-13 with 1:2); that all the various members of this one spiritual Body should assemble themselves together in local churches for worship, prayer, fellowship, teaching, united testimony, and the observance of the ordinances of our Lord (Heb. 10:25, Acts 2:41-47), among which are the following: The Baptism of believers by Triune Immersion (Matt. 28:20), the Laying on of Hands (1 Tim. 4:14, 2 Tim. 1:6), the Washing of the Saints' Feet (John 13:1-17), the Lord's Supper or Love Feast (I Cor. 11:17-22, Jude 12 ASV), the Communion of the Bread and Cup (1 Cor. 11:23-24), and Prayer and Anointing for the Sick (Jas. 5:13-18).

Separation from the World

We believe in separation from the world; that since our Christian citizenship is in heaven, as the children of God we should walk in separation from this present world, having no fellowship with its evil ways (Phil. 3:20 ASV, 2 Cor. 6:14-18, Rom. 12:2, Eph. 5:11), abstaining from all worldly amusements and unclean habits which defile mind and body (Luke 8:14, 1 Thess. 5:22, 1 Tim. 5:6, 1 Pet. 2:11, Eph. 5:3-11, Col. 3:17, Eph. 5:3-5, 18, 1 Cor. 6:19-20), from the sin of divorce and remarriage as forbidden by our Lord (Matt. 19:9), from the swearing of any oath (Jas. 5:12), from the use of unbelieving courts for the settlement of disputes between Christians (1 Cor. 6:1-9), and from taking personal vengeance in carnal strife (Rom. 12:18-21, 2 Cor. 10:3-4).

Appendix B

Educational Philosophy

The first institution-wide philosophy of education was created alongside revisions to the general education curriculum during a process that took place between 1995 and 2002. These efforts were representative of a desire by President Manahan to sharpen the sense of identity for the college and seminary and were led by Skip Forbes. In 2010, the general education curriculum was again revised and implemented as the "Grace Core" and the current philosophy of education was created. Adopted in the spring of 2010 and reproduced below, this document was written by M. M. Norris, who chaired the committee that created the "Grace Core," and Jared S. Burkholder. It also draws from Forbes' 2002 philosophy and includes previous contributions from James Bowling.

As faculty members at Grace and individuals who are committed to a life of worship and spiritual growth, we actively look for reflective and practical ways the Christian faith intersects with our disciplines.[1] The integration of faith and learning is based on the shared understanding that our faith "sacralizes" the pursuits of the Christian academician. That is, to the extent to which we do our work consciously as Christians, our professional lives become an offering of worship to God, and our faith "gives the questions we struggle with in our work and in our lives larger significance."[2] In other words, we are whole individuals and recognize the deficiency of a compartmentalized life.[3] Based on this foundation, our faith informs our work and makes it distinctive.[4] This distinctiveness may be further enhanced by the richness of our Grace Brethren heritage, which is rooted in the Pietist, Anabaptist, and evangelical traditions, and we value the contributions these historical streams have to offer.[5]

As we strive for greater integration of faith and learning, our Christian faith prompts us to facilitate a rich sense of collegiality and community among faculty and students.[6] This is largely made possible through the fruit of the spirit. Humility prods us to consider our own biases and presuppositions. It calls us to listen to competing voices and perform our work in dialogue with colleagues and others within the broader discipline. Integrity requires that we accurately represent the views of others, resisting generalizations and caricatures. It also requires that we strive for Christian excellence in all that we do, maintaining the highest standards of professionalism. Love prompts us to encourage and challenge each other as faculty members while caring for and serving our students. In an atmosphere permeated by the fruit of the spirit, our community will be a grace-filled place for us and our students to think critically, ask questions, and wrestle with the challenges of our world.

God has called us to be a certain kind of people (BEING), for example, humane, communal, compassionate, redemptive, honest, just, hard working, etc. Further, God has called us to a life of learning and has invested us with the requisite skills and resources to learn (KNOWING), such as the mind and its cognitive capacities, the Scriptures, academic institutions, life experiences, peoples and nations, etc. Finally, God has asked us to convert our being and knowing into service to others (DOING) as a way of expressing our love for and service to him. Therefore, Grace College and Grace Theological Seminary and their faculties are committed to integrated learning as a necessary component for empowering people to create lives that are whole, full, balanced, and rewarding.[7]

There are a myriad of specific ways to accomplish the integration of faith and learning in our study and in our teaching. They will vary depending on the context and discipline, but will always move beyond mere indoctrination.[8] At times, they may be of a reflective nature, having more to do with the questions that we ask and less about our conclusions. We might ask ourselves and our students, "How is the understanding that God created and sustains the world relevant to the material in question?" or "How does my belief in the fallen nature of human beings affect my world view?" or "How does the belief that all of humanity is loved and

valued by God influence the way I consider those of other cultures?"[9]
Other times, the integration of faith and learning will be of a more ap-plied nature.[10] *This will happen in many ways, not only in the classroom, but also as we mentor and advise students. We may prod ourselves and our students to consider ethical questions related to medical, scientific, or business practice. We may bring discussions of justice and caring for the oppressed into our classrooms and offices. We will no doubt consider specific portions of the Bible. And we may engage students in questions concerning the most effective ways of ministering, expressing themselves artistically, or serving Christ in local industries or within a chosen field.*[11]

At Grace, we believe that an education that emphasizes the integra-tion of faith and learning lays the foundation for and is in perfect concert with the institutional mission. Our mission statement reads: "Grace is an evangelical Christian community of higher education which applies biblical values in strengthening character, sharpening competence, and preparing for service [emphasis added]. Our curriculum and delivery system are designed to achieve these goals.

Character is the sum of distinctive dispositions, traits, qualities, at-tributes, and behaviors that constitute the nature of an individual or community. People of good character are marked by a desire to be learn-ers. The goal of a Grace College education is to create people of deeper substance who understand and desire the more noble and healthy values. They are able to make discriminating judgments between truth and error, merit and demerit, the substantial and superficial. They possess a develop-ing sense of self and place in God's world and purpose. They are people who have maturing skills and a growing sense of confidence that they can contribute and make a positive difference. People of strong character appreciate (give place to) and engage (think through, even debate) the pe-rennial and often controversial questions of life in a civil and reasonable way. People of character possess an elevated work ethic, care about work-manship, and are committed to a productive life, careful performance, and excellent products. As Christians, we best demonstrate this charac-ter when we live intentionally and consistently through our calling and profession of faith and biblical/theological commitments. Therefore, the undergraduate curriculum at Grace is designed to strengthen character.

Competence is the pursuit of proficiencies and credentials that enable one to be a contributing member of society. A competent person possesses the requisite capacities and skills essential to a personal, professional, and community life. A competent person increases knowledge bases and sharpens abilities and dispositions to put this knowledge to use in productive ways. A person who is competent is one who can gather data, think, discern, analyze, synthesize, and create solutions to problems. Such a person is one who suspends personal prejudices, who uses wise judgment, and who negotiates the world of ideas, grasps issues, wrestles with argumentation, interprets and traces implications, and makes connections to others and their ideas and expressions. A competent person is a literate person who is empowered to take in more and contribute more with his or her mind and life. A competent person is creative, enterprising, and confident—one who exercises initiative, takes risks, exhibits leadership, and commands respect. A competent person is thoughtful, articulate, expressive, and able to communicate in knowledgeable and persuasive ways. Such a person is one whose curiosity is wide ranging and one who can conduct a substantive conversation on a variety of subject matters, someone who is interesting to be around. Therefore, the Grace undergraduate education is designed to produce people who are sharpening their competence as persons, Christians, citizens, and professionals.

Service is a central imperative of the Christian faith. It is the natural outgrowth of loving and worshiping God. It is an outcome of a life well-lived. People of character serve competently. One ought to use one's personal and professional competencies to serve one another and the larger society, thus fulfilling one's service to God. Learning for the purpose of service is an act of stewardship and worship. Learning is a prerequisite that empowers service. A Grace education contributes to both the practical and moral dimensions of life. Practically, it empowers people to gain the proficiencies that make them marketable and employable. One's professional life produces the resources and contexts for service. However, this is not the total goal of education. Life is more than work for personal gain. The Grace education should inspire students to build lives and careers that will be turned toward advancing the cause of the One whom we ultimately serve. The mode of Christian servanthood can be expressed in several specific imperatives, each located somewhere in the curricular and co-curricular educational activities (e.g., go make disciples, call God's people to a renewed vision and energy to serve Christ and his kingdom, defend and perpetuate the truth of God's revelation, work for the moral health of society, and pursue peace and justice in the world). The investment of our time, skills, intellect, and energies will leave an effect on our *families, communities, work places, churches, the market place, and all of society. Therefore, at Grace, we have an education designed to foster service.*[12]

In summary, as faculty, we strive to do our work as faithful worshippers of God, to embody the Fruit of the Spirit, and to prod ourselves and our students to reflect on the ways our respective disciplines [13] *intersect with the depths of the Christian faith. This is an issue of character that enhances competence and empowers us for service.*

Notes

1. See Richard T. Hughes, *How Christian Faith Can Sustain the Life of the Mind* (Grand Rapids: Eerdman's Publishing Co., 2001) and Arthur F. Holmes, *The Idea of a Christian College* (Grand Rapids: Eerdmans, 1987). Holmes writes (46), "Integration should be seen not as an achievement or a position but as an intellectual activity that goes on as long as we keep learning anything at all."

2. Robert Wuthnow, "Living the Question," in *Christianity in the Twenty-First Century: Reflections on the Challenges Ahead* (New York: Oxford Univ. Press, 1993) 211-112, quoted in George M. Marsden, *The Outrageous Idea of Christian Scholarship* (New York, Oxford Univ. Press, 1997), 65.

3. On living an integrated Christian life, see Grace Brethren author Kary Oberbrunner, *The Fine Line: Re-envisioning the Gap between Christ and Culture* (Zondervan, 2009).

4. For more on Christian distinctiveness, consult Marsden, *Outrageous Idea*, 68-70.

5. For examples of how others within the Anabaptist tradition have wrestled with the integration of faith and learning, see J. Denny Weaver and Gerald Biesecker Mast, eds. *Teaching Peace: Nonviolence and the Liberal Arts* (San Antonio: Rowman and Littlefield Publishers, Inc., 2003) and David Weaver-Zercher, ed., *Minding the Church: Scholarship in the Anabaptist Tradition* (Kitchener, ON: Pandora Press, 2002).

6. On the important link between learning and Christian community, See Claudia Beversluis, "Community as Curriculum," *Council for Christian Colleges and Universities,* Online Resource Center (http://www.cccu.org/resourcecenter). Consult as well, Holmes chapter seven, "College as Community" in, *Idea of a Christian College,* 77-85.

7. From, Forbes, *et. al.,* "Philosophy of Liberal Education," Appendix B.

8. According to Arthur Holmes (*Idea of a Christian College*, 46) "prepackaged answers" will never satisfy inquiring minds. "Students need rather to gain a realistic look at life and to discover for themselves the questions that confront us. They need to work their way painfully through the maze of alternative ideas and arguments while finding out how the Christian faith speaks to such matters. They need a

teacher as a catalyst and guide, one who has struggled and is struggling with similar questions and knows some of the pertinent materials and procedures. They need to be exposed to the frontiers of learning where problems are still not fully formulated and knowledge is exploding, and where by the very nature of things indoctrination is impossible."

9. On the significance and usefulness of theological questions within the context of Christian higher education, see Denise Lardner Carmody, *Organizing a Christian Mind* (Valley Forge, PA, Trinity Press International, 1996).

10. In *The Outrageous Idea of Christian Scholarship*, George Marsden observes that faith can and should be integrated within even the most applied disciplines. He writes, "Even mathematicians or technical scientists will be able to point out some faith-related considerations that have relevance to the foundational questions affecting the frameworks of their disciplines or the application of their work. It simply does not follow that, because there is no special Christian view of photosynthesis, there is therefore not a Christian view of biology." George M. Marsden, *The Outrageous Idea of Christian Scholarship* (Oxford University Press, 1998), 6.

11. For the way faith and learning might be integrated within a variety of disciplines, see some practical examples from several Grace faculty members in James E. Bowling and Joel B. Curry, *Values in a Christian Liberal Arts Education*.

12. The definitions of Character, Competence, and Service are from: Forbes, *et. al.* Appendix C.

13. See James E. Bowling and Joel B. Curry.

Index